About the author

I wrote my memoir some twenty years ago, after leaving an abusive, dictatorial, lonely marriage of seventeen years. Having lived for years with anxiety and depression and having always lived my life 'through a partner' from the age of thirteen, I never really had the time or confidence to discover who I was and be 'just me'.

Even though I experienced some things that I would never have dreamed I would have done, during 2002/3, I have absolutely no regrets and that year turned out to be the best year of my life. I became liberated, answerable to no one and felt happy, happy, happy and, best of all, no depression or anxiety.

I would like to thank Pegasus for believing in my work and publishing my book. I am going to donate 5% of my royalties from every book sold towards much underfunded mental health charities.

Thanks for joining me on my journey and I hope you enjoy the ride.

This is a work of creative nonfiction. The events are portrayed to the best of the author's memory. While all the stories in this book are true, some names and identifying details have been changed to protect the privacy of the people involved.

MY MIDLIFE CHRYSALIS

GAYNOR MOORE

MY MIDLIFE CHRYSALIS

Vanguard Press

A CIP catalogue record for this title is
available from the British Library.

ISBN 978 1 80016 309 6

*Vanguard Press is an imprint of
Pegasus Elliot MacKenzie Publishers Ltd.*
www.pegasuspublishers.com

First Published in 2022

**Vanguard Press
Sheraton House Castle Park
Cambridge England**

Printed & Bound in Great Britain

Acknowledgements

With special thanks and appreciation to

Dave Trott

Mike Chapman

Chips Hardy

Jack Rubins

Lynne Norman

Bunty Banbridge

Contents

AUNTY'S NIGHT OUT

Saturday, 20th April, 2002

"I HATE empty holes!" I said, feeling my ears and lack of earrings. I was off out, with Nancy, Lara, Nina and Kelly. I had met all Nancy's mates before. Together they are a beautiful group of girls, all around twenty-eight years, all buzzing with life and what it's got in store for them. Kelly, blonde, tall, the best legs on the planet. Nina, the most extraordinary blue eyes you've ever seen with eyelashes that reach her eyebrows. Lara, only 5ft but perfectly formed with long brown hair and the cutest butt. She was like a little doll (and was usually surrounded by action men). Nancy, well, she has large smoky blue eyes, the cutest giggle and a smile to die for. She is also my friend, confident, niece and a true light, in my life.

The evening had been planned for about three weeks and the boyfriends had been left to their own devices, while the girls, went out with Nancy's 'Aunty Gaynor' — Moi. I'm sure the lads took some comfort from that. After all, a forty-seven-year-old, was hardly going to be a bad influence, so therefore 'Aunty Gaynor' would be a bit of a 'safety net' and keep the wolves at bay. Nothing would get 'out of hand'.

Of course, they hadn't seen me. I had arisen like a phoenix, from the ashes, of a miserable, controlling, emotionally abusive, loveless marriage, where I had come to believe I was stupid, boring, and unattractive with an aging, sagging body. Gone was the dictated brown hair, high necklines mid-calf dresses and no make-up. Instead, I was now blonde, low necklines, pink lipstick, dresses above the knee, make-up and lots of perfume. And, as the weeks had passed, I came to realise, I had turned into a bit of a 'blonde bombshell', who was constantly turning the heads of men and some women. I think I was exuding some sort of super energy or something. It was both odd and lovely because I had felt invisible for so long.

All the girls were wearing their clubbing gear, mainly black except for me who was wearing a low-cut white dress. We hit The Globe Bar for some Champagne, where we talked, mainly about men, pubic hair, orgasms, lack of orgasms, and how one rarely has one, with a partner, and something unfamiliar to me… vibrators. We discussed why we had all pretended to have orgasms in the past, there were three reasons. 1) Because we wanted our partners to feel they had done really well and we wanted to keep their confidence up, and, because women are, in the main, kind, empathic and compassionate (making wives and girlfriends climax, was sooooo important to them), and 2) Because 'It', had gone on for too long, hence us going "Ah, ah, ah, ah, ah, ah, ah, ah, ahhhhhhhh." That would mean to our partners, they could relax in the knowledge they had 'done their job'. Our partners were, unknowingly, invariably reaching for a goal they would very rarely achieve. 3) Ladies didn't want their partners to think they weren't 'normal'. Most men, had had their sex education via porn films so they wrongly believed, they just had to shag a woman 'hard', to make her orgasm. I wondered whether these lady porn stars realized the terrible damage and disservice they were doing, by sending out these totally false, misleading ideologies, which would often lead to psychological problems.

It's a fact that less than one in five women ever climax during vaginal intercourse, alone, no matter how long the penis, how long it lasts or how much you like the person you are with. The clitoris is the key. The girls blamed the porn business for misleading information by way of film. It was no wonder that men had been misled and thought it would be 'easy'.

I disclosed to the girls. "Personally, I'm more of a wham, bam, thank you, mam, kind of a girl. I was never into long sessions that went on for ages."

"I agree!"

"Me too! I like a quick shag!"

"And me. I find a quickie on the kitchen table, much more thrilling!"

"And I like the feeling and excitement of allowing entrance!" I added.

"Allowing entrance!" squeaked Nancy.

Everyone fell about giggling.

14

"You're so funny, Aunty Gaynor."

Cobden Club was next for some more Champagne, then off to 10room where the real fun was about to begin. I loved 10room. So much energy, no judgement on the way one looked, and everyone was out for a good time. Drinking and dancing. And possibly, a sexual encounter.

I had joined 10room just a few weeks before and had introduced myself to most of the people that worked there, manager included. My confidence had returned in abundance.

It was a busy night as usual, and the queue was long — even for members. That wasn't going to stop me. I asked to be let in to use the loo and immediately went to find the manager. Greeting him with the biggest smile, two pert breasts (thanks to the wonder bra) and a hug, I told him I was in the queue, outside, with my pals.

"Outside? Queuing? No, you're not!" he said, beckoning me back to the queue, to wave my girls in.

Straight to the bar, I ordered a bottle of Champagne and the manager asked if we would mind sharing a table. To my delight, a waiter took us to an area where five handsome men were seated. The waiter introduced us to one of them. "This is Hasan. It's his birthday."

I leant across the table and gave him a kiss on the cheek. "Happy birthday, Hasan! How old are you?"

He was quite taken back but gave me the loveliest smile. A beautiful young man with stunning eyes and fabulous soft 'hazelnut-brown' skin. "I'm twenty-eight."

"Aaahhh," I said, stroking his cheek, with my finger. "I could be your mum!"

"I don't think so!" he said, subtly checking me out.

I thought to myself, So young... so far to go... who knows where... I'm so glad I'm not where you are. I'm so glad I'm forty-seven.

I was about to take a seat and a big black hand came toward me. At the end of it, was a huge guy, with the biggest chest and arms you ever did see.

"Hi! I'm Garth!" he said, in a strong American accent. He was sitting on the sofa at the end of the table. To make more room for the girls, I decided to sit next to him.

"Hi, I'm Gaynor. Where are you from? USA?"

"Yes, mam, Washington."

"First time to London?"

"No, second, and I'll be back again," he said, with a cheeky smile.

We had a great evening drinking, talking, dancing, flirting, although Nancy, at one point, seemed to be having a rather intense conversation with Hasan.

As we were about to leave, Garth asked how he could get hold of me. "Just ask for Gaynor at 10room," I said candidly. I was too pissed to start writing down telephone numbers. As I was leaving, someone told me he was one of the Washington Redskins. I looked back at him wondering if it was true. He was 'giant size' so it could be a possibility. Catching my eye, he gave me a gentle finger wave and a wink. Smiling, I waved back.

We were collecting our coats and I asked Nancy, if she was okay. "I am," she said, "but Hasan is sad and not really enjoying himself. He seems so down and depressed."

Before I had a chance to respond he was standing next to us asking which way we were all going because he had a car.

"West Hampstead."

"I'll drop you off, it's on my way home."

That's sweet, I thought, and grabbed hold of his arm.

"Your perfume is lovely," he said, leaning into my neck. Not that depressed then, I thought.

"Come on, ladies, we have a lift! Hasan is going to drop us at mine!"

I looked back, to see Nina, Lara, Kelly and Nancy chatting to two large black guys outside the club. I back tracked.

"Hi. I'm Richard. Hi, I'm Solomon," they said in unison, reaching out their hands to shake mine. Finding it hard to separate the group, despite encouragement, I invited them all back to my flat for a smoke. I'm not usually accustomed to inviting strangers back to my flat but they seemed like nice guys, well turned out, nicely spoken, very polite, and, there was safety in numbers. They followed in their car.

I sat in the front with Hasan, while the girls crashed out on the back seat. On arriving home, Hasan got out of the driver's side to open the car door for me, then the two back doors, for the girls. Nina did a runner up the street, followed by the girls, to do a private vomit, whilst Nancy held

16

her hair back. Me, Hasan, Richard and Solomon, went into the flat and were greeted by my extremely excited cocker spaniels, Daisy and Flo. I got the boys a coffee then sat on the floor, rolling a joint and happily chatted away, waiting for the girls to appear.

After fifteen minutes, I decided to find out where they were... not in the kitchen... or the bathroom. I opened my bedroom door to find them all lying on my bed, all in different directions, fully clothed, make-up still on and 'out to the world'. I left them in peace and returned to the group of lads.

Richard turned out to be in finance, and worked in the city. He was a lovely unassuming sort of person.

Softly spoken with a wide, white smile. Solomon didn't say much, preferring to lie back in his chair and observe. I kept subtle eye on Hasan, feeling for him and wondering if he was in a depressed state. I understood the feelings well.

After some general chit-chat and a few spliffs, Richard and Solomon headed for home and I was left with birthday boy. We hadn't really spoken much because Hasan had also taken a 'back seat', while I chatted away with Richard.

"Right, I suppose I should be off now, too," he said, getting up from his seat. He really is rather nice, I thought, he has a such a gentle air about him... or was that his depression?

As we got to the door, for me to see him out, he put his hands around my waist, leant into my neck again, more closely this time, until his lips touched my skin. "Your perfume really is lovely," he said, again. Actually, it was more of a breathy whisper. The gentle touch of his lips on my neck, along with the softly spoken compliment, was enough to do it. I felt extremely flattered.

"As it's your birthday and you are feeling a bit down..." I said, putting my arms around his neck, "Would you like to stay the night?"

He jumped on my words. "I'd love to, even if I only lie next to you," he replied. Fat chance, I thought and took his hand.

With the girls crashed out on my bed, we returned to the sofa-bed in the living room, made it up, clothes off, underwear on, and got in. All the time, my heart seemed to be beating faster and faster. This was going to be my first sexual experience with a new man, for seventeen years.

17

Boom, boom, boom. It felt like my chest was going to burst and I could see my bosoms rising and falling quickly, out of the top of my bra. Then, the adrenalin really kicked in, fear and excitement all at once. I could hear myself breathing heavily, like a madman running through the woods after he had murdered someone. God, he's going to think I'm an insatiable, sexual monster, I thought. I tried thinking of dead dogs — my saddest thought.

I calmed myself with some slow, deep breaths, then lifted his arm up, so as to rest my head on his chest. We chatted. And chatted. Had a drink. And giggled, and chatted. And then it was four a.m.

"I really think I should go to sleep," said Hasan. "I have to get up at seven." He put one arm around my waist and the other under my neck and pulled me gently towards him, in 'spoons'.

Pause.

Continued pause.

Shag? Yes? No? Will he? Won't he? Should I? Shouldn't I? Too late. No chance. Hasan was asleep within seconds… or pretending to be. Was I surprised? Yes. Was I disappointed? Yes, but not really. He was too nice to be disappointed with. I told myself it just wasn't meant to be, besides, he was only twenty-eight… and I didn't want to turn into 'Mrs Robinson'… or did I?

I lay there, thinking how lovely it was to be cuddled.

My husband used to draw an invisible line down the bed, which I wasn't allowed to cross because it made him 'too hot'. Cuddling had been quite out of the question. At that time, I was grateful to have my bear. I had to be careful though. If I turned over in my sleep, towards my husband with my bear in my arms, he would grab it at the first available opportunity and throw it out of the bed.

I fell asleep with Hasan's arm around my waist, in a deep, warm, protective cuddle. How odd. Feeling safe with a stranger. And one so young.

***

Seven a.m., alarm. I felt a gentle kiss on my shoulder and then, Hasan, slipping his arm out from under my neck. "Morning, Gaynor."

"Morning, lovely."

"I can't feel my arm, it's gone dead."

I giggled, under my breath, then realised I was dribbling. We had been in the same position for three hours. I had probably cut off the blood supply. Opening my eyes, I pretended to be fresh and wide awake, so went to get out of bed. Then, I realised, I too, had an injury. Sleeping on Hasan's arm had given me a very stiff neck and it felt quite 'locked', on one side. I waited for Hasan to go to the bathroom and gently heaved myself up. Sitting, I tried to stretch neck out. Bloody hell! THAT IS SORE! I could hardly move it. Then, head on one side, shoulder raised and feeling like 'The Hunch Back of Notre Dame', I went to make Hasan some tea. Lara was standing in the kitchen, leaning against the sink holding onto a mug of coffee with two hands. "Morning, Gaynor," she whispered. "Sorry we hijacked your bed last night... What's wrong with your neck?"

"No problem. Stiff. Slept awkwardly," I whispered back.

"Hasan is in the bathroom... he stayed the night."

Lara raised her eyebrows, giggled and trotted off back into my bedroom, presumably to tell the others. It turned out that none of the girls could remember much after the car journey home, and I was told, later, that upon hearing the news that Hasan had spent the night with me, Nancy sat bolt upright, in bed, with a startled look on her face and said, "But he's depressed!"

After handing Hasan some tea, with a tilted smile, I went back to the kitchen so he wouldn't notice he'd spent the night with 'Quasimodo'. I stayed there until he was ready to leave, trying to stretch my neck by rolling my head.

"Morning workout?" he said, entering the kitchen. I lifted my head, very slowly, with a smile.

"I'm off now. Thanks for a great evening, it was lovely."

"Yes, it really was," I said, giving him a one-sided hug and a piece of toast.

With a wave, I closed the front door and shuffled, all lop-sided, back to bed.

BOXING ON THE BIAS

I stepped, this time alone, back through the doors of The Globe Bar to join the assistant manager, Mark, in celebration of his fortieth birthday.

Another 'v neck' dress, I was once again showing off my cleavage to full advantage. Not that that would be relevant for this evening because Mark was gay, so I imagined most of those in attendance would be gay too. I just wanted to look sexy, I was enjoying the experience.

I spotted Mark, as he spotted me and we walked towards each other, open armed and beaming. "You look sensational, darling!" he said, kissing my cheek.

"So do you!" I responded, leaning back, to check out his beautiful purple silk shirt and white jeans.

All his pals had turned their heads to look at us. I gave a broad smile. "Good evening, gentlemen!"

"Hello."

"Hiya."

"How ya doin'?"

"Hi."

"Hi," came back, in unison.

"This is my dear friend, Gaynor, I'm just going to grab her a drink." Mark grabbed my arm and led me to the bar.

"Champagne?" asked Elton, the bar manager, as he lifted a glass.

"Of course!" said Mark, leaning back, looking at Elton with raised eyebrows, as if to say, 'How impertinent!' I giggled and headed, with Mark back to the group of gentlemen.

Three glasses of Champagne later, I was dancing around the floor, on my own, having the time of my life. Occasionally, a willing 'party-person' joined me for a few minutes, or maybe, they just felt sorry for me, I'm not sure as no one stayed for longer than one dance. Not that I cared, 'Fun!' was my new middle name and I was going to live up to it.

As the minutes passed and the alcohol kicked in, more and more people joined the dance floor.

"I'm so hot!" I said, to a man who started dancing in front of me. Sweat was trickling down my back

"Yes, you are," he said, throwing his head back and laughing.

He was very attractive. About thirty-five to forty, not particularly tall, around the same as me 5'7", but with very wide shoulders and big, muscly arms, rather like Popeye's nemesis, Bluto. He had closely cropped black hair and was wearing a black vest with jeans.

"I'm 'Dodge'. Who are you?"

"You're what?"

"Dodge."

Dodge the todge, came to mind

"Why Dodge?"

Dodge suddenly dipped into a boxing position, lifting both fists up, then 'dodged' to one side as if to avoid an oncoming punch.

"Hi, Dodge, I'm Gaynor," I said, turning my back to him, then spinning back around.

I beamed and we carried on dancing, for not one, but three dances!

Feeling very merry and rather boisterous, I continued dancing and drinking until I was the only one left on the floor. It was about midnight and most of the party people had gone home, so I joined the other hanger-onner's at a table, for Mark to open his presents.

I pulled up a seat next to Dodge. I wondered if he's gay?

He looked up at me and smiled. Then don't ask me why, I just came straight out with it. "Are you gay?"

He looked down at the table, smiled again and shook his head. "No."

"Are you single?"

He looked up from the table still smiling. "Yes…"

In with a chance.

We chatted away while Mark opened his gifts and then it was time to go home.

"Great party, Mark! Would you like to come back to mine for a coffee?" I said, with a smile. "I've invited some other people too." I turned to Dodge. "Would you like to come for a coffee, too, Mr Dodge?"

"My place is literally around the corner, why don't we all go there?" he said, reaching out his hand to me. Big hand, to go with big shoulders.

We all grabbed our jackets, left The Globe Bar and I linked arms with Dodge to walk up the hill.

"You've got lovely big shoulders, Dodge," I said, hanging on to one of his big arms, with both hands.

"I used to box," he said, smiling.

"Used to box," I repeated. "So, what are you doing now?"

"Masters, in Business Studies," he said. "I finish in about three months, then I get my life back."

"And after that?" I said, wanting him to continue.

"After that, well, what I really want, is to be a deal-maker."

Haven't come across anyone like this before, I thought. A deal maker. The boxing might come in useful.

We all crashed on to the sofas and Dodge went to sort out drinks. Upon his return, he handed out the drinks, then immediately picked up the remote control and put on a 'blue movie', channel. I was immediately uncomfortable. I tried and pretended not to be embarrassed or old fashioned.

I piped up. "I saw my first blue movie a month ago. In fact, I saw three in one evening. I was lent them by a friend. I saw, 'Provocateur', 'Lesbians 3' and 'Debbie Does Dallas'."

"Blue movies? Do you mean porn?" asked Dodge, laughing.

"Yes, porn," I said, triumphantly, as though I had enjoyed the experience, even though I hadn't. In fact, I had only put on 'Debbie Does Dallas'. I watched it for about twenty minutes, then turned it off. It was something that just had to be done, to bring me into the new millennium.

"Where's the loo?" I asked.

"I'll show you," said Dodge, reaching out for my hand.

I followed him into his bedroom and he pointed to the bathroom door. "It's in there… the loo handle's broken, so leave the door ajar."

Good job I don't need a poo, I thought.

When I came out Dodge was sitting on the extra-large, super king size bed in front of me. "You look lovely in that dress," he said. "Not many women can get away wearing a bias-cut, like that."

"Oh, thanks," I said, then wondered how he even knew what a bias-cut was.

"I worked in the fashion industry for ten years," he said, as though reading my mind.

"Had a turnover, of £50,000,000."

I didn't say anything but walked towards him and sat on the bed.

Dodge asked me if I was okay and when I assured him, I was, he rolled me over on to the bed and gave me a lovely, long, gentle, lingering, kiss. Then he disturbed the moment. "I've just got to pop to the bathroom for a moment," he said, jumping up, enthusiastically.

I didn't move. I just lay there, knowing what was going to happen next.

He came out of the bathroom, grabbed both my hands and pulled me up on to my feet. "Let's go and get another drink," he said, leading me out of the bedroom. That was odd, I thought. That was very odd.

We went back to the living room, where everyone was chatting and 'half-looking' at the porn. I spotted the TV remote, so deliberately sat on it and with my hand under my bottom, I frantically started pressing buttons to change the channel. I didn't like looking at people's 'bits', close up. Or from three meters away, let alone on the biggest TV I had ever seen.

"Ooops," said Dodge, noticing the channel had changed. "Where's the TV remote?"

No one responded but instead, carried on chatting. I turned to look at him with an innocent smile, knowing it was under my bum.

"Why don't you put some music on, Dodge?" I suggested.

"Good idea!"

As Dodge headed for the hi-fi, I skilfully retrieved the remote and pushed it down the side of the sofa cushion, until it wasn't visible or available. I was grateful no one had come up with my idea, of pressing a button on the TV, to make 'lost' remotes respond, by beeping.

Half an hour later, friends were grabbing their jackets to head home. I stood up and put mine on. We all said our goodbyes and headed for the door.

As we walked out, I heard Dodge call to me. "Oh, Gaynor, can I have a quick word?"

Mark turned around and winked at me as I headed back through the front door.

"Yes?" I said, waiting for a response. He took my hand and led me back to the living room.

"Yes?" I said, again.

"Would you like to stay?"

Oh, so he really was attracted to me after all. Or, was he just desperate for some 'rumpy-pumpy'?

"Okay," I said, tentatively.

"EXCELLENT!"

He responded with great enthusiasm, as though he had just won something. I smiled, amused, then, to my surprise, he leaned over me, scooped me up in his big, strong arms and carried me off to the bedroom, where he gently lay me, on his bed.

"Just popping to the bathroom," he said, pulling the belt from his trousers.

I wondered, Is he going for a poo or preparing to strip off? I took a chance with the second option so quickly removed all my clothes and jumped into his bed, pulling the duvet over me so just my face was showing. I ran my fingers through my hair, to an 'attractive shape' and quickly removed my earrings. My heart was beating very fast again.

Dodge, exited the bathroom naked. Phew. I was right. Not a poo. He sure did have a big chest. I imagined him walloping the red punch bag which I had noticed in his spare room. He looked very solid from his neck all the way down to his feet. Okay, baby, box your way over here, I thought, giggling and pulling the covers over my head.

"Why are you hiding under the covers?"

"Because I'm shy."

"Don't be shy, you have a really beautiful body."

I allowed him to slip the covers from over my breasts. They hadn't been looked at for a long, long time.

24

"Fab boobs," he said, nestling into them. Distracted, and not really in the moment, I thought about my husband. He wouldn't look at my breasts, or anything else. In fact, if he ever caught me in the bedroom without my clothes on, he would pretend to wretch and immediately walk out the door.

***

I returned home at around eight a.m. with very tender bits and felt like I'd just completed two and a half furlongs in the Grand National, on a very large horse. Dodge sure did have stamina. I'd never been moved around a bed so much. He had been a Trojan in his love making, constantly picking me up with his big arms and folding me into different positions. At one stage, we were in a position, I've only ever seen contortionists do. I had no idea I was still so bendy. Extraordinary.

It had been a wild, fun night but on the way home in the cab, I decided I wouldn't be sleeping with Dodge again. He was too fast and furious for me. He was also too fit and too young. I crashed into bed and fell asleep, very quickly.

Upon waking up and leaving my bed, I felt as though I was walking like John Wayne, with a large horse still between my legs.

KNOCKED OUT

Tuesday, 30th April

Seven p.m. I was getting ready to go back to the Globe for another party. While looking through my jewellery, I remembered that I had returned home from Dodge's, minus my earrings. I wouldn't have been bothered but they were really pretty with red opal stones, so I decided to text him.

Hi Dodge, hope you are good. I left my earrings at yours, have you found them? Love Gaynor

I went out and forgot about the message. I was upstairs in the ladies at The Globe, when my phone bleeped. I saw the little envelope.

Hi Gaynor. I have your earrings. Do you want me to pop them round? Where do you live?

Oh dear, bit eager, I thought.

Oh, it's not urgent, just want you to keep them safe.

It's okay, I'm not busy.

Okay then, yes please, if you wouldn't mind, I'm actually at The Globe — again. Another party!

I'm safe at The Globe, I thought, so relaxed.

I'll be there in ten mins xxxx

Hope I wasn't sending out a misleading message. Should have just said I was out. Hope he didn't think I wanted more.

Ten minutes later he came through the door. He caught my eye and gave me a lovely big smile. Distracted by no one or anything, he headed toward me, leant over and kissed me on the lips.

I stood up to hug him. "Hi, Dodge, how are you?"

"I'm fantastic! I've got your earrings," he said, all pleased with himself.

"That's great, thank you for popping them around to me."

He reached into his pocket and handed them to me. I smiled inwardly at the irony then grimacing, bit one side of my lip. The earrings weren't mine.

"Ooops, they're not mine," I said, handing them back to him with a smile, trying not to embarrass him.

"You're kidding!" he said, expression changing.

"No, they're not mine... really."

As his face turned slowly, to one of horror, I couldn't contain myself any longer and laughed.

"Oh, they are yours," he said, looking relieved.

"No, I swear to God, they're not. Mine were small, fire opals."

"Oh my God. I'll kill my fucking cleaner."

"Oh, don't worry," I said, still smiling. "It's not like we're a 'couple'."

"I'm so incredibly embarrassed. I'm so sorry."

"Really, don't worry about it," I said, feeling sorry for him. He gazed, head down, at the floor, like a child that had been chastised.

Grabbing his arm, I led him off to the bar. "C'mon, it's not a problem," I said, rubbing his back.

We sat and talked for a few hours. I discovered Dodge owned his fabulous flat in Belsize Village and he had money in the bank, all thanks to his time in the fashion business. His mum was a socialite, and dad was a millionaire who had made his money through many ventures including, restaurants, fashion, theatre and plasma televisions. Dodge, also disclosed that his parents had separated when he was just four years old and that he was an only child.

As the evening went on, I listened, more than talked and I could see Dodge wasn't really a very happy person. He tried to hide his pain with constant jokes and frivolities but I could see he had issues and also that he was very insecure. I felt performance on every level, was incredibly important to him and that meant always coming first or being the best. I wondered whether that was the reason that he had been so extraordinary in the bedroom.

"Was I okay in bed last night?" he asked.

"Colossal," I said, feeling it was the appropriate and correct answer for him. He smiled and seemed to sigh a breath of relief.

"It was quite crazy though," I said.

He looked slightly surprised. "That would be the Viagra!"

"VIAGRA!" I responded, astonished.

"Yes, I took some last night."

"WHY?" I squeaked.

He chuckled, then got up from his seat and asked me if I wanted another drink.

As he walked to the bar, it hit me right between the eyes. The Trojan in bed, had in fact been 'Viagra Man' in disguise. And that was the reason he had popped into the bathroom after kissing me. He'd gone to take the tablet and that was why, after, he had led me back to the living room. He wanted to wait until it 'kicked in'. As I hadn't refused his kiss, he must have felt it was a signal.

He returned with the drinks and sat down.

"Even if it had only lasted ten minutes, for me, it's not about performance, more about two adults sharing some fun... on equal ground... do you know what I mean?" I said, feeling slightly unsure and screwing my nose up, like a child.

"You had a good time, didn't you?" he said, confidently, rocking his head from side to side with a grin.

"Yes, but I'm sure we could have had just as good a time without the Viagra," I said, placing my hand affectionately on his knee.

I looked into his face. He suddenly looked upset. Oh, shit! It occurred to me that maybe he had some kind of physical problem and needed to take Viagra.

"Sorry, Dodge. Do you need to take it for medical reasons?" I asked, warmly.

He looked horrified. "NO!" he said, raising his voice, "OF COURSE I DON'T HAVE TO TAKE IT FOR FUCKING MEDICAL REASONS!"

Oooo, ouch, crikey. I could see Dodge was extremely insulted and that he had taken my question as an attack and an insult. I recoiled into my shell.

"Only asking," I said, quietly, removing my hand from his angry knee.

Very sensitive, I thought, as I sheepishly took a sip from my vodka and orange. But then again, it was perhaps, a question too personal, to ask. Mind, I think a secure person would have just smiled and said 'No, I don't need to take it.'

I apologized again and then he changed the subject.

"I'm going to tell you a really funny joke, you'll love this," he announced, sitting upright in his seat.

Now, I don't really like jokes very much anyway, and for me, there is nothing worse than someone saying at the start of a joke 'You'll love this…' because I never do.

He told his joke, I smiled dutifully and chuckled at the end. I wasn't listening to a word he was saying, I was studying his face and trying to work him out. He sure blew hot and cold. He's very angry about something, I thought. Knowing that anger is often a symptom of pain, I felt sorry for him and wondered whether I might be able to help. I could see danger but I could also see someone hurting badly. And despite Dodge's furious outbreak, he did keep telling me I was lovely and kept asking me if he could take me on a proper date.

I considered what I had witnessed over the last twenty-four hours, then I remembered what my pal, Callie, had said to me, 'You can't save all the wounded birds, Gaynor.' That was followed by an image which came into my head, of me and Dodge on Daddy's luxury yacht sailing around the Caribbean, at sunset.

I shook my head and came to my senses. Did I really want to go there? No, on reflection, I didn't. I had been trying to deal with my own pain and trauma over many years, even before my marriage and was still struggling with that. To get more 'involved' would just be too bloody sore, in every respect. I decided that now was my time for being free, having fun and being in charge of myself and to do that, I needed to be at ease. I knew with Dodge, I couldn't be.

Dodge left shortly after his joke. "I'm off now."

"Okay, Dodge, take care."

A quick kiss on my cheek, he got up and walked towards the door. En route, he 'half' turned around, not looking at me and said, "Call me, yeah!"

Oh shit. What about my bloody earrings? Not worth the trouble. I'd have to sacrifice them.

THINGS THAT GO BUZZ IN THE NIGHT

Thursday 2nd May

Having been given a precise verbal introduction to the wonderous benefits of vibrators, at The Globe, from my niece and friends, I decided I would purchase one for myself. The 'Rampant Rabbit' had been given a five-star rating and was highly recommended by all the girls.

Things had really changed from the 70s. I had only ever heard of a dildo, which a young male friend of mine had found in a shoe box, in his mother's wardrobe. Her husband was 'doing time' in HMP Wormwood Scrubs. He had told me it was a 'rubber willy'. Shoe boxes hidden in wardrobes were no longer necessary. Times had changed and vibrators were usually kept in bedside drawers.

Too embarrassed to go into an Ann Summers, I rang their head office to see if I could order one over the phone. Yes, I could. Excellent! It would take up to five days for delivery. Cool.

Tuesday, 2nd May

8.20 a.m. I was fast asleep when the door buzzer rang. I dragged myself out of bed and picked up the answerphone. "Hello?"

"Package for Miss Moore."

I woke up sharply remembering the Rabbit. Can't be the Rabbit, only ordered it yesterday. I wasn't expecting any other packages. I hadn't considered the postman. I just imagined the Rabbit landing on my door mat. I prayed that there was no evidence of what the package contained as I buzzed the door open. The postman handed me a plain brown paper package, with a smile. Why is he smiling? Did he know something? No. No clues. Good. Phew. I signed for 'the item' then carried it off to the bedroom.

I felt like a kid at Christmas as I sat in my jimmy-jams tearing at the package. Under the brown paper, a bright and cheery box with a large cellophane window. Inside, part of the Rabbit exposing itself. The first thing that hit me was the colour. The Rabbit was pink. Bright pink. Very bright pink. The whole thing was presented as a thing of fun. There were no apologies, no embarrassment. This 'Rampant Rabbit' was hip and proud. I opened the window and as I pulled it out of the box, it seemed to grow. I was so glad, it wasn't 'willy', coloured.

I held it up in front of me. It was much bigger than I had imagined. At least nine inches long. It suddenly looked extremely big and overwhelming… Oh, hang on… no, it's okay, three inches of the Rabbit is the bit you hold. Phew.

I studied it more carefully.

Apart from the 'handle' or 'base', the 'willy' bit was made from firm rubber. At the top was a standard 'willy shaped' head. As I turned the head round, I spotted a discreet smiling face sitting just below the 'V' bit. Travelling down the willy shaft, under the head, was a transparent section exposing lots of little pearls. Under the pearls, the willy turned bright pink again, and in this section, was an extension. Ahh, here was the actual 'rabbit' bit. The extension existed of two firm rubber ears sticking up, and underneath the ears, the 'rabbit' had a face.

I held the shaft to study the control buttons. Top button, ON, OFF, ROTATION. I pressed it, the top of the willy rotated in small circles, rather like a seal with a hoola-hoop around its neck. At the same time, the pearls jiggled around. It seemed quite noisy. I would have to have to use it under the covers to keep it quiet. Top button off, I looked at the button underneath. ROTATION. I pressed it. Nothing happened. I pressed the top button again, followed by the second button. Action, same as top button, but willy head rotation, anti-clockwise. Mmmmm? Would the direction make any difference? I turned it off. Next button, underneath the top two, on the left, ON/OFF. I pressed it. The friendly little bunny ears started vibrating intensely… kind of electric toothbrush speed. I pressed the button sitting next to it, HIGH. The ears picked up speed. GOSH! I held it to my mouth, the sensation made me speak out loud, "BLIMEY!"

The little rabbit's ears vibrated against my lips. Very fast and very tingly. I then put the vibrating ears on the tip of my nose. It made me sneeze, almost immediately and then I remembered that I had read somewhere, 'The 'build-up' to a sneeze, is the closest sensation, to the 'build-up' of an orgasm'.

Okay. Right, full throttle, I turned all the buttons on. A seal with a hoop, jiggling pearls, smiling faces, rabbits, vibrating ears, there sure was a lot going on. I turned all the buttons off, then stood my new ornament on the bedside table.

As I lay there looking at it, the little face smiling back, I thought it would be like 'learning to drive'. So, as I had passed my driving test first time, I decided to 'go for it' and take an immediate test drive. I was about to take my pyjama-bottoms off, then noticed the blank TV screen staring at me. I got up and pulled the plug out from the socket. You never know if there's a camera inside, recording your every move, then I instinctively took a condom from the drawer and put it on the rabbit. Weird? I don't know. I propped a cushion under my bottom then thought 'Lubrication!'. I grabbed some Vaseline from the drawer. Moistening the area and slowly pushed the smiling face in, positioning the rabbit's ears where they needed to be, on Miss Clitoria.

Not being able to work out the controls, I had to pull it out again to see what I was doing. Top button, ON. I gently pushed the circling willy back inside me. Easy. Just like slowly drilling a hole in the wall. The pearls rattled away as they bounced and danced in the crowded space. I then pulled it out again, to locate buttons two and three. In position, the rabbit was now upside down. Finger poised over button two and thumb over three, I pressed button two. Ahh yes. The same as button 1 but anti-clockwise. Again, I circled the willy back in, thumb ready to hit button three.

It was not so much like learning to drive a car, more like learning to play the recorder between your legs. Rabbit's ears, again positioned, I pressed button three. I nearly hit the ceiling. "BLOODY HELL!" I quickly tilted the ears so they just 'whispered' on the spot. "WEYHEY! HOUSTON, WE HAVE LIFT OFF!"

I applied a little more pressure with the ears. Suddenly my legs jolted, and as I kicked out, my bare feet slid along the sheet and my bent knees collapsed. I hadn't come, but the intensity of the rabbit, all consuming, meant I needed help to hold my position.

Rabbit pulled out, again, I turned it off and lay it on the bed. I need to put my slippers on for more grip, I thought, so leant over the side of the bed and picked them up. I checked the soles. No grip. No good. I looked under the bed hoping to see my trainers. No trainers. I went to my wardrobe. Shoe section. No trainers. Only shoes. And Wellington boots. They've got grip, I thought, picking one up and turning it over. Loads of grip. Like a Michelin tyre. No point in searching for the trainers. Wellies win. I pulled them on. They were a 'girly' lilac colour. The sense of fun in them, seemed to go well with the pinkness of the rabbit. I caught myself in the mirror, pyjama top and lilac wellies.

I got back on to the bed, cushion under my bum and firmly fixed my 'wellied' feet in position. Perfect.

Buttons... ON, willy circling, pearls jiggling, ears vibrating... Entry and holding position. I closed my eyes and applied the ears with suitable pressure. In less than a minute, I was building up rapidly to a 'sneeze'. I decided to slow the rabbit down and take more time with my initial experience. I pressed the button. Suddenly, my back arched. Wrong button. I had pressed 'manic-ear' button. It was too late. I started coming. I desperately grappled with the rabbit's buttons trying to 'cut off' its energy so that I could feel myself coming, in uninhibited glory. Too late. Those delicate and throbbing pulses deep inside had been blighted by the fairground between my legs.

I pulled the frenzied, whirling dervish out and chucked it across the bed. It lay on the duvet buzzing and 'doing its thing'.

'BLOODY HELL! THAT WAS QUICK!' I picked the rabbit up again and looked it in the eye. I was quite simply gob-smacked that this fun pink toy, had delivered what it had. An orgasm in under two minutes. It was a marvellous feat of engineering. A fantastic invention. This was the best £30 I had ever spent and I was really looking forward to mastering it. This was, indeed, an item every woman should unashamedly own. Coming with a partner, is most often unlikely, and at my age, my fingers don't have the energy or flexibility they once had. If I were to masturbate, my fingers would arthritically lock and my hand end up looking like a frozen version of 'The Claw', from the 'Silver Streak Comics', 1939.

As the years have gone by, I have believed, more and more, that masturbating is really good for you. It's a positive release of energy, with a feel-good factor and it's natural. Also, during orgasm, researchers have found, that the genital sensory cortex, motor areas, hypothalamus, thalamus and substantia nigra all light up during orgasm. And, more importantly, through a younger generation, I have come to learn that wanking is not 'just a blokes thing'. Ladies were now embracing it, enthusiastically too, especially with the assistance and cooperation of a rabbit.

Now that I had experienced a vibrator, instead of thinking of it being something rather vulgar, unnecessary and for ladies that didn't have a partner to speak of, I had now totally changed my opinion. I would now be an advocator. One minute with Mr Pink, had turned any misleading preconceptions on their head.

On to the soap box. Gather round.

Ladies and gentlemen. The rabbit should be seen as an enhancement during sex, alone or with a partner, and not as an enemy. Many of the more fashionably younger women among us, know this to be true. Apparently, men wank much more than women. I think the need to release is there in both sexes, it's just that it's much harder work for a female, especially if you are only using your hand. It's easy for guys. Their willies stick out like pan handles and can be grabbed easily, and in comfort. We have nothing to grab hold of and worse still our hand has to go over and under, to a far less accessible place. Rampant Rabbit is the answer. I think they should be available on the NHS.

And for any of you chaps who might feel threatened by a rabbit, don't be. Having sex with a warm, loving man will always win hands down, come or no come. Do not think of Mr Pink as a threat, more of an enhancement.

If your missus doesn't have one, consider buying her one. Let her master it and wait to be invited in. She might be horrified initially, so just tell her, it's all the rage and you're going to leave it in her knicker drawer. And for God's sake, don't suggest you want to use it on her (that can come down the line, if she's willing), let her get used to it first. Tell her

35

it's a gift and a bit of fun. If she calls you a dirty old bastard, don't get upset. Just stick it in her knicker drawer, anyway. I'm sure she will lift it out one day, when you're guaranteed to be out of the house for a few hours. And another thing, don't ask her, "Have you tried it out yet?" Wait until she mentions it. And if she does, be extremely encouraging.

Ladies on your own, who are prepared to meet up with Mr Pink, you won't be sorry. And don't forget, lubrication and safety grip soles. PS. You don't have to insert Mr Pink, it's the 'V-shaped' rabbit ears, that are the integral component.

A SURPRISE CALL

My mobile rang… HASAN!

I was thoroughly surprised to hear from him.

"Hi, baby! How are you?" I squeaked delightedly.

"I'm fantastic! How are you?"

"I'm great!"

It went quiet for a moment so I jumped in. "It was lovely to meet you on Friday."

"You too. I had a really lovely time, thanks."

"So did I. You are a lovely man."

It went quiet again.

"So, are you at work, Hasan?"

"Yes."

"Where do you work?"

"I work for Emmody."

"Emmody? What's that?" I asked, imagining it was probably some swanky, high profile fashion business, that I hadn't heard of.

"Emmody, Ministry of Defence."

"OH!" I shrieked, "M… O… D!" Ministry of Defence!"

"Yes, MOD."

I was a bit stumped to say the least. Hasan didn't seem like an 'MOD' type. Mind, not that I knew any. I was judging him against the old black and white spy films.

"The reason I am calling, is to ask you if you would like to meet up again? I'm going away for a week but will be back on the 13ᵗʰ, so I was thinking of a week Friday, the 17ᵗʰ. Would that suit you?"

Oh, bless him, I thought, then blurted out, "I'm forty-seven, Hasan."

"And…" he responded, politely.

I paused.

"I don't care how old you are, Gaynor, you're just a lovely person to be around."

"Ahhh, you are so lovely, Hasan. Yes, okay, see on the 17th."

"Great! I will pick you up at eight and take you to dinner."

"Oh, don't worry about dinner, we can meet for a drink."

'No," he said, firmly, but kindly, "I'd like to take you out."

"Oh, okay, how nice. I'll look forward to seeing you then, then. Nice to hear from you."

"Great! I'll call you nearer the day," responded Hasan, enthusiastically.

I put the phone down and thought about Hasan's call. Well, he doesn't just want a shag or he wouldn't have invited me to dinner... or maybe he does want a shag and is being polite about it... or, maybe I'm fun to be around. Yes, that's it, I'm fun. and he must feel a connection. Yes, that has to be it because he is a very handsome, charming and polite young man, so he could choose to go out with any number of beautiful young ladies in his age group. Mmmm. Maybe he simply wants to thank me for cheering him up on his birthday. Whatever. Aahhh. What a poppet.

I amused myself with 'Emmody'.

LARDER

Friday, 10th May

The Champagne had kicked us off to a good start. Three very merry birds in the back of a taxi looking Hot! Hot! Hot! Everyone one was wearing a cleavage revealing top, jeans, heeled boots and smelled gorgeous. It was Amy's birthday, grand old age of twenty-six and we were off to our favourite haunt, 10room.

"SHIT! I forgot to put my earrings on, AGAIN! Must have 'shag-brain' again," I murmured, to myself.

"No one's going to be looking at your ears with that cleavage, Gaynor," piped Callie, sticking her finger between my breasts. I smiled, knowing she was right but I still wished I'd put some on.

Amy and Callie on one sofa, me the other, we sat at right angles to each other in the best corner in 10room. Three lovely ladies, Champagne and lots of attention. It wasn't long before we were all up shaking it. As much as I love and always have loved dancing, I still couldn't help looking at us all strutting our own stuff, along with all the other punters, and thinking how odd the whole dancing thing was. Whenever I had this thought, I reminded myself of a group of babies I had once seen on TV who had automatically moved, rhythmically, to music, without ever having been exposed to it before. I took comfort in the knowledge that it was, in fact instinctive. We all had an excuse.

If they hadn't seen the programme and were oblivious to these documentary facts, what did they think the whole dancing thing was all about? Did they ever bother thinking about it at all? Do they feel it's 'in them' to just move to the beat but not know why, or do they feel it's like joining a club, a bit like table tennis? And, then, what about the ones that don't like dancing? Are they fighting their natural instinct? I realised I'd gone off on one in my head and was thinking far too deeply.

39

Resting with my legs over the arm of the sofa after a few dances, a nice-looking young man came over, leant over the drinks table and spoke to me. "Are you all right, madam?"

I detected an accent.

"I'm fine thanks, just very, very hot."

"Yes, it is very 'ot in 'ere tonight… I will fetch you some water, madam."

Sweet man, I thought as he wandered off. He returned a moment later.

"Ere is your water, madam… on the 'ouse."

"Oh, bless you, sweetheart," I said, as he placed the large glass of iced water in front of me.

I looked more closely at the way he was dressed. "Do you work here?"

He sat on the arm of the sofa, as I swivelled around to grab the water.

"Yes, my name is Francois, and I am in charge of the bars."

"Oh, I don't remember seeing you before… sorry."

"I 'ave been here for four months and you 'ave never noticed me before. I 'ave noticed you though… you always 'ave good shoes on your feet."

He looked down at my pointy, beaded, stilettos.

"And you always look very sexy."

"Thank you. Sorry I didn't notice you before. What's your name?"

"Francois, I told you."

"Oh yes, sorry, I'm Gaynor."

I put out my hand to shake but he lifted it and kissed it.

"Where are you from, Francois?"

'France."

"France? I know Francois is a French name, but you look more Italian."

"Many people have said this but I am French."

"Well, it's nice to meet you, Francois," I said, not knowing what to say next.

"May I come back and 'ave a dance with you later?"

"You may," I said smiling, as he departed with a wink.

Six or seven winks later, amongst lots of eye contact and smiles, Francois came over and led me to the dance floor, like a gentleman. Not the first 'close dance' of the evening, but the one I had been waiting for. Along with the soft French accent and gentle manner, Francois was an incredibly fit young man. He had been on his feet all evening. I'd seen him dashing from bar to bar, organising, ordering and he didn't even have a bead of sweat to show for it.

Taking me in his arms, our similar height enabled us to get very close, very quickly. He was a lovely mover and in no time, we were sliding up and down each other's hips. My thought of the bizarreness of dancing was 'dead and buried' until I thought, Is this instinctive, or a contrived sex dance, manufactured by humans, to allow the closeness of bodies to touch one another? Mmmm, I couldn't imagine 'ape-man' dancing with his ape-girlfriend like this, nor tribal dancers who tend to jump up and down on the spot, in their own space. Although dancing was instinctive, dancing with another person 'united as one', I decided, was probably not instinctive. Good ploy though.

I got back into the sliding. As he twisted his hips, more toward the front of me, still sliding, but now also pressing, it felt like he had a bottle of beer down his trousers. I was flattered and not offended. He was a young, fit, handsome, and bursting with testosterone. I was forty-seven, he must have been mid-twenties.

At the end of the dance, Francois pulled back and looked at my sweaty face. He still looked cool as a cucumber.

"Come with me, Gaynor. I will take you to the fresh air and to get some water."

I held his hand as he led the way. He swung open some double doors which I had never noticed before and we stepped into a wide corridor where the temperature was about twenty degrees cooler. The air felt fab. Still being led by Francois, I wiped the beads of sweat, running down my forehead. I hoped he wouldn't turn around to look at me because we were under those horrid, unflattering, florescent tube lights. They were so harsh. I kept my head down and continued to follow. Through a large black single door, we arrived in a large 'idle' stainless-steel kitchen. I looked around. No people. It felt like everyone had jumped ship. They probably had.

We were swamped in that dreadful florescent lighting again.

"Sit 'ere, Gaynor," Francois, said, pointing to a high three-legged stool with no back. I climbed on to it and wriggled my bum into position. Francois moved toward a huge industrial fridge and returned with fresh, cooler than cool, ice-water.

"Thank you so much. Bless you. I really need this," I said, taking the glass from him.

"You are a great dancer, Gaynor."

"So are you, Francois," I said, beaming.

"It is very 'ot in the club tonight."

"Yes, it is," I said, wiping my forehead again.

"Ow would you like to 'ave some soft, fresh, cool, sweet, strawberries?" he asked, gently stroking my sweaty cheek.

The description of the strawberries was too delicious to refuse. "That would be lovely," I said, smiling again.

"Follow me," Francois instructed, helping me down from the stool.

By the time both my feet were on the ground, one was shoeless. "I've lost a shoe!"

Francois dropped to his knees in front of my legs and retrieved my shoe. I then tried to balance, as he struggled to get it back on for me.

"That's it, thanks Francois. It got caught on the bar!"

"It's no problem! Let's go and get the strawberries."

Taking his arm, he took me through more double doors to another large kitchen. This one was busy. Two staff members playing cards on a work surface. They both looked up as Francois shouted something to them in French. They nodded respectfully and then carried on with their cards.

We headed for the back of the kitchen. "The strawberries, are in 'ere," said Francois enthusiastically, as he opened yet another door.

I peered in, as he stepped back, to let me look. "It's a little larder!"

"What is a little 'arder?"

"This is!" I said, "and it's a very little larder, compared with the size of the kitchen."

"I don't understand 'little 'arder'."

I giggled, realising he wasn't familiar with this 'old-fashioned' word, 'larder'.

"What do you call this little room, Francois?"

"'This is the cool room... just for fruit... go in and choose your strawberries."

I felt a bit disappointed. I didn't really want to 'pick my own'. I had envisioned a silver bowl, ready laden with hand-picked strawberries. And an elegant silver spoon to match.

I then reconsidered and thought maybe he was just trying to be sweet. People might well have different ideas about the perfect strawberry. Maybe he just wants me to have what is 'my' best.

Smiling reluctantly, I stepped into the little 4ft x 4ft larder. To my left, was an unnecessary stool. Above it, sat a few large glass bowls full of strawberries, and above that, dozens of crisp, white, china bowls. Francois lifted down one of the large bowls from the shelf.

"I want a little bowl," I said, reaching up on tip-toes to grab one. Ahh, that's why the stool is in here, I thought, for 'shorter' staff members.

As I reached out, I suddenly felt Francois putting his arms around my waist. "Do you want some too, Francois?" I asked, reaching for two bowls.

"No, Gaynor, I want to kiss you. You are such a beautiful woman."

He kissed my neck.

"Darling, I am forty-seven. Old enough to be your mother."

"Darling, I am twenty-eight, and I don't give a shit. You are so beautiful and I want to make the kiss to you."

I felt frozen in time for a split second, not knowing which way I was going to go. I decided to drop my guard. I wouldn't mind a nice kiss. As I slowly turned toward him, I confirmed to myself, There's nothing wrong with a beautiful kiss... it would be nice, besides, it would stop there because there wasn't enough room to do anything else.

Our lips slowly came together. Maybe it was the thought of the strawberries that was making my mouth water, Naah, it was definitely Francois. His tongue worked like an elegant snake. Tempting, teasing, seducing.

I was really enjoying our beautiful kiss and as my mouth searched for more, Francois gently pulled away and whispered in my ear. "Can I make the love with you, Gaynor?"

"Naughty!"

"It's not naughty, I really want to make the love with you."

"Well. maybe… sometime…" I said, trying to bring his lips back, to kiss.

We started kissing again. The kissing became more intense. Both myself and my knickers became really excited. My mind was racing. Do I want to do this? Don't I want to do this? Yes. Okay. I want to do this. And actually, I want to do this, right now, but how? Where? How could we keep it 'in the moment'?

Francois whispered again. "Gaynor, I want to make the love with you now, I want to kissing you and loving you…"

"Okay, but how? Where?" I said, searching for an instant solution. I knew if we had to go in search of a new location, I could, very easily, change my mind en-route.

Francois very gently lifted up my dress and pulled down my knickers. I tried to step out of them elegantly in the tight, tiny space. I got one leg out. That would have to do.

"Sit on the stool," whispered Francois, helping me on. Then he kissed me again, at the same time gently pulling my knees apart.

OH MY GOD! He's going to shag me in here!' The larder. Well, that is to say, he's going to 'attempt' to shag me, in the larder. I personally think it will be a physical impossibility.

Francois opened my legs and slowly placed one over each of his shoulders. It felt awkward. They weren't dangling right. He sensed my discomfort and lifted my legs down until my knees were lined up with his chest.

"Put your legs at side of me and your feet on the wall, Gaynor. It will be more comfortable for you."

He's done this before, I thought, quickly checking the evidence. The stool, and 'wall positioning' were for comfort and to make the process 'easy'.

I wondered how many bottoms had sat before, where I was now sitting. The whole set-up was quite ingenious.

He slid his hand gently across me and knew I was ready. Without wasting another second, he whipped out a condom, whacked it on and then entered me. The smooth entry confirmed that this young man was an expert in the larder.

It quickly turned into a shag fest with the pair of us frantically rocking the bollocks out of the stool. I hoped the larder was 'sound-proofed'. It was over within a couple of minutes. Wham, bam, thank you, mam.

"I'm sorry I 'ave come too quickly. I 'ave been so excited about you for weeks, Gaynor," said Francois, looking slightly embarrassed.

"What are you talking about. That was fab!" I had a great time! Thank you! Thank you! Thank you, Francois."

Francois looked surprised at my seemingly 'over the top response'. I suddenly thought he might think I was being sarcastic so went on to explain. "The thing is, Francois, I am forty-seven years old and I have never had sex anywhere, apart from the bedroom, before…"

"Are you joking? Seriously?"

"Yes, it's true, only in my bed."

"What about in a car… or on a train… or the kitchen table?"

"No, not yet, I still have those experiences to look forward to."

I clapped my hands in anticipation.

"I 'ave a car! Oh, Gaynor, you *really* are such a beautiful woman. I feel very honoured that you 'ave shared yourself with me. I didn't really think you would make the love with me."

"Nor did I… until your naughty tongue started to weave its magic, but I'm really glad I did. I feel liberated."

Francois held up my chin and kissed me on the lips again… not in a sexy way… a bit like a father to a daughter. He then managed to bend down and feed my foot back through my knickers and pull them up. What an absolute poppet. He checked that my dress and hair were all re-aligned and then handed me a bowl of strawberries as we left the larder.

"I 'ave to check the bars, Gaynor. Is it all right if I come and find you later?"

"Sure," I said, feeling all 'tickety-boo' with the 'new, improved' me.

He squeezed my hand as we approached the double doors which lead back to the dance floor. I tried to sneak back through them without being noticed. It worked. Francois would follow in a minute or so, but headed off in the other direction. He could not afford to get caught coming out of a 'NO ENTRY' door with me.

The girls were dancing, so I just plonked myself on the sofa, threw my head back and laughed. Callie spotted me and came over, followed by Amy.

"What are you laughing at?" she asked, as she plonked herself next to me. "Where have you been?" I shoved a strawberry into my smiling mouth then just came straight out with it. "I've just shagged someone in a larder!"

"YOU'VE WHAT?"

Callie's face contorted between a smile and shock.

Amy's mouth fell open as she leaned forward.

"I had a shag in the larder, in the kitchen…"

"WHAT! WHERE? WHEN? HOW? WHO?"

"Just a few minutes ago, in the larder."

"IN THE LARDER? WHO WITH?"

I thought Callie's eyes were going to pop out of her head.

"Francois."

"WHO THE FUCK'S FRANCOIS?"

"He's the bar manager."

"What? Do you mean that young guy in the black shirt you were talking to earlier?"

"Yes, him."

"How old is he?"

"Twenty-eight"

"He doesn't look twenty-eight, he looks nineteen! No, there's definitely no way he's twenty-eight."

"Actually, there is a way, but you'd have to get him into the larder to find out. He's very sweet. He even put my knickers back on for me, afterwards."

Callie squealed with delight. "What a gentleman!" then she threw her head back, fell on to her side laughing, and grabbed my hand. "Brilliant! I would never have believed that the person sitting next to me now, is the same Gaynor I knew three years ago. That person was afraid of everything. That person was afraid to 'live'. That person didn't even like leaving the house. I'm SO glad you left HIM!"

"Just shows you," I said, with absolute conviction. "It really is, never too late… no matter what it is."

"Here's to you, Gayn's," said Callie, clinking my glass.

"Cheers, Gaynor. Well done," said Amy, giggling and taking a handful of strawberries.

"Another box ticked, and not just 'sex outside of bed' but most interestingly, in a larder, in 10room with the bar manager!" I squeaked, excitedly.

"I think you have balls! I think you are great, Gayn's," said Callie, responding enthusiastically to my accomplishment.

I sat feeling all pleased with myself, then my mind changed from fifth gear into reverse. Of course, I realised, there were many ladies out there, who would not be in the least bit impressed with my 'larder love-in' experience, especially if armed with the knowledge that the man in the larder with me was half my age. I knew this to be true from my own personal perspective in the 'not-so-distant' past. I, myself, had been one of those 'stiff-knickered' women, riddled with fear, insecurity, sadness, vulnerability, hurt and unworthiness. Judging others was always a good distraction to take the focus away from me. I could still hear my old voice 'squawking', along with all the others that were still in that place. 'Tart', 'tramp', 'slapper'. 'She's far too old to be behaving like that!' 'It's disgusting!'

I returned to the moment and cheerfully, started singing Mrs Robinson, by Simon and Garfunkel. I decided I had been blessed. Unbelievably, last year, against all the odds and despite my continuing depression and sense of gloom, to my surprise I was finally able to recognize that there really was more than just one path open to me.

And ultimately, at that time, there really was only one question that had to be answered. Was I prepared to leave my husband and subsequently, face my biggest fear. Being on my own? The question answered itself when I realised there was no way on Gods earth that I could ever possibly have felt any lonelier, than I already did. I had been feeling pretty 'dead' for years. Any spark that I may have once had, seemed to have been extinguished long, long ago. So, what did I have to lose? A nice house. A very comfortable lifestyle. Lovely holidays. My husband constantly calling me 'a sad old bastard' or 'a mad old bitch'. The list was endless.

I realised that 'going it alone', would be a real challenge for me. Within the anti-depressants, which I had been on for eight years, I would have to try to find 'myself'. My 'real' self. The part of me which had never been mine because I had always handed it to a man.

To be honest, before I left my husband, I didn't feel that I really knew who I was. I had no friends of my own, except Callie, who I had met three years previously when we were both walking our cocker spaniels in the park. We often sat down together for a coffee and a chat. She rarely came over to my flat when my husband was there. He didn't like me having visitors.

Lost between my old world and my new, I was bought back to the moment again, by Francois, whispering in my ear. "You 'ave free drinks, all night, on the 'ouse. What can I get for you?"

"Champagne!" squealed Callie and Amy in unison.

"Champagne, it is."

"Bless you, Francois," I called, as he weaved his way speedily across the dance floor.

An hour later, it was time to go. I looked for Francois to say goodbye but couldn't find him. We collected our coats from the cloakroom and as I pulled mine on, a hand travelled under my coat and around my waist. I knew it was Francois.

"Are you coming 'ere next week, ma Cherie? May I 'ave your number?"

"I'll be back next week, Francois," I said, hugging him briefly, in case higher management were watching.

"Okay, goodbye, Gaynor. I 'ope I will see you next week. Take care of yourself and 'ave fun."

Me, Callie and Amy, left 10room, arm in arm and bundled into the back of a black cab. Once seated, Callie threw her arms around my neck and kissed me on the cheek. "I'm so proud of you, Gayn's!"

I giggled and started singing *Mrs Robinson* again.

GUMBALLS

Wednesday. Middle of the week. Past the beginning but not near enough to the end. In limbo, so invite Callie down to 10room. Amy, was already going on a date. We popped into The Globe first for a couple of drinks, then arrived at 10room, about ten thirty. The place was buzzing.

Appreciating how short, but sweet, our encounter had been in the larder, I arrived at 10room hoping that when I spotted Francois, he would greet me with joy. Even though I realised, there was the possibility he wouldn't.

I ordered myself a cocktail then stood by the bar and slowly scanned the room. Couldn't see him. Then I suddenly felt a soft kiss on my neck. "Hello, beautiful." A recognisable, soft French accent.

I swung around and threw my arms over his shoulders with delight. "Francois!"

He spoke softly, in my ear. "It's so good to see you back. I 'ave thought about you all week. You are a beautiful and such fun woman."

"Ahh, you are *so* sweet. How are you?"

"I am very good but very, very, busy tonight... but I will make time for you. I will come and see you later and bring you strawberries."

I giggled as Francois kissed me on the neck again, then he smiled and walked away to tend to business. As I wandered off to find a sofa, I thought maybe Francois had had the idea of taking me to the larder again. I wasn't going. However, depending on how the evening went, I might be tempted to upgrade to my bedroom.

Flirting eyes, a touch here and there, whispers, raised heartbeats, me turning down the larder, Francois looking disappointed, me offering an alternative, my bedroom, later, Francois looking thrilled. We couldn't wait for the next three hours to pass for Francois to finish his shift, at two a.m. Callie, had met someone in the club, who she rather liked, so would be going home with him.

It seemed an eternity before we tumbled through the door to the flat. The dogs greeted the Frenchman, who greeted them back, then Francois followed me into the living room.

"You 'ave a beautiful 'om! and you 'ave two beautiful dogs."

"Thank you, darling, sit down and make yourself comfortable. I'll get us a drink."

"Where is the bedroom?"

"Down there, on the left."

"May I 'ave a look?"

"Help yourself."

I wondered if he would come back. He didn't, so I chewed some fresh gum and took the drinks to the bedroom, where Francois had turned the bedroom lamps on and was now lying naked, apart from his underpants.

"I am so 'ot, I worked so 'ard tonight."

"Yes, it's very warm. I'll open the terrace door," I said, placing the glasses on the bedside table.

"You 'ave a terrace?"

"Yes, here." I pulled back the curtains to reveal.

"Yes, you really 'ave a beautiful 'ome, a beautiful 'ome for a beautiful woman."

Suddenly I felt like I was in a scene from 'Allo, Allo' and giggled.

'Come 'ere and tell me why you are laughing."

"Because you are so lovely, Francois."

I sat beside him on the bed.

"You 'ad fun in the small room with me, then?" he asked, holding my hand.

I giggled again.

"Small room… it was a larder! Yes, it was great fun. First time for me… doing it somewhere unusual like that… felt very naughty. Glad I've done it. Can you see where the thrill comes from?"

"Are you ready for me to thrill you again, ma Cherie?"

"I certainly am," I said, throwing myself backwards onto the bed waiting to be ravaged.

And ravaged I was. We were both insanely rampant after the long wait. Francois had every item of clothing off me, in under a minute. A few minutes of French kisses later, despite the gum which I still had tucked down the side of my inner cheek, Francois suddenly got up on his knees, swung around and aimed his penis at my mouth. I suddenly reached into my cheek with my tongue, to retrieve the gum. I wasn't fast enough. His penis lunged at me with such speed and power, that as I opened my mouth, his penis went in. Pictorially, it was rather like a large python darting into a hole. I saw it as the camera would, from inside the hole. Not wanting to spoil the moment, I wiggled the gum to the front of my mouth, moved my hand in and tried to discreetly retrieve it with my fingers. The gum was quite sticky and a large part of it stuck to my lips. As I tried to pull it away, it left a thread-thin trail across my fingers. I went back, a second time, for the piece still attached to my lips. In doing so, what with the lunging and all, the gum somehow attached itself to Francois' pubic hairs. I pulled at it gently but just made more threads. I began to feel like a fly trapped in a web. I started to wrap the threads around my fingers. Lunge, lunge. I didn't give up. Good job girls can deal with two things at once, I thought. Still not wanting to spoil the moment, I stuck what I could on the headboard and got involved in the action. And excellent action it was, after the rather bizarre start.

After an hour of fit fun and ravaging, Francois was lying on his back in a deep sleep. I looked at his fit, firm young body. Not a big guy but beautifully formed. His skin colour was definitely more Italian than French. His face also. No, he definitely didn't look French.

I suddenly remembered the gum. I quietly and carefully turned the lamps up and leant over to check out Francois' pubes. Hairy gum. There it was. All caught up. A piece in his groin and a piece closer to the base of his penis. What should I do? Tell him in the morning? I would have to tell him. What if he had lied about not having a girlfriend but really did, and what if she had found it! Hard one to get away with. But, then again, if he had a girlfriend, he wouldn't have spent the night, would he.

Not feeling as tired as Francois, I sat up in bed and rolled a joint. Puffing away, I looked more closely at the gum. Should I attempt to cut it out? It looked easy enough to deal with. I decided I would have a go, at the groin area first so quietly and gently, I lifted a small pair of nail scissors from the bedside drawer.

With Francois still fast asleep, I got onto my knees and hunching over, started carefully trimming the hair containing the offending gum. Snip… snip… snip… should I get my glasses? Yes, I should probably get my glasses. Glasses on and ready for the expert surgery. I knelt again, slowly but surely, snipping away, until the stretchy gum was freed. It was a job well done.

I peered at Francois over the top of my glasses. Still in a deep sleep. I checked his pubes again. One piece left in the most sensitive of areas. Could I get to it? It would save the bother of having to deal with it in the morning. However, it was going to require a great deal of skill and a very steady hand. Was I up to it? I decided I was.

I couldn't get enough access to the gum from my side, so I had to creep around the bed and kneel on the floor, to make an entry. I caught sight of myself in the floor to ceiling mirrors. Naked, crazy ravaged hair, make-up smeared, armed with a pair of nail scissors. Scary. But still in control.

Too low, kneeling, I raised up on to my knees and lined the scissor point up, with the hairy gum. Moving in gently, I started to part the soft, black shiny hairs. Horror. It was worse than I thought. Several stretching tentacles were coming from this piece and were spread across a wider area. There were at least half a dozen tentacles. I decided I would remove those first. Delicately, delicately, I cut out the hairy threads, like an expert surgeon, all the time checking over my glasses, that Francois was still sleeping. Slight bald patch but no one would notice.

Even though the de-threading only took a couple of minutes, it was intense work and I needed a break before I tackled the main piece. I headed for the terrace with my vodka and orange, had a sip and breathed in the warm air. Revived, after a little naked star gazing, I had mentally prepared myself for the main operation.

I eyeballed the main piece of gum. This was going to be a real test. I got into position, lined up the scissors again and took a big breath. Just as I was about to go in, Daisy jumped onto the bed. SHIT. I froze. Please don't wake up. Please don't wake up. Then she licked his face. Francois lifted his head slightly and half opened his bleary eyes. He glanced at me hovering above his penis with the scissors in my hand. I didn't know what to do so I just smiled. Then, he just laid back down again without so much as a murmur. How odd, I thought. he must be well out of it.

Francois bolted upright with a jolt, looking totally confused. "What the fuck are you doing with the scissors?" he said, totally startled, trying to focus his eyes.

"Don't panic… It's a long story… sorry, didn't mean to scare you. I'm not going to 'Bobbitt' you."

I couldn't help giggling. Poor man.

"Thank my God, for that, but what are you doing with the scissors?"

"You have chewing gum in your pubes."

'I 'ave what?" said Francois, rubbing his eyes.

"You have gum in your pubes, and I was cutting it out for you…"

"Poobs? What is a poobs?" Francois doubled over, to take a look. "'Ow did THAT get there?"

He squeezed it for confirmation, not realising how much worse he was making matters.

"It is the chewing gum! 'Ow the fuck did THAT got there?"

"It fell out of my mouth."

"It fell out of your mouth and into my dick 'air?"

I started giggling at his funny and beautiful accent.

"Yes, sorry."

"When?"

I started to giggle, again.

"It happened when we were making love."

"Why didn't you say this to me?"

"I didn't want to spoil the moment."

"Very sweet but it would 'ave been better to 'ave said something. I did not know what was 'appening. Sometimes I 'ave noticed that women can be a bit crazy…"

I tried to keep a straight face. "I wasn't being crazy. I was being practical, and I thought I'd save you the hassle."

Francois softened and realising he was going to stay intact, smiled.

"Sorry, Francois."

"It's okay. It was a shock but it is a funny story for my friend, 'e will 'ave a laugh."

Francois relaxed and took a sip from his drink.

"Shall I carry on?" I enquired. "There's only a bit left and I already successfully removed some of the other gum."

"Okay. But you 'ave to be very, very careful."

"Do you trust me?"

"But of course. Enjoy yourself. But be careful. 'Ow much 'ave you 'ad to drink?"

"Enough to carefully have removed this much," I said, showing him the previously trimmed, hairy gum. It looked like something from an early episode of 'Star Trek', only more gruesome.

"Okay, I try to relax. Off you go…"

Francois lay back tentatively, all the time keeping an eye on me while I performed the rest of the surgery.

A few minutes later, all the gum had been extracted. "All done, Francois," I said, kissing him on his balls.

"Ahh. No pain and no blood. You are a good surgeon!" He looked a bit more closely and ruffled his pubes with his fingers.

"A bit of an 'ole, but it's okay… it will come back."

"The gum was in deep. I could trim the rest to match," I suggested.

"No, no, no, it is fine, really, it is a good job. Come and give me a cuddle."

I put the horrible sticky hairy ball in the bin and went to lie next to Francois. Opening his arms to let me in, he wrapped them gently around my naked body, then spoke softly in my ear. "Thank you for taking the gum, you are a very nice lady. Very thoughtful. You did the good job."

"Ahh bless you, no problem, Francois."

"You know, it is so nice to be close to such a woman. You are so warm and kind. It is so 'ard to find a girlfriend in London. The young women all ask the same questions. "'Ow much money do you make? What is your work? What car are you drive?"

I listened caringly and sensitively to Francois' words. Times had definitely changed. I didn't feel it was so much the fault of the 'Thatcher Years' but more the culture of 'Footballer's wives'. A lot of 'sisters', didn't seem so keen on 'doing it for themselves' these days.

"Francois, you are a lovely, warm, funny, sensitive man. And you are *so* young, darling. You will find somebody."

"It is 'ard to meet someone because I only sleep and work at the 10room."

"Don't worry. It will happen."

I felt there was nothing more I could say so just stroked Francois' hair, until he fell asleep. I decided there and then, that I would love, but would not be intimate with Francois again. I would be there for him as a friend or confident, if required. If Francois lost all interest in me, knowing we wouldn't be intimate again, no problem.

I had a vision of Francois at 10room leading another lady through the swing doors. The great thing was, I felt no anger or hurt. I did not feel compromised or threatened. I would always treasure the memory of my time with Francois for what it was, a crazy, naughty, delightful time with a lovely, warm, handsome young man. I hoped that any other ladies that were taken through the swing doors and into the larder, would have as much fun as I'd had.

THE MOD, THE AA AND THE MOTHER

Friday, 17th May

Eleven a.m. Hasan, called to confirm our date for tonight. I was ready at seven forty-five just in case he came early.

Eight p.m., I'm looking out of the window, for his car to pull up. Eight fifteen, I'm still looking. Eight thirty, I take my coat off and fix myself a drink. Eight forty-five, I roll a joint and put my feet up. Nine p.m., To text or not to text? Nine twenty, I was just about to text him, when he texted me.

Am outside x

My disappointment faded away and I grabbed my coat and rushed down to his car. He stepped out to greet me. "I am SO sorry!" he said, kissing me on the cheek.

He continued, "My fucking car wouldn't start."

That's a bit lame, I thought, but smiled sweetly.

He continued. "You would never believe the 'luck', I have, Gaynor. I don't know what I've done to deserve it."

I climbed into the car.

"Always call or text rather than keep a lady waiting."

"I know, I'm sorry."

I lifted my school mistress stance.

"Where are we going?"

"To a lovely restaurant, in Knightsbridge."

"Cool," I said, at the same time thinking, If one works for the MOD, surely one needs a reliable vehicle.

I let it go.

"Honestly, Gaynor, when I tell you some of the bad luck I have, you won't believe it, and it never seems to end!"

"Don't worry," I said, curling back into the seat.

I took a breath. "So, what do you do for the Ministry of Defence?"

"At the moment, I'm designing helicopters to land on ships at sea."

'Wow!" I said, believing him and not knowing what to say next.

I stopped talking, to let Hasan drive in peace as we made our way down the Edgware Road and onto Park Lane. Park Lane, dark blue. It was the one place I always wanted to buy when playing Monopoly.

"It's not far now," said Hasan, as we drove around Hyde Park Corner and off to the left. "Are you hungry?"

"Sure!" I said, pleasingly, not feeling hungry at all.

I was in a bit of a daydream as the car slowly came to a halt. I looked out of the window to see lots of huge concrete blocks. "Are we there?" I asked enthusiastically.

"FUCK! FUCK! FUCKING FUCK! OH FUCK!" yelled Hasan, appearing very disturbed.

"NO! the fucking car has cut out again."

"Oh," I said, believing his earlier story.

"Where are we?"

"WE'RE OUTSIDE THE FUCKING AMERICAN EMBASSY!"

I took another look at the concrete blocks then thought about the appalling, relatively recent terrorist activities. My head leapt into overdrive.

"I hope they don't thing we are terrorist car bombers," I said, turning my head to look at Hasan's features and skin colour.

He started swearing again, and turning the ignition key frantically, backwards and forwards.

"FUCKING START YOU BASTARD! FUCKING START!"

"Don't worry," I said, turning to him. "It's not a problem."

"It bloody is!" he said, throwing his head back onto the headrest. "We really don't want to be stuck here!"

Suddenly there was a knock on the window on my side. I turned and saw two heavily armed men dressed for combat, both carrying guns. I wound my window down. They threw a torchlight onto my face and held it for a second. Then they lit up, Hasan.

"Why have you stopped here, sir? You can't park here, this is the American Embassy," said one of the armed officers, in an American accent.

"I KNOW IT'S THE AMERICAN EMBASSY!"

Hasan couldn't contain himself and opened the car door and leapt out. The 'soldiers' stepped back quickly, one pointing his gun, at Hasan.

"WE'RE HERE BECAUSE MY FUCKING CAR HAS JUST BROKEN DOWN," he yelled, as he repeatedly kicked his front bumper.

I quickly jumped out of the car to try to calm things down. "We were on our way to have dinner and the car just cut out and we came to a stand-still. No power. It's just gone dead."

Hasan carried on kicking the car.

"Well, you can't park here, mam," repeated the soldier.

"We haven't parked here, we've broken down. The car just stopped!"

"Well, you need to move your car, mam."

"Okay, okay! I'll sort it. I'll get a tow truck organised. HASAN! Get in the car!"

The soldiers backed off and stood beside one of the mammoth concrete blocks.

I tried to calm Hasan. "See! I told you nothing ever goes right for me. I CAN'T EVEN TAKE YOU OUT FOR DINNER."

Now, I really felt for him.

"Okay, calm down. It's not a problem. I wasn't very hungry anyway. Let's get the car moved," I said, reassuringly. "Are you a member of the AA?"

"No, I'm not," responded Hasan, repeatedly banging his head on the steering wheel.

"Well, I am," I said, "and I think I have a policy where they will sort things out, even if I am in someone else's car that has broken down. I think they will send out a tow truck to tow me, and the car I'm in."

Hasan got out of the car again and lifted up the bonnet, while the soldiers, guns at the ready, observed him closely. I rang the AA while he fiddled under the bonnet. I started thinking… MOD. Unreliable car… Not a member of the AA… Not very organised… What if there's an MOD emergency? All very odd.

Twenty minutes later, very efficient, the lovely man in the comforting yellow jacket turned up with his tow truck. The soldiers approached him and asked for I.D. and then he loaded Hasan's car onto the truck. We climbed into the cabin to join the AA man and headed for Finchley, which was where Hasan lived.

"Not a good place to 'break down', mate," he said, to Hasan. Hasan looked at me and raised his eyebrows. I had to stop myself from laughing out loud, so bit my lip hard. Hasan just held his head in his hands, for most of the journey. He had no conversation so I just stroked his back until we arrived in his street.

"Just pull over here please, mate," said Hasan, raising his head, then he turned to me. "I've got a headache from hell."

We jumped out of the truck and the car was unloaded.

"I really am SO sorry, Gaynor. My life is always like this. Thanks for getting my car back home."

"No problem. Shit happens," I said, grabbing his hand. "Can you call me a local cab to take me home? I feel really knackered."

"No problem, but I'll have to go into the house as my phone's out of juice."

I began thinking again. MOD? No car, no phone? What if war breaks out?

I started to follow Hasan, up the street. "Can you wait here?" he asked, politely, turning toward me.

I was shocked. Surely, he's not married!

"Why?"

"Because I live with my mum."

"You live with your MUM?"

"It's a long story... I'll be back in a sec."

Lots of things seemed to be attached to 'long stories'.

Actually, he didn't really need to say any more. After all, I was probably the same age as his mum.

He returned a few minutes later. "Gaynor, I have to go away for a few weeks, can I call you when I get back?"

"MOD. business?" I enquired, thinking he went away, a lot.

"Classified."

I giggled.

"Okay, call me upon your return. We might have better luck next time!"

"Thanks, Gaynor, really sorry about tonight."

"Stop apologising," I said, as a large black Mercedes pulled up. We hugged each other goodbye and I headed off, toward the security of my flat and reliability of my large comfy bed.

MOD INSPECTS THE RABBIT

Tuesday, 18th June

Hasan was due at eight p.m. He wanted to attempt to take me out for dinner again.

At nine p.m., I texted him.

Have you crashed?

Sorry. Be there in twenty mins x

He pulled up in a borrowed, blue sports car. It was a lovely warm summer evening and I was hanging over the balcony with my camera. He came strolling towards the house. Those fab shoulders, his olive skin against a white T shirt, black jeans and shades. I called to him, camera at the ready. "Hi, Hasan!"

He looked up, spotted me, lifted his sunglasses from his face, and gave a big beautiful smile.

Click, click. Click, click. He threw back his head and laughed.

"Hi! How are you?" he called back.

"I'm a lady-in-waiting," I responded, smiling and forgiving his lateness, again.

"Sorry I'm late."

On first meeting, my two dogs, Daisy and Flo, greeted Hasan like a long-lost friend, jumping up at his knees, desperate for attention. He obliged, while I patiently watched, all the time thinking, What about me? What about me? Look at me! He finally lifted his head and smiled. I opened my arms and hugged him. It was hard to let go but I managed to tug myself away after about four seconds. He smelled all clean and yummy.

Having consumed three quarters of a bottle of Champagne while waiting for Hasan, I told him I couldn't be arsed going out to eat so we opted for a 'bring to you' pizza. We knelt on the floor next to each other and tucked in like a couple of hungry kids at a picnic. I could feel the grease from the cheese running down my chin. That'll look nice, I thought and quickly grabbed a napkin.

Pizza finished. Hasan started telling me a few of his 'bad luck' stories. It was easy to understand why this guy thought he was jinxed. This is a man who:

1) Share certificates got lost in the post before Black Wednesday

2) Lent £10,000, to a mate who did a runner

3) Broke down after rescuing someone else who had broken down (key snapped in his ignition)

4) Was locked out of his mum's house (forgot his keys and his mum was in Turkey) and got stuck in small window. A passer-by had called the police while shouting at him, "Serves you right, you thieving, hooligan bastard!"

5) Innocently used someone else's Domain name and was called to trial in the USA.

Well, as the stories got worse and worse, I started to see the funny side of Hasan's tragedies and about an hour later, I was doubled over with laughter, tears rolling down my face. I could not stop laughing. It took me about ten minutes to calm down and I had the sorest tummy muscles. Thank God, Hasan could see the funny side of it and the more I laughed, the more he would feed me those sad, sad stories. A man hadn't made me laugh like that since I was at school. He was hilarious.

Having recovered, Hasan changed the subject and asked if he could see the Rampant Rabbit, I had told him, I had bought.

"Have you seen one before?" I asked.

"No, I haven't."

I popped into the bedroom to get it. Hasan lifted it carefully from the box. "So how does it work then?"

Presuming he didn't want a personal demonstration, I started pressing various buttons.

"This one, makes this go around, this one makes it go the other way, these balls rotate all at the same time, this button makes the rabbit vibrate at this speed and this button makes it go faster, then even faster!"

"Mmmm," he said, lifting his hand to his chin, like a thinking professor.

He held the vibrator in his hand and looked down it lengthways, then inspected underneath and then held up to the light.

"Right, so that means the vibrating Rabbit is running independently from the shaft, although they are running from the same power source. You see this wire here, it's connected to this one here. God I'd love to take it apart!"

Mmmm. Maybe he does work for the MOD, certainly interested in mechanics and engineering.

"It's yours for £30," I said.

"How much?" he said, somewhat surprised, handing it back to me.

"Best £30 I ever spent," I said proudly.

Hasan had a real innocence about him. He didn't even ask if I'd tried it out. What a gentleman.

Back safely in the box, I decided to spread myself along the sofa. Hasan, who was still sitting on the floor, let his head fall back until it touched my thigh. He turned and climbed carefully and slowly onto the sofa, next to me. Putting his hand behind my neck and lifting my face towards him, he kissed me softly and on doing so, the CD jumped. The more he kissed me, the more the music kept jumping. I giggled with Hasan still in my mouth, he knew why, then started giggling himself.

"See what I mean," he said.

Then he turned ninety degrees towards me, so his head was by my knees. He lifted up my purple silk dress to reveal my white cotton knickers.

"Now let's see what's going on down here," he whispered.

I shrieked, giggled, and pulled my knees up and together. I felt shy. There was a lamp on the side that was throwing light onto my knickered vagina.

"Can we go to the bedroom?" I said.

I was aware that I must have sounded like an innocent schoolgirl. The sophisticated forty-sevenyear-old had gone straight out of the window. I realised at that moment that I still have a bit of a problem with men looking at my bits. It's not so bad if it's very subdued lighting or I'm under the sheets but with that lamp, I felt like I was going to be inspected. It would be like having a cervical smear without the stirrups.

"Come on then," he said, taking my hand.

I jumped onto the bed enthusiastically after removing just my dress then laid down and grabbed a cushion from where to peep behind. Still with no urgency from Hasan, I watched him undress down to underpants in slow motion. I wondered whether he moved so slowly because he had the same metabolic rate as a sloth or, perhaps because his brain worked in a different way from other people's. He always seemed to have more than one thing on his mind at a time, a bit like ladies having to concentrate on two things at once, except, ladies were able to move quickly even when in this phase. Hasan climbed into bed and with all interest in my body parts having disappeared then cuddling me, he dozed off.

DIRTY SHEETS

It was the following morning and I could hear Hasan moving around. I opened my eyes and caught site of myself in the wardrobe mirror. I looked like a scarecrow on acid. I quickly calmed down my hair and grabbed my night slip. The duvet was half on and half off the bed and as I lifted it to give it a shake, I was shocked to see a brown 'leakage' stain on the white bed sheet. Where the fuck did that come from? was my first thought. It was, where I had been lying for most of the night, although Hasan, had been there earlier. It can't be me, I thought, quickly feeling the back of my knickers. Of course it's not me! I don't 'leak' from my bottom. I said to myself. Crikey, maybe it was Hasan... maybe he doesn't know.

I removed the sheet like lightning, threw it into the laundry basket and jumped back into bed as though nothing had happened.

Hasan came strolling into the room and smiled. "Hi... How are you?"

"Great!" I said, with a broad smile.

He grabbed a towel and strolled back into the bathroom. My mind returned to the stain. What I was confused about, was that Callie had told me about 'leakage' stains but I couldn't understand why they were in my bed when neither of us had been anywhere near each other's bottoms. Now, I may be wearing my 'stiff knickers' but my bottom is a one-way exit only. No entry allowed, under any circumstances.

Daisy jumped up onto the bed to greet me good morning and after she had licked my face, she turned around for me to scratch her back. As my hand went towards it, I spotted a brown stain right under her tail. Both shocked and delighted (because it hadn't been either one of us), I ushered Daisy out onto the terrace. On the way, I noticed a little trail of diarrhoea spots on the pale carpet. I grabbed a can of spray and squirted the little bastards with Vanish Power Shot, until they fizzled into near oblivion. I finished them off with a quick rub with a cloth.

"Daisy's got diarrhoea," I called to Hasan, in the bathroom.

"Oh, it's her, is it?" came back the reply.

God, he's been in the bathroom for the last ten minutes thinking it was me.

"Yes! Do you remember? She climbed into bed with us last night. She's on the terrace, I need to shower her."

"Ahh, poor Daisy," said Hasan, sympathetically, as he left the bathroom.

"She's never had diarrhoea, before," I said, trying to apologise for her.

Suddenly I thought that Hasan might think I was blaming Daisy for the leakage, so I grabbed him and took him out to the terrace.

"Look at Daisy's bottom," I said, gently lifting her tail up a little.

"Awww, poor Daisy," he said, again, stroking the top of her head.

Good. Confirmation complete, via evidence.

Hasan left after some tea and toast and as soon as I waved him off, I went and washed Daisy's bum. All sparkly and clean, I crashed back onto the bed and grabbed my mobile phone and sent a text to Hasan.

Lovely to see you, Hasan X

I put the mobile down, closed my eyes and lay back on the bed. Then, I heard a muffled, unrecognised, tune. Diddle, diddle, squeak-squeak, diddle, diddle, squeak-squeak.

FUCK I thought, He's left his bloody mobile phone. Diddle, diddle, squeak-squeak. Such a strange tune, I'd never heard one like that before.

For the next half an hour, when I should have been reliving the joys of the night before, I was instead thinking, what will he do without his phone… how the hell can I get it back to him… someone important from the MOD might call… should I pick it up if it rings? I should, in case Hasan tries to contact me… But what if it's his mother! I wondered if Hasan would have made a note of my number anywhere. No, don't be daft. Boys aren't that organised.

His phone rang again. I lifted it from its case and opened it. I pressed the answer button. "Please state your name for voice recognition, followed by keying in your code."

FUCK! IT'S THE MOD! I quickly hung up.

I was just drifting into a sleep and my mobile rang. It just displayed 'CALL' so I didn't know who it was. No number recognition. I took the call anyway.

"Hello."

"Hi, it's Hasan. I left my mobile phone."

"Of course, you did," I laughed. "How did you get my number? Don't tell me you are the 'one in a million' blokes who sensibly copies numbers into an address book!"

Hasan laughed.

"No, I told you, I remember numbers. I'd asked you your number and you told me what it was."

He was right, I had, and he HAD remembered. Although I felt he had an interesting and at times, remarkable mind, I hadn't realised, he was one of those people with a special gift for numbers. I was impressed. Mmmmm. Maybe the MOD *would* be likely to hire someone like him.

Daisy jumped onto the bed with her cleanly washed bum. She doubled over and started licking it. Lovely I thought, as I was reminded that she had been licking my face after I'd woken up.

BUNTY'S BIRTHDAY

Friday, 28th June

Seven p.m. It was my dear friend, Dorothy Banbridge, aka 'Bunty's', fortieth birthday and she had come to stay with me in London for a break.

With presents open, Champagne toasts and latest gossip exchanged, we decided to go to the Groucho Club, for more Champagne.

Jumping out of the cab, we entered through the swing doors to be greeted at reception by the manager. "Good evening, ladies."

"It's Bunty's birthday!" I announced, excitedly.

"Happy birthday, Bunty! First bottle on the house."

"How lovely. Thanks, darling," she responded, as he led us to a lovely comfy semi-circular seat. Champagne delivered and poured, we picked up our glasses and clinked.

"Cheers, darling, up your bum," said Bunty.

"Up yours," I responded, as we both giggled.

As we drank and giggled, old friends and acquaintances popped over to us to say hi. We hadn't been in the Groucho for months and it was nice to see all the regular friendly faces. I announced to everyone that it was Bunty's birthday and bottles of Champagne kept appearing on the table. Looking at the seven bottles, Bunty turned to me and whispered in my ear. "Stop telling people it's my birthday, Gaynor."

"Why? It is."

"Because we have more than enough Champagne to keep us going. I'm going to have to leave most of these behind the bar."

"Okay," I said, sitting back realising my announcements were filling up our little round table, fast.

We were just finishing the second bottle and I needed the loo. As I went to uncross my legs, my knee lifted the table, tipping it onto its side. Bunty shrieked and jumped out of the way, causing heads to turn. All the unopened bottles clanked loudly, then bounced on the carpet, rolling off in different directions. Our half-filled glasses followed. All the chatting stopped and the Groucho fell silent. The floor resembled a bowling alley and I couldn't help myself from shouting, "STRIKE!" After a brief pause, a few people started laughing and then the chatting resumed.

Two waiters hurried over with napkins and paper towels. "I'm sorry about that," I said, grimacing.

"No problem," they responded in unison, while frantically picking up the green skittles. The floor definitely looked like a bowling alley.

Embarrassed, Bunty followed me to the loo.

"I think we should go for a dance now," I said, enthusiastically.

"Where?"

"10room. It's a great club with great music and it's just around the corner."

"Okay, great. I haven't had a bop for ages."

Champagne saved behind the bar, we trotted off, arm in arm to 10room.

The place was buzzing. I had a quick search for Francois but couldn't see him. Bunty wasn't aware of our brief encounter. It wasn't long before we were up on our feet, giving it all, to Destiny's Child. I closed my eyes and got lost in the music, except for occasionally, when I would open my eyes to see if I liked the look of any of the men, who came to dance in front us. If I didn't, I would close my eyes again and just lose myself. I ended up dancing, most of the night, with my eyes shut.

It was about one thirty when Bunty and I crashed onto a sofa for a ciggy and some ice-cold water. What appeared to be a rather nice group of lads had just come into the club and were sitting a few tables away.

"They might have potential," said Bunty. "I wonder what they look like close up?"

It was pretty dark in 10room so I decided to walk to the toilet the long way around so I could get a better view. The closer I got, the better they looked. Two of them glanced in my direction but before I had a chance to smile, they looked away. Bum, I thought, as I watched the potential fade.

We decided it was time to go back home and headed off to pay the bill. Bunty stood by the exit as I 'cheek-kissed' various waiters goodbye.

I turned back to Bunty, who was standing by the exit. She had a stunningly beautiful black guy chatting in her ear. Excellent, I thought, and on closer inspection was more delighted to discover it was one of the lads from the group we had been checking out. He gave me a welcoming smile as I approached. He's bloody lovely, I thought.

Bunty introduced him. "This is Chris and he wants to know if we would like to go with him and his friends to Elysium for a glass of Champagne, they have a table booked."

"Great," I said. "Where's Elysium?"

"Just around the corner, on Piccadilly," responded Chris.

"The only trouble is…" said Bunty, as Chris wandered off to tell his friends, "I like the look of his mate, the guy over there in the white T-shirt. He's got such lovely arms."

"Don't worry about that," I said confidently, "I'll distract Chris."

Walking around the corner to Piccadilly, Chris was constantly at Bunty's side chatting in her ear while I walked with the other four. This is going to be tricky, I thought.

We hadn't been to Elysium before and on arriving, we wound our way downstairs through a large bar with lots, and I mean lots, of men. Beyond that, we zig-zagged amongst the dancers until we were shown to our table. The atmosphere was fab.

More Champagne was ordered and Chris plonked himself next to Bunty. I went and sat next to the guy in the white T-shirt. "Hi, I'm Gaynor."

"Hi… I'm Mac," responded the softly spoken man.

He seemed quite shy and a bit unsure of himself.

"Hi, Mac," I said, reaching out to shake his hand, while studying his face.

He was a good-looking man. Soft, sexy brown eyes which were kind of sleepy, lovely eyelashes which curled upwards, a pleasant smile, dark hair and yes, Bunty was right, he did have fabulous arms. He reminded me a bit of John Cusack.

"Bunty thinks you're lovely," I said with a big smile.

"I think she's lovely… but my best friend likes her too, and he got in first."

Admirable, I thought, then went straight over to Chris and whispered in his ear. "Chris, please don't take this badly, you're totally gorgeous but my friend has had her eye on Mac, ever since she spotted him in 10room."

He looked at me, slightly surprised, slightly disappointed, then went to get out of his seat.

"Don't want to talk to me then?" I spouted, as he rose to standing position.

He leant towards my ear. "It's not that, and yes of course I want to talk to you. It's just, I wouldn't dream of being so discourteous, as to make a move on you, when I've just made a move on your friend."

Then he went and sat next to Mac for a chat. I could see Mac shaking his head. He obviously felt awkward that Chris had made a move on Bunty first. I could see from their body language that they were close and after a bit of encouragement from a most gracious loser, Chris, Mac went and sat next to Bunty. What a lovely bloke, I thought getting up from my seat as Chris took my hand and led me onto the dance floor.

I danced the next three tracks with my eyes open. Chris was a lovely man to watch. Tall, smashing physique, beautifully shaved head, great smile and a lovely mover.

We sat down and started chatting. He was nicely spoken with a mellow, husky voice and cheeky, husky laugh.

"So, what do you do?" he asked.

"My marriage broke up six months ago, so at the moment, I'm a social butterfly. I'm spreading my wings and thoroughly enjoying myself."

Before he had a chance to respond, I threw the question back at him. "So, what do you do, Chris?"

"Criminal lawyer."

"Criminal lawyer?" I felt my eyebrows rising.

"Yes, we *all* are."

Bloody hell, I thought, a whole heard of criminal lawyers. How bloody marvellous.

Mac and Bunty were now sitting face to face and holding hands. Aaah, I thought, I must make sure Bunty feels comfortable enough to bring Mac back to the flat.

"Fancy coming back with Mac to our place for a smoke?" I asked Chris, then remembered they were all criminal lawyers. He looked surprised but tried to hide it.

"Sounds good, not just a smoke I hope," he said.

Now, I was somewhat surprised but pretended I hadn't heard him. Bit presumptuous, and cheeky, I thought. He had just said he wouldn't dream of being so discourteous as to make a move on me. Mind, I could quite happily throw him onto my bed.

We got back to the flat at three thirty a.m. and had a cup of tea. Not because we wanted one but because there was no booze left in the house and it seemed the polite thing to do. Chris went to the loo, Bunty was in the kitchen so Mac asked me if he could have a look round the flat. After a quick tour, we returned to the living room.

"Great flat," said Mac, to Chris.

Chris sat up in his seat eagerly and went to speak. I spoke first. "Would you like to see it, Chris?" I said politely, wanting him not to feel left out.

'I'd love to," he responded, enthusiastically.

Mmmmm, especially the bedroom, I thought.

I showed him the kitchen, terrace then my bedroom.

"If you lie in the middle of the bed and look out the window, all you can see is the church," I said, pointing at the spire.

"I can't get onto the bed with my shoes on," he said, slipping them off.

He lay down and looked out of the window. "That's really nice, isn't it," he said, then slowly reached for my hand. I was still standing and stepped towards him. He gently pulled me until I was seated on the bed. I suddenly remembered I was having my period and realised, I had to say something.

"Um... er..."

For some reason I found it hard to say.

"What is it?" asked Chris, intuitively.

"Well... the thing is... I'm sort of having my period at the moment."

He smiled and pulled me closer toward him. He lifted his arm and placed my head on his chest.

"I suppose you must be used to crime scenes, being a criminal lawyer and all that," I said.

He threw back his head and laughed and then pulled me even closer. I lay there quietly for a minute enjoying his arms around me.

Then he kissed me. And it was a kiss to die for. So soft, so pure, so sweet. This is going to be fab, I thought. And it was.

***

Chris fell asleep about six a.m., so I got up and went out to the terrace for a cup of tea and a joint. It was a beautiful morning and I watched the changing shadows on the church spire as the sun moved across the sky. It felt good to be alive.

Returning to the bedroom, I looked at the warm summer light spilling across everything. I sat on the chair and looked at Chris. He stirred, then opened his eyes, as though he knew. He smiled and as I smiled back, he lifted the covers inviting me back into bed. He slipped his hand around my waist and went back to sleep. I lay there thinking about my life for about an hour, then snuck out of bed again. This time I needed food. I was starving. In the kitchen all I could find was an avocado pear, cheese and onion crisps and Rice Krispies. I settled for the Rice Krispies and for some reason, my senses felt heightened as I became very aware of the snap, crackle and pop in my bowl. Tummy satisfied, I snuck back into bed and fell asleep.

It was nine a.m. when we woke up, and Chris asked me to call a cab for him, to arrive in fifteen minutes. He stepped out of bed and I looked at his toned body.

"Do you play any sport or work out?" I asked. "You look very fit."

He smiled.

"No, not really… haven't got the time… just football on Saturday afternoons."

He pulled on his clothes, went to the bathroom, came back, and then leant across the bed to give me a kiss goodbye. I jumped out of bed to give him a hug. When I stood next to him, I realised he was taller than I had thought. Then I remembered, I'd been wearing 3" heels the night before and I hadn't kicked them off until I got into bed. I looked up. He gave me a lovely smile then put his arms around my waist in a way that made me feel 'all woman'. And he, was the most definitely, undeniably, unmistakably, categorically, 100% all man.

He asked for my telephone number before he left, and also gave me his. He said if I fancied going out again, to give him a call.

RACISM, SEXISM AND ADVERTISING

Sunday, 30th June

The following morning, Bunty jumped into my bed.

"Have you ever slept with a black fellow before, Gayn's?"

"Yes, last night."

"No, I mean *before* last night."

"Have you ever slept with a criminal lawyer, Bunty?" I laughed.

Bunty jabbed me in the side.

I went on, "No, but only because when I met some, I was already in relationships. I HATE racism!"

"Me too," said Bunty.

"Do you know, when I worked in advertising, there were around 500 people in our agency and only ONE black person! I remember writing a television ad, in around 1986, which had all black people in, no whites. It was just rejected out of hand without so much as a second thought. I vaguely remember, someone in our creative department had done poster ad, which contained loads of people. I think the poster had to include one black person, for every ten white people... It was something like that, anyway. Also, I was only one of two females in our creative department which consisted of fifty men. Creative departments have always been extremely sexist AND even though 80% of advertising is aimed at women, the ads are invariably written by men! Do you remember a TV ad in the sixties, called Unzip a banana? Written by a man, of course! And, twenty years later, *that* Flake ad, again, written by a man! In the eighties, despite other departments such as account handling, media buying, production, research, all having around fifty-fifty split of males and females, creative departments were totally male dominated. I think across London agencies there were just one, or maybe two, female creative directors. It took me fucking ages to get my foot in the door. When I went for interviews, I was told things like, 'What's the point, you'll be having kids in a few years'. Some bastard from CDP said to me, 'Don't think that just because you're good looking, you'll get a job here!' He hadn't even looked at my work and my portfolio of ideas was EXCELLENT. I'd had the best creative, award winning, legendary 'Ad man', teacher… a guy called Dave Trott."

Bunty listened intently.

"Dave Trott had returned to London, from an agency in USA, and had realized that very few people understood 'good advertising'. It wasn't about 'execution' it was about IDEAS."

"So, who hired you, then?"

"A creative director called Mike Chapman from a top London agency, after I'd been interviewed by him and his copywriter, Chips Hardy. Mike and Chips had the intelligence to put gender to one side and just look at my ideas. They loved my folio so I was given a three-month trial. I worked my ass off and was then employed. I am forever grateful to Mr Trott Mr Chapman and Mr Hardy. I was at that agency for ten years and loved every minute of it."

"So why did you leave, then?"

"I didn't leave, I was 'let go'."

"Why?"

"They were looking at cutting back, in all departments to cut costs. I couldn't believe it. I had won many awards and that particular year, I was nominated for more awards, along with my writer, than any other team in the creative department."

"Why you, then?"

"I'll tell you why, Randy Cracknail, the new creative director, had heard I was going through IVF. He called me into his office one lunchtime, and said, 'Hi, Gaynor, you know we are cutting back on people at the moment across all departments, well, I've heard you are doing IVF and trying to get pregnant so I'm afraid I'll have to let you go'. I sat there and couldn't speak. My throat had closed up completely. He carried on, 'Well, I have to tell you, I have never seen someone taking *that* information with such dignity'. I still couldn't speak. I was in fact, in total shock. I felt totally traumatized. I had had no intention of leaving advertising, even if I'd had children. I left his office without saying a single word. AND, worse still, my male copywriter was not 'let go' he was allowed to stay. Randy Cracknail was a horrible man, a sexist bastard. I remember walking into his office on one occasion and he said, 'So, what colour knickers are you wearing today, Gaynor?' I felt sick, didn't reply and dismissed his unacceptable, impertinent, outrageous question, out of hand. I had always felt he hadn't taken me seriously, ever since he had joined the agency, a year or so, previously.

Bunty was horrified. "What a horrible, fucking, dirty, sexist bastard!"

"Also, all the other people that were let go of, were expected to pack up their stuff and leave the agency that day. I did go home that lunchtime, but as I lay on my sofa, I thought, I am NOT walking out of that agency with my tail between my legs as though I'd done something wrong. I hadn't. I had worked extremely hard for the agency and was incredibly loyal. I hadn't been 'fired' I had been 'let go'. Anyway, I had lots of friends there and wanted to have a leaving party."

"Carry on," said Bunty.

"Okay, so the next morning, I got up and got ready for work as usual. When I arrived at the agency, I was stopped at the door by the elderly security guy, who had been there for years. We had always been very friendly toward each other. Most people just walked past him but I had *always* said, Good morning or Goodbye."

"You can't come in."

"What are you talking about? I can't come in. I work here, until the end of the month anyway."

"I've been told not to let you in."

"I'm coming in," I said, pushing him to one side.

I went up to the third floor to my desk and sat down to work, as usual. A few of the people walking past, who had obviously heard the news, stuck their head in the door and said things like, "Really sorry, Gaynor, it shouldn't have been you."

"What are you doing here, I thought that bastard had fired you."

"Gaynor! I thought you had been fired!"

"I'll be leaving in four weeks. It's in my contract, so Mr Bastard can't just chuck me out. Also, I'm having a leaving party, so please come."

After that, no one in authority approached me. I was pleased with myself. I had shown I had style and balls. And, do you know what, about 200 people came to my leaving party."

"That's quite a story," said Bunty. Now, about last night, did you have a nice time?"

"It was beautiful. He is lovely and a total gentleman… and, he gave me his phone number."

"Did he?" responded Bunty, trying not to look surprised.

"Did Mac give you his number?"

"No, he didn't. Maybe we should swap partners!" she said, with a cheeky smile.

"You had your chance," Bunty, I said, smiling more.

We pulled the duvet over ourselves and slept through until about eight p.m. Bunty went to get a bowl of Rice Krispies, while I texted Chris's mobile.

Hi, Chris, just wanted to say thank you for a lovely evening and wondered if you and Mac are up to anything on Thursday evening? If not, you might like to come to a birthday cabaret at The Globe Restaurant with me and Bunty? It's the manager, Neil's, fortieth birthday. Let me know asap in case I need to book a bigger table, cabaret nights are very busy! If you can't make it, no worries. Bye. x

WINALOT

Monday, 1ˢᵗ July

Four p.m. Can't wait any longer and ring Chris to see if they're coming, I need to get the table booked.

Chris picked up the phone. "Hi, Gaynor," he said, enthusiastically. "I was going to call you later. (I could hear people in the background and kicked myself for not being patient.) I spoke to Mac and we would like to come on Thursday."

"Excellent, if you come here at about seven thirty we can have a glass of Champagne before we go," I said chirpily, in return (wondering whether he still had a thing for Bunty).

"I'll call you in the week," he said.

"Okay, bye, Chris."

I yelled to Bunty, excitedly, "They're coming to the cabaret on Thursday! Hurrah!"

She walked into my room. "Are they? Great! That'll be fun."

She returned to the kitchen with a broad smile.

***

It was 8.20 p.m., and me and Bunty were going through all the fantastic photos we had taken on her birthday. I must say Bunty and I were looking rather gorgeous, in most of them. The candy pink, 'Jackie O' dress that I had bought, made me feel quite fab and I remembered that Callie had squealed, 'It's Lady Penelope!' when she had first seen me wearing it.

I was distracted by my mobile phone ringing and raced round the flat looking for it. It could be… anyone, I thought. Found, I lifted it from the bed and read the name 'HASAN'.

"Hi, Hasan."

"Hi, Gaynor, how are you?"

"Fantastic! How are you?"

"Tired… and I've got a headache."

He's rung me up, to tell me he's tired and has a headache, I thought, bless him. I told him about the lovely shots I had taken of him when he stayed over.

"Why don't you pop around to see them. You can stay over if you like…"

Bunty pushed my knee.

"I'd love to but I'm really tired," he said.

"You don't have to shag me," I said. "We can just have a cuddle and you can go to bed whenever you're ready. I promise to be a good girl."

Bunty pushed my knee again, wide mouthed.

"Okay then… but I am really tired… I'll be around in about an hour."

I turned to Bunty. "He's coming over in a couple of hours," I said, remembering his 'time keeping'.

"God! Rather you than me. Aren't you knackered?"

"No, but don't worry, he is."

Keeping in mind, the conversation with Hasan, that he was too tired for sex, I decided I would respect what he had said. Then, I ran a quick bath and shaved my legs, just in case.

Two hours later, I saw Hasan pull up outside, through the kitchen window. I grabbed Daisy and Flo and put them in the bedroom. I had decided that I was going to get the attention first, this evening.

He rang the buzzer. I let him in and peered over the banisters. He was holding on to the rail and was pulling himself up the stairs at half speed. I beamed as he came around the corner.

"Hi, Babe."

"Hello," he said, slightly flatly.

After climbing the last few stairs, he fell into my arms. I changed my tone immediately.

"Ahhh, are you knackered, darling?" I asked, sympathetically.

I felt like a mum whose son had just come back from camp and patted him on the back.

"Fucking knackered," he sighed. "I've worked about seventy hours this week."

"MOD are busy then…"

I kissed his cheek and held him up for a moment. He was looking over my shoulder and I could hear Daisy and Flo whimpering at the bedroom door.

"I've got treats!" he claimed, with a bit more enthusiasm.

"Oooo, how exciting!" I said, as he put his hand in his jacket pocket. "Shall I close my eyes?"

"No, it's okay," he said, lifting a bag of Winalot Allsorts out. "I bought these for the dogs."

"Oh, how sweet of you," I said, wondering where my gift was. "Do you have anything for me in your pocket? A Mars Bar, perhaps?"

He looked up and laughed, then said, "How about this…" engaging me in a sensitive, lingering kiss.

"That'll do nicely," I said, meaning it, but also feeling a bit jealous of Daisy and Flo.

Hasan looked towards the bedroom door. He wanted to see the dogs and the dogs wanted to see him. I let them out.

"Hi, girls," he said, enthusiastically, as they jumped up at his legs. He looked over to me and smiled, then carried on patting the dogs.

I made him tea and then got out the photographs.

"Look at this, you look like Andy Garcia," I said, excitedly handing him the first one, "and every girlfriend of mine that has seen these, has gone PHWOAR! WHO IS THAT?"

Hasan laughed and agreed he did look rather good.

"Actually, Hasan," I said. "You look really good in all the shots. You are very photogenic."

While looking through the photos, Hasan seemed to revitalize… slightly. Placing the last one on the floor, he lay back on the sofa with his hands over his brow.

"Would you like to go to bed?"

"Yes… Do you mind? I really am exhausted."

"Off you go then," I said, pulling him up from his seat. "I'll bring you another cup of tea."

"Thanks, Gaynor."

I came into the bedroom with tea for two and some toast. I thought I'd make toast as we weren't going to have sex. It was probably a comfort thing. Hasan wasn't hungry so I ate the four triangles myself. Mmmm, that was yummy, I thought, but then I looked at Hasan and thought but not as yummy as you. I leant over to kiss him goodnight and as I moved away, he pulled me gently, back.

"Okay, I'll stay for a quick cuddle," I said, turning away from him so that we were spooning. I took his hand and put it around my waist. I tried to do it in a way that was friendly but not sexy. I knew he was exhausted and didn't want him to think that I just wanted him there, to 'service me'. I was happy, even only with his company and cuddle, and I wanted him to know that.

He talked quietly in my ear stroking my tummy over my T-shirt. Now it was getting tricky, because I was beginning to get turned on. I was thinking, oh please don't do that, if you're not going to do anything else... I can't bear it. He carried on, stroking and talking in my ear. I could feel my back arching and wanted to stick my bottom against his hips but fought against it. I could feel my breathing changing. Must get up immediately, I thought, as I lay there. No, let's wait and see where this goes, I decided. I tried to calm my breathing, then felt my clothes move and he slowly lifted up my T-shirt. I arched my back as he ran his hand from my tummy up over my chest, then he gently buried his fingers in my cleavage. Sex? No sex? Sex? No sex? Pause. Then he went to sleep. He really didn't want sex. He just wanted comfort.

CRIMINAL ACTIVITY

Thursday, 4ᵗʰ July

It was Neil's fortieth birthday party at The Globe. Chris hadn't called me back and it was now six p.m.

"We've been dumped! How bloody dare they!" said Bunty, indignantly, looking at the clock.

With no Chris and no Mac, Bunty and I decided not to attend Neil's birthday cabaret. I wasn't really bothered anyway because I wasn't very close to Neil. I considered, that Chris was, perhaps, still really into Bunty and not me and that was the reason he had decided not to call. Either way, or whatever, it was all fine. Besides, Chris was lovely and we'd had a great night together.

Blown out, we decided we would stay in, drink, get a lovely take away, get totally stoned and watch lots of great videos — Catch Me If You Can, A Beautiful Mind and The Colour Purple. It was a fantastic second option and we were all excited about the prospect of our imminent 'girly' night in.

Settled, and in comfy jimmy-jams, Bunty rolled a big, fat, joint, then we clinked our first glass of Champagne.

"Who needs men anyway!"

BANANA MAN

Saturday, 6th July

Into Globe Bar for a few drinks, then Bunty, Callie and I, cabbed off to 10room It had been one of those evenings where no matter what I had put on, I hadn't been comfortable in it. To make matters worse and despite having just spent £20 on a wash and blow dry, I wasn't happy with my hair so I stupidly decided to give myself a bit of a trim, on the front sides.

Big mistake.

"BUNTY! I'VE DONE SOMETHING TERRIBLE TO MY HAIR," I yelled, as I realised just how short I'd cut it.

I was holding onto two short sections, either side of my face as she came rushing into the bedroom. "What do you mean?" she said, prising my hair from my hands.

"Ooo fuck! How much did you cut off?"

"About three inches."

"THREE INCHES! ARE YOU MAD?"

"I was trying to make them even," I whined.

"Don't worry, give me the scissors," she said confidently.

"Just thin it out a bit, so it's not so 'blocky'," I responded, nervously, handing her the scissors. She took her time and was very careful. It turned out okay-ish.

On arriving at 10room, I went straight to the loos, to check out my hair. I tried 'stretching' it by pulling it hard, down the sides of my face. Bollocks. There was nothing I could really do to make any difference so I decided to forget about it. I made my way around the dance floor until I spotted Callie and Bunty seated at a table. We weren't there for long. Dancing had very much been on our minds that evening so we left our seats and boogied around the floor for a couple of hours until we were exhausted.

An hour later, after lots of water and pop, we were about to leave, when a smartly dressed man in a suit with open necked shirt, came toward to me. "You are a great dancer, may I dance with you?" he said, softly, holding out his hand and smiling.

I turned to Bunty and Callie. "Is that okay? Just one dance?"

"Yes, go ahead."

He carefully led me to the dance floor.

We danced apart at first and I really enjoyed the way he watched me. I felt there was a man who appreciated women. Then we danced closely. I liked the way he held me. I liked the way we moved together. I liked the way he smelled. He didn't rub his body against mine. I felt like I was dancing with a gentleman. He was also closer to my age too... I'd say around forty.

I looked across the room. The girls were waiting for me.

"Gotta go now, thanks for the dance," I said.

"What's your name?" he asked.

"Gaynor."

"Can I call you, Gaynor?" he asked, politely.

I paused, not because I wasn't taken with him but because he seemed like a decent man and I didn't want to end up hurting him. I thought that might happen in view of the fact that, at that moment, I'm a free spirit in every sense of the word. He seemed to be the sort of man that might be looking for more than a night under the covers. As he waited for a response, he looked at me, like a puppy waiting for a biscuit. I couldn't resist and gave him my number.

"What's your name?" I yelled, as the girls grabbed my arms and marched me out.

"Max."

"Bye, Max."

"He was nice," I said, as we stepped into a cab.

"Who was that?" asked Bunty.

I was just about to answer when Callie piped up. "That's Max, I shared a banana with him earlier."

POP. The little bubble burst. What a charmer! First Callie and then me. He must have seen we were together. I felt conned even though our encounter had been extremely brief.

"I thought he was a really nice bloke," said Callie.

I didn't say anything but wondered how and why they had ended up sharing a banana together and why she hadn't ended up giving her number to him.

Bunty looked at me. "Did you give him your number?"

"Yes," I said quietly, wishing I hadn't. "I won't answer his calls though."

THE RAT

Sunday, 7th July

Bunty, Callie and I had stayed up talking until eight a.m., and then decided to go to bed. I heard kitchen noises at around six p.m. and got up to find Bunty and Callie knocking out a late breakfast fry-up. Callie handed me a tea and I cradled it back to my bed.

I turned on my mobile and saw two little envelopes, I opened the first. It read:

Morning, we met last night. Wondering if you're busy today, if not, would you like to be taken out to lunch? If not, have a great day X (msg sent @ 9.56 a.m).

Oh, the text must have come from Max. God, he must think I'm extremely rude, not responding, I thought. Then I remembered Callie and the banana.

Then I opened up a second text message.

So this isn't your number! If you get this message call me x (msg sent @ 1.45 p.m.)

Now, I didn't like the tone of the scond message at all. Untrusting and demanding. I was confused. I checked the number. Unfamiliar.

Who are you? I texted back.

C'mon Barbie! How many blokes did you give your number to last night? came back the reply.

Cheeky bugger, I thought, and what does he mean, calling me 'Barbie'.

Did I dance with you? I asked.

If you had, you would definitely remember, he texted back.

He's SO full of himself, I thought. I texted back.

Are you Max?

No but I was with him last night.

Who are you? I enquired.

It's Ken. Max's mate. Can I take you out one evening XXX ?

Oh, that's why he called me, 'Barbie'.

Then it came to me. Max didn't have his mobile with him at 10room and so he had put my number in his mate's phone. That's bad form, I thought, and decided Ken wasn't Max's mate at all. Ken was a rat.

Sorry, Ken, Max beat you to it.

Oh, okay, no worries. Have fun!

I wondered if both Max and Ken, were 'Players'.

But then, I decided Ken was being mean, so I texted Ken, asking for Max's telephone number. Number forwarded, I text him.

Hi, Max. We met last night. How are you?

Hi, Gaynor. Great to hear from you. Am good. Hope you enjoyed your evening. Would love to meet up sometime X

I drank my tea and then decided to throw the cat amongst the pigeons. Why? Well, firstly, I thought, Ken was out of order, and secondly, I wanted to see how Max would respond. The 'banana' was still on my mind. Would he slip on it?

I sent the text.

Ken is texting me too.

A little envelope returned very quickly. Should be interesting, I thought and opened it up.

All this attention. Great to be popular. Enjoy. speak to you soon. Max X

I was surprised at Max's response. Soooo, accepting. No comment regarding Ken's misdemeanour, no questions, not even a spark of irritation or annoyance. Maybe Ken was always misbehaving. My barricade came down with Max's last reply and I felt myself waving a white flag. I don't think he could have sent a better text. It spoke volumes. He was confident, unthreatened by his mate's behaviour and his message had been very polite and unintrusive. I decided I would definitely like to see him again. He had won me over with his text messages. I decided to forget about the banana, for the moment. I felt if I took a chance with Max, it could turn out to be a very tender trip. I texted Mike back.

I'm off to the country for a few days, with my friend Bunty. I'll call at the weekend. X

OK I'll look forward to it X came back a speedy reply.

I lay back on my bed thinking about the messages from Max and Ken. I really was quite amazed at how, even from words, I was able to see the vast difference in character between the two of them. From the texting alone, anyone could see they were like chalk and cheese.

WHAT'S A BANANA BETWEEN FRIENDS?

Monday, 15th July

10.25 a.m. Text from Max. I was still in bed.

Good morning. Hope you had a good week in the country. I will be in town today on business. If you don't have plans, can I take you to lunch? Max X

I was delighted to hear from him but it was too short notice for lunch. Besides, it was a glorious day and I wanted to do some sunbathing on the terrace.

Can't make lunch. Would you like to come by for a cup of tea after work?

He called. It was the first time we had spoken since the night at 10room.

During our brief conversation, I was surprised to hear an accent. I could hear the accent, more than the words. Max was an Essex lad and sounded like a bit of a 'geezer'.

I found myself getting caught up in all this 'bollocks' about Essex girls, Essex shoes, Essex geezers, Essex people, Essex dogs and cats. Essex schmeshicks! I refused to be influenced by Bunty's posh accent, then heard her in my head. 'Goin' out wiv an Essex geezer, are ya?'

I reminded myself I was actually a 'Norf' London girl myself but my accent had changed over the years.

Max told me that he would be over at around four thirty but would call to let me know when he was ten minutes away. He may be a bit of a geezer, I thought, but I think he might be a bit of a diamond geezer. He was, in the very least, a gentleman. (Get out of my head, banana.)

I was standing in the kitchen when Max's car pulled up outside. I had spent two hours making myself look as gorgeous as possible, in a casual sort of way. Pretty little black summer dress, low at the front, light and soft to the touch with shoestring straps, pink sequined flip flops, and soft pink lipstick.

His car was medium size and silver. I'm not sure what make, might have been a Mercedes. He was wearing a dark suit, white shirt and tie. He pressed the buzzer and came up the stairs. It was the first time I had seen him in daylight. I wondered where his family roots were from, looking at his olive skin and dark eyes. He gave a pleasant smile.

"Allo," he said, beaming in a way that begged a response.

He reminded me of a younger, slimmer, better looking, olive skinned, very sharply dressed, 'Del Boy'.

"Hello, Max," I responded, warmly.

"It's nice to see you."

"It's nice to see you, too."

I gave him a hug and realised he was the same height as me. He had appeared smaller when I was wearing my heels.

"Lovely aftershave... How do you like your tea?" I said, heading straight off to the kitchen nervously. What is the matter with me? Breathe, slowly, quietly, calmly... in... out...

"White, no sugar, please," he replied, following in my footsteps.

"Strong, weak or medium?"

"As it comes."

Thank God he's easy going, I thought.

"You go and sit on the terrace and I'll bring the tea," I instructed feeling somewhat like a teacher.

"Sure. Where's the terrace?"

I showed him and went back to the kitchen. Breathe... Breathe...

I composed myself and arrived on the terrace with two teas and a smile.

Max took off his jacket and exposed a lovely silver and pale blue tie. I like a nice tie and this one was very nice.

"Nice tie... I love buying ties for my dad," I said.

"Have to wear one for work," he said, undoing his collar and loosening the tie from around his neck.

Max looked very relaxed sitting on the sun lounger. We made polite conversation and he was very easy to talk to.

I threw one into the pot. "Well, what about Ken texting me, then?"

He smiled and seemed amused.

"I don't make enemies," he said.

Another good answer. I decided to tell Max why I had agreed to see him.

"I wasn't going to see you again but your text messages were so nice... charming... warm... accepting... and generous."

Max smiled again. he didn't say anything and took a sip from his tea.

I paused. Then I had to ask. "Did you share a banana with..."

"Yes, Callie. I hadn't eaten all day and I was starving. I hadn't been to 10room before and my mates told me I could get something to eat from the kitchen there. The kitchen was closed. The best they could come up with was a banana. Callie ate most of it."

"I had strawberries there a few weeks ago. They must keep the fruit stocked up," I said, wondering why I had mentioned it.

What a nice man, I thought, he shared his banana with Callie even though he was starving.

We chatted some more.

"I'm forty-four, next year," he said, (excellent, I thought, a grown up) "and all my mates say I'm going through a mid-life crisis."

"Are you?" I enquired, smiling.

"Well, I might be. I've turned into a bit of a boy."

"What do you mean?"

"Well, I've just bought myself my dream car."

"Good for you. What is it then?" I asked, hoping I'd recognise the make.

"A Porsche 911."

I didn't know exactly what model that was. I'm not well up on Porsches.

I nodded knowingly. "What colour?" I asked.

"Midnight blue, with light grey interior."

The car of my dreams would be midnight blue but a Jaguar.

"Great colour choice," I said, enthusiastically.

"I ordered it ten months ago. I should be getting it soon."

"That's a long time to wait."

"They're made to order."

"Aaah," I said, and sipped my tea.

I wasn't going to ask, but Max offered some information about his work. He said he was 'head of sales' and supplied offices and companies and was out on the road a lot. Must be a good salesman to be able to afford a top of the range Porsche, I thought. But then again, he did have a lovely personality. I wasn't surprised that he would be very popular with his clients.

"Where do you live?" I asked.

"Welwyn Garden City."

"Not married then?"

"I'm separated. She's got her own house but she comes over a lot. We're very good friends."

'That's good. I left my husband six months ago, after seventeen years."

"So, how is it going?" he asked.

Not answering his question, I added, "He wouldn't wear his wedding ring. He said he found it annoying." Then I reverted back to his question. "It's going really well. I feel like a new and very different woman. I'm very happy."

"Any children, Max?"

"No. We couldn't…"

"Me neither," I disclosed, then changed the subject.

"So where are your offices?"

"Ware at the moment but we've got great new offices in Hemel Hempstead, they'll be ready soon. Can't wait to move in."

"That'll be very convenient for you."

I looked at him in the sunshine.

"Are you too hot?"

"No, you're joking, with my skin, I love the sun."

"Where are you from?" I asked.

"I was born in Britain but my parents are from Turkey."

Just like Hasan, I thought.

He paused for a moment. "Gaynor, I think you are a really lovely woman but I can't offer you anything more than friendship at the moment. My life is so busy with work, especially with travelling around the country and arranging the company move to my new offices."

Your new offices? I thought.

"Your new offices? Is it your company then?"

"There are three of us, partners."

If Max just wanted to be 'just friends', why was he sitting on my terrace having tea when he should be working, especially if he so busy? Also, why had he pursued me in the way he had, if he wasn't interested in being more than 'friends'. I dismissed but respected what he had said. Maybe Max wanted to be friends, with 'extras'? Max had presumed I wanted to be more than friends and actually, I wasn't looking for a serious relationship anyway.

"I'm taking some of my clients on a golfing day out tomorrow, followed by a trip in town."

"That should be fun. Are you any good?"

"No, not really but we have a good laugh."

Tea finished, Max left as gently as he had arrived. We hugged and he told me he'd call. I kissed him on the cheek and then went to the balcony at the front of the house to wave goodbye. Mmmmm I hummed as he disappeared down the street toward his car. What a nice person, I thought, I can be his friend…

POSHUS TOTTUS

It was nine thirty p.m. on a warm summer's evening when Callie, Bunty and Amy, Callie's new friend, dragged me to Primrose Hill in search of food. There was nothing in the house except five different tubs of Haagan-Dazs ice cream, dog treats and Champagne. It would have suited me but it didn't suit them.

"Must have some greenery… must have green food," said Bunty, breathily, as though she was dying from the sheer exhaustion of it all. Everyone had a bad case of the munchies.

"I don't know if I can carry on, Caruthers," quipped Bunty, in a posh 1940s BBC accent.

"Almost there now, sir," I responded, supporting her leaning body.

We were all wearing low tops again so there was a magnificent array of fabulous cleavages on display. Bunty had decided that while we were eating, we would sit outside somewhere and watch the passing gentlemen, picking out our favourites.

"There's an Italian with tables outside," said Bunty, pointing at a restaurant across the street.

"Yes, but there are no seats," said Callie, still looking around.

"We'll soon change that," I said, then walked across the road and swanned up to the desk toward the smartly dressed waiter.

"Can we have a table outside for four fabulous ladies?" I said, with the biggest smile.

The young man laughed and went to speak to the manager who turned to look at all of us.

Abracadabra. We were sitting outside.

Bunty decided we'd have a code. "Right. In front of me is twelve o'clock," instructed Bunty. "I don't want anyone pointing. And we'll just call them, Totty."

"Totty at three o'clock," I chirped.

"And ten o'clock," said Amy

"Too young," said Bunty.

I found myself repeating something totally appalling and shocking, that I had heard a bloke say to his mate, some years before. "Too young? If there's grass on the pitch, you can play."

I knew my comment would cause the outrage it had done with me. It had been one of the most shocking 'bad jokes' I had ever heard. I waited to be severely reprimanded.

Callie looked totally shocked, Amy squealed with delight and Bunty did the right thing, and slapped me.

"Come on, they're at least sixteen," I said, waiting for the next slap.

"You are SO naughty, Gaynor!" said Bunty, putting her napkin over my head, so I couldn't see.

As I lifted it up, I saw the lovely young man from the desk heading toward us. Excellent, I thought, he's going to be looking after us.

"I am Francesco. What can I get for the four fabulous ladies?" he asked, with a big smile.

"Hello, Francesco," I said, getting up from my seat.

I took his head in my hands and planted a lovely big kiss on his cheek. His eyes glazed over and he giggled.

"I'm Gaynor."

"I'm Francesco,' he said, again, proudly.

Then Bunty grabbed my sleeve and pulled me back down, into my seat. "Leave the poor boy alone," she said.

I looked up and he was smiling at me.

"Water with ice, please, Francesco," I said, smiling back and... I looked towards the others to make their choices.

"Gin and tonic, please."

"Glass of house white, please."

"And I'll have a glass of Champagne, please," said Bunty.

Menus in hand, we ordered lots of food to share and watched the 'totty' as we consumed it.

"Poshus-Tottus at six o'clock," I chirped, because he was wearing a very smart, well-fitting suit and a silk tie."

The girls giggled.

"Mannus-Bloke-us at three o'clock," responded Amy, because he was wearing a vest and Dr Martin's.

Nine o'clock, one o'clock, ten o'clock. The clock was very busy that evening. Totty was everywhere. We made up names for all of them. Richus-Mannus, Fittus -Mannus, Tightus-Arse-us, Broadus-Shouldus etc, etc. My favourite was Bunty's name for a king... Royallus-Erectus.

After sitting and laughing and being naughty for a couple of hours, my mobile bleeped. It was a message from Max.

Hi, it's Max, where are you? X

I texted back.

I'm at a restaurant in Primrose Hill with girlfriends. Are you with your lads or alone?

Either, or, came back the reply.

Another great answer, I thought. His social skills are exceptional.

Preferably alone x I texted back.

Would you like me to meet you?

Meet at my house in an hour. Bring Champagne, I said.

The girls thought that was a bit cheeky. It probably was, on reflection, but I was testing his keenness.

I put the phone down and ordered the bill.

"We've got to go. Max is coming over in an hour and I haven't shaved my legs!"

The girls realised the urgency of the situation and quickly finished their drinks.

Francesco came out with the bill and discreetly pushed a piece of paper into my hand with his telephone number on. Little Tinker, I thought, he must be all of nineteen. I threw it into my bag and squeezed the little tinker goodbye.

Arrive back home. Have bath. Shave legs. Dry off. Wash hair. Dry hair. Cream on. Deodorant on. Make-up on. Perfume on. Clothes on. Wrong clothes. Clothes off. Different clothes on. That'll do. That looks cool.

Max texted.

I'm on my way. Got Champagne. It's a bit warm X

No problem, I can murder it with ice x

What a sweetie, I thought.

Eleven forty-five p.m.

I laid down and tried to do some deep breathing. In… out… in… out…

Why was I feeling so nervous? Was it because I really liked him? STOP! We were going to be MATES! Why was I so keen to impress? I told myself to stop being so bloody ridiculous and pull myself together.

Midnight. Then I heard a car pull up outside. I quickly put Daisy and Flo in my bedroom, then buzzed him in. He flew up the stairs, two at a time.

Breathe slowly in… breathe slowly out…

I opened the door.

"Allo," he said, pecking me on the cheek and holding up two bottles of Champagne.

"Hi, Max. Come in."

"You look nice."

He complimented me on my dress and then followed in my footsteps to the kitchen. He placed one bottle of Champagne on the work surface and passed me the second. I tried to hide the fact that my hands were shaking.

Breathe in… breathe out…

"Let me do that, Gaynor," he said, taking the bottle. I grabbed two glasses and handed them to him.

"Where's the ice you're going to murder it with?" he chuckled. I pointed at the freezer then went and sat at the table in the living room.

Max strolled in and handed me my glass. We clinked glasses and as I lifted mine to my mouth, Max saw my hand visibly shaking.

"Are you okay?" he said, looking rather concerned.

I shook my head. "No, I'm really nervous."

"What are you nervous about?"

"You."

"Why?"

"Don't know. Just feel nervous."

"Don't feel nervous," he said, reaching out for my free hand, across the table.

"I'll be fine, just a bit nervous that's all."

I lit up a cigarette still shaking.

Breathe the nicotine in… breathe the nicotine out…

Max broke the ice. "I've dropped my clients off at Spearmint Rhino."

"Spearmint Rhino!" I responded, knowing it was an expensive, private, gentleman's club. In other words, a strip club. I tried not to look too surprised while I was saying it.

"Yes, they've come from around the country and they wanted a night in town."

"How was the golf?" I asked, changing the subject.

"Played well today, considering I haven't played for a month."

"That's good," I said, only half listening.

Spearmint Rhino?

"They'll be coming by cab to pick me up about two a.m., I've got to get them back to their hotel as we have a nine a.m. meeting in the morning."

We small talked for a while, against the background music of Aretha Franklin and then Max stood up and reached for my hand. My tummy turned over.

"Let's dance," he said, pulling me up and placing me in a position that suggested a waltz.

My legs turned to lead.

"I can't dance, I'm too nervous," I said, releasing myself from his arms.

"Are you all right?"

"No, I can't move my legs."

"Do you need to sit down?"

"No. I need to lie down. I feel really dizzy."

I felt like a child as I plonked myself on the sofa.

"Jesus," I said, "I don't know what's the matter with me."

Max sat on the floor next to me. "You just need to relax. Would you like a cuddle?" he said, as he watched me slowly gathering myself.

"Okay," I said, not really wanting one.

"I've got my shoes on."

"It doesn't matter, I'm not precious about things like that."

"No, I can't."

"Okay then, take them off."

99

He did and climbed onto the sofa next to me. I needed to hide under his arm so lifted it and placed my head on his chest. We lay quietly for a few minutes.

"How are you feeling now?"

"A bit better," I lied, as the adrenalin rushed through my veins.

I felt myself getting bigger and smaller at the same time. He stroked my arms and kissed my hair trying to calm me.

Just at that moment, Max's phone beeped 'Message'. I felt his annoyance.

He picked up the phone and called someone back.

"Where are you?... It's number 53... Ok, see you in a sec." He hung up.

"FUCK. My clients are almost outside. I'm sorry, babe, I'm going to have to go. They left Spearmint Rhino now and want to go to a club."

"It's okay," I said, trying to ease his guilt and at the same time, feeling relieved.

He jumped off the sofa, pulled his shoes on and kissed me goodbye on the forehead.

"I'll call you later," he said, grabbing his jacket and hurrying through the front door and down the stairs.

I peeped out of the window to see a minibus-cab with about six men inside.

Laying back down on the sofa, I closed my eyes and went back into the feeling of Max gently stroking my arm and kissing my head. Five minutes later, a text came through.

Hi. I'm really sorry about that. Are you okay? Can't believe I'm in a car and not with you! I'll call you tomorrow. XX

Tea. I need tea. And a joint.

BYE-BYE, BUNTY

Wednesday, 17th July

Ten a.m. Bunty knocked my bedroom door. "Do you have company?"

"No, come in, he went home, half an hour after he arrived."

"A quickie, then?"

"Absolutely not! He couldn't stay long, and just wanted to say hi."

"At midnight?"

"Yes, at midnight, Bunty," I said, peering at her from under my frown.

"I've got to leave in about thirty minutes. I have to go home to sort myself out then come back to London for an audition."

"NOOOoooooooooo! I don't want you to go."

"Have to! My agent told me I needed to be there. It's a nice role."

"OOhhh," I winged, like a child that couldn't have any sweets. Then I jumped out of bed and hugged her.

"You stay in bed, Gaynor, I'll see myself out."

"Are you sure?"

"Yes, of course. I've arranged a car."

We kissed each other on the cheek.

"A car? Okay. I'm really going to miss you, Bunty. It's been such fun!"

"It has, it's been a great break. I'll call you."

"Okay, darling. Love you."

"Love you too, Gayn's. Bye."

"Bye. Take care. Good luck with the audition."

Bunty, gone, I went back to thinking about Max. Why had I been in such a state? Why was I shaking so much? Why so much adrenaline? Was it because I found myself really attracted to him? Really liking someone or even ending up loving someone, meant danger. DANGER, in big red, flashing letters.

I thought about the disastrous experiences I'd had with men in the past.

I wandered around aimlessly for the rest of the day with my phone in my pocket waiting for a call from Max. Every time it rang or bleeped my heart skipped a beat. Each time, it wasn't Max. By seven p.m., I began to feel quite cross that he hadn't made contact. By ten p.m., I was feeling angry and frustrated. At eleven p.m., I very nearly rang him, but thought NO! STOP! DON'T DO IT! BE STRONG!

I stayed strong and didn't call. I made some tea and toast instead then rolled a joint and put the TV on. I hope he doesn't think I'm going to let him in for another midnight visit. I made the decision that if he did call, I wouldn't pick up nor respond to any texts. His actions, or lack of, were totally unacceptable. It is NOT the way a friend behaves and it is definitely NOT the way to treat a lady. I bet he wouldn't treat his clients so disrespectfully. I absolutely hate it when someone states they are going to do something then doesn't follow through. He's old enough to know better. If you say you're going to call, CALL! And if you can't call, TEXT! I don't care how bloody busy he is. It takes one minute to text someone. So bloody rude. Wanker.

My mind travelled back in time to disastrous past relationships.

I lost my virginity in 1969. I was aged fourteen and my boyfriend was fifteen. Young, I know but it was the 'sixties'. Free love, flower-power and all that. I wasn't alone, at least half of the girls in my class were 'at it'. We had been together for about a year. He was also a virgin and we had gone on to have a relationship for eight years. I had been totally faithful and loyal. However, around the age of eighteen, friends and associates, started telling me they had seen my boyfriend out and about at various pubs, clubs and parties, with various girls. I constantly challenged him about these 'stories' but he always swore blind, that it wasn't him and that he must have a look-alike.

I started having very debilitating panic attacks at this time and although I didn't want to believe the stories, I stupidly took him at his word because I was so desperate to trust him. I loved him and wanted to believe he wouldn't do that to me. I didn't get concrete evidence of his 'affairs' until I was twenty-two and when that evidence came through, I left him.

A year later, when I was at Art school in Watford, I discovered that a student in the year above me also lived in my home town of Hatfield. So, instead of catching the coach to Watford and back, every day, I asked him if he would give me a lift. He agreed and within a matter of months, I was in love with him. A few months later, despite our relationship being fractious (possibly due to my trust issues, he was a very good-looking man), we decided to move in together, closer to the college, so moved to Bushey. He drove an old sports car and occasionally, in the evenings, he would go for a drive. I always asked him where he was off to, but he would say he had to keep the battery charged up because the short drive to and from college wasn't charging it enough.

My panic attacks continued during this time. About a year later, I ended up with an infection around and in my vagina and he was suffering with a terrible itch and soreness. We ended up in the VD clinic. We were seen separately and both asked if we were sleeping with people outside of our relationship. Of course, we weren't. We were given antibiotics which sorted us out.

A few months later, after one of his drives, he didn't return. He didn't return until two days later. I was out of my mind with worry and my panic attacks were at an all-time high. He hadn't turned up at college either. When he finally returned, we had a massive row and he wouldn't tell me where he had been. I was so angry I threw a pair of shoes at him. He then picked up a mirror and threw it at my head. It cut my head open, not bad enough for stitches, but it made a dent in my skull which I still have to this day. After his disappearing act and the following violence, I left him. A couple of weeks later, his sister called me and told me he was having an affair with a friend of his. A male friend. I was totally shocked but it explained why I had ended up in the VD clinic.

The following year, I was working as a designer in Oxford Street. Only a small company, eleven men and me. I eventually went out with one of the other designers, a man that was constantly pursuing me. He was just a year older than me and although I hadn't found him particularly attractive, in the end his charm, personality and appreciation of me won me over. After being with him for a few months, I absolutely adored him. We decided to get a flat together in Shepherds Bush. In his spare time, he was a drummer in a band. He left the design company and went to work as a typographer in an advertising agency in Chelsea. Often going to meet him after work, I got to know the various ad people and was frequently invited to agency parties and days out.

I began to get a real buzz about the whole advertising thing. I decided I didn't want to be a designer any more, but instead, an art director or copywriter. I eventually got a job as a 'creative' at Dorland Advertising. I was loving every minute of it. A few months later, there was a summer party arranged by his agency. He was going to be drumming with the agency band, which practiced regularly. I dressed up in my new silver trousers and went along to the venue. I couldn't see him upon arriving so went on a search. Ten minutes later, I discovered him, backstage with a female on his lap. It was the singer from the agency band. She had her arms around his neck, and his arms were around her waist. They were having a jolly old time until they spotted me. Looking totally shocked and 'caught out', I knew immediately what was going on. Their body language was extremely intimate. I turned, ran outside, vomited and had a massive panic attack. He didn't come after me.

When I had semi-calmed down, I stuck my head through the entrance door to see him happily playing his drums. We didn't speak for the rest of the evening but when we got home, I went nuts. He said it was 'all in my head' and she was just a friend. I didn't believe him one bit despite his protests. He swore he was telling the truth, over and over again.

I eventually said, "If what you are telling me is true, then I need help, serious help, I need to see a shrink!"

It was only then that he owned up to the fact that he was having an affair. I packed my bag and left.

A few years later, I was married. I married a man who was actually, already married to the pub. We had been living together for three years and he rarely came home 'on time', instead, choosing to go drinking with his pals after work. He often didn't arrive home until midnight. More panic attacks. Then, when he suggested we got married in a pub one evening, I ran outside and vomited and followed up with another massive panic attack. Should have listened to my body. I had stupidly and naively thought that after we were married, his behaviour would change. WRONG! Actually, in retrospect, it did change, for the worse.

Why did I always end up with the wrong man... the one that would break my heart? I sure did pick 'em. It was little wonder that I always felt so insecure, had serious trust issues and years of debilitating panic attacks. My panic attacks embedded themselves so deeply in my psyche that I would have them without a reason. I would just get a tingle up the back of my neck and knew what was going to happen. I could be anywhere. On a bus, in a supermarket, in the park, having a meal. I was living in a hidden hell with no respite.

A TRUE AMERICAN GENTLEMAN

Thursday, 18th July

Woke up. Fed up. Felt miserable.

4.08 p.m. Message from Max.

I hope you are okay. Work crazy. Call u later xx

Don't bother. I won't respond.

Callie and Amy came around at eight p.m. I told them about my hour with Max and how I couldn't stop shaking. I told them that I was really nervous because I was really attracted and drawn to him then I told them that he said he'd call and he didn't. They could see I felt terribly let down and was 'hurting'.

"It all sounds very odd to me," said Callie. "I don't trust him. What did he mean, when he said 'I just want to be 'friends'. He's definitely up to something."

"Bloody men," added Amy. "It's so hard to trust them."

Ten p.m., Callie felt too tired to go anywhere so she went home. Amy and I, however, decided to leave 'men misery', behind and hit 10room for a few drinks and a dance.

11.10 p.m. A bottle of Champagne and two double 'Twist my melon' shots later we had forgotten about dishonourable men and started looking around the room at all the 'Dancus-Blokus'.

"Four at twelve o'clock," I said to Amy, as her head span around like something from the exorcist.

"Don't look! They're looking this way," I said, through a ventriloquist's grin.

11.20 p.m. Champagne and two more 'Double Twist my melon' shots. Feeling very merry, we got up for a spot of dancing.

"I'm feeling merry very," I said. "I think it's the 'shots'! I don't usually drink spirits, let alone shots."

"Merry very! Me too!" responded Amy, laughing and grabbing my hand to pull me up for a dance.

For the next forty minutes we danced our cotton socks off, sipping drinks in-between tracks then stumbled back to the safety and steadiness of the sofa.

"Water, I need water," I whined, through a breathless sweat and spinning head.

A broad, black man, aged about forty-five to fifty, with a wide, sunny, smiley face leant forward from a seat across the table and spoke, in a lovely deep, soft, warm, 'Barry White' type accent. "Would you like me to get you some water?"

"Oh, yes pleash, how kind," I said, trying not to sound pissed.

He returned with glasses of iced water, one for me and one for Amy.

He then sat back down in his seat. That was nice, I thought. I noticed he was sitting by himself so I leant forward. "Are you here on your own?"

"Yes, I'm over from New York on business. James Milton."

"I'm Gaynor."

"How are you doin', Gaynor?"

"Hot. Jamsh. It's so bloody hot in here. This is my friend, Amy."

"Hi, Amy. Nice to meet you both."

"Hi, James," she said, as her eyes followed a Mannus-Dancus, walking past, behind him.

Amy grabbed my hand. "Come and dance with me," she said, pulling me off the sofa.

"Are you all right about him?" she asked, through her white teeth with a smile.

"Sure, he's just on his own," I replied, feeling a little sorry for him. "He seems very nice, very polite."

"He's a bit old, isn't he?" she said, smiling sarcastically.

I laughed.

By midnight, I was feeling a little steadier, so, Champagne and another double shot.

"Would you like to dance, Gaynor?" James asked.

"Sure," I said, leaning very slightly sideways.

James was around 6'2" and was a great dancer and like all black people had great rhythm. In my opinion, black people were always the best dancers. I had never seen a black person without rhythm but I had seen plenty of white people. This became more apparent in older people. Elderly white men tend to do 'Dad dancing', whereas elderly black men still looked incredibly cool when they were in the groove.

One a.m. I collapsed on to the sofa again and James joined me. Amy was still dancing in the middle of a group of male admirers. I turned to James to listen to his lovely voice. I could tell he was a charming man. Polite, courteous, intelligent, interesting. As I listened to him talk, the heat, or should I say the booze, really began to affect me. I couldn't focus. I felt more 'out of control' than I had ever done. I hadn't ever been much of a drinker and I rarely went to pubs. Even enjoying a few glasses of Champagne on evenings out, was new to me.

"Air, I need air," I said, feeling a little nauseous. Leaving my seat in a swagger I nearly toppled over. The road to the 'Ladies' was going to be a long one. I held my hands out at my side, partly to balance and partly to steady me, in the event that I would need to find a passing pillar or post, to lean on. Halfway, along the swimming, curving, swaying path, my knees turned direction, and my body circled on to a large, empty (thank God) sofa. As I lay there not knowing what position I was in, or which direction I was facing, I felt beads of sweat oozing through my leaden body. Suddenly, I was free-falling spinning fast, all control lost.

A sweet man came over and asked me if I was okay. It was hard to get the words out. "Waaarrter... I need waaarrter."

I desperately called for Amy, in my head.

"Are you all right baby?"

Thank God. The comfort of her gentle hand and a soft female voice. It was Amy.

"Noooo..." I whined. "I feel heavy and spinning. I can't move. I am really, really drunk."

"Come on," she said, lifting me up to sitting position. As soon as she let go, I rolled back down again.

James appeared and pulled me up again, not letting go. With James taking most of my weight, he and Amy lifted me from the sofa and steadied me through one of the emergency exits, and balanced me down the stairs.

Something felt like it was pulling my head and shoulders backwards. The feeling was incredibly strange and incredibly strong. It was as though 'gravity' and 'alcohol' had made a bond.

On to the street, leaning backwards at 45%, I started laughing as soon as the cool air hit me.

James hailed a cab.

"Do you want him to come too?" Amy whispered.

"Yesh. He's really schweet bloke and I might need him to get me up the sstairs to the flat."

"Are you sure?"

"Yes, I'm sure, I am in need of ashistanch."

"Are you okay, Gaynor?" asked James.

"Yesh, but you need to help me. Come."

James opened the cab door and carefully posted me in.

"Aaah, you're really schweet," I said, accidently poking him in the eye.

With Amy and James sitting either side of me to keep me upright, we had been in the cab for about five minutes when I realised, I was going to vomit and nothing was going to stop it. I unzipped the bag and tipped the contents onto Amy's lap, then threw up in it. Thank God it wasn't projectile. It spilled, carefully in short bursts, into the convenient container.

A voice, bellowed from the front. "YOU'RE NOT BEING SICK IN MY CAB, ARE YOU?"

"No, it's okay," responded Amy, in a calm and coherent manner.

"She's doing it in her hand bag… no mess…"

Finished, Amy zipped it up and put all my stuff in hers, then she sat the bag on the floor and patted my chin with a Kleenex.

After a couple of minutes, I started to feel much better. I smiled. Then I started to chuckle.

"What are you laughing at, Gaynor?" asked Amy, smiling and stroking my leg.

"This is the first time," I slurred, "that I have EVER been drunk in my entire life. And I have NEVER been shick from drink before."

"Are you serious?"

"Yesh, it's true," I said, then sang "I love you, I love you, Amy poo, boop-oop-di-do," then laughed at my 'joke'.

As we pulled up at the house, my smile had faded and I was starting to feel sick again. James and Amy helped me out of the cab and supported me at the sides.

"One step... two shteps... three shteps, four... oooops. Gravity spun me around and I fell into a bush then vomited. When I'd finished, I looked up at Amy and James with a smile then they carefully tried to lift me from the greenery.

"Ow! My hairsh stuck in the branches."

Hair untangled, I started giggling again.

James put his hands around my waist and gently pulled me up.

"You're sho, sho, schtrong, James," I slurred.

"Amy, my shoe has gone off my foot. Pleash get it."

James carried me up to the front door then gently leant me against the wall.

"You've got the keysh, Amy," I said, trying to point at her handbag.

Amy put the contents of her handbag on the door step and searched through. "The keys aren't here," she said. "Only your make-up, wallet, hairbrush and mobile."

Even in my pissed state, two things occurred to me. The keys were either on the floor of the cab or, euk, still in my handbag. I prayed for the disgusting latter.

"They might be lost... or shtill in my bag."

James tried to grab the bag. "Here, let me have a look."

There was no-way I was going to let him do that.

"NO! I'll look!" I slurred loudly, clutching the bag to my chest.

James grabbed the bag in an instant and unzipped it. Amy had to look away as he fished around until he lifted out the keys. That is sooo schweet, I thought, he touched my shick.

James opened the front door with one hand, still holding me and my bag in the other. "Where's her bedroom?" asked James, carrying me up the stairs.

"Just in there," said Amy, pointing left.

She followed us in as he gently laid me on the bed.

"Thank you sho much, Jamesh," I whispered, trying to focus on him as he swam in and out of focus.

"Jamesh, you are a true gentleman and a lovely man and a kind man and a shweet man and such a shtrong man and all men should be like you."

He leant forward and kissed me on the cheek. "Can I call you next time I'm in London, Gaynor?"

"Of coursh you can! Amy, can you give Jamesh my number, pleash."

"Great. I'll be back in two or three months so will call you then. Take care of yourself."

"Thanksh again."

Amy showed James to the door, as I lay there thinking Bless him, he paid for the cab, carried me up the stairs and all he had got for his trouble was a hand-full of vomit. What a gentleman.

"Is it okay if I head home, Gaynor, will you be okay?"

"Of coursh, my darling. Thanksh for a great evening and for looking after me and getting me home."

"Would you like me to undress you and put your jimmy-jams on? Okay, I'll just get you a glass of water, then I'll be off."

COIN WASHING

Woke up. No hangover. Couldn't believe it, thought that was part of the deal. Took two Nurofen, just in case it decided to surprise me later. Bloody hell. I had finally joined the ranks of those who'd had a booze puke. Euck! Never again. Poor James.

I suddenly remembered my handbag. That'll be nice, I thought. I wondered whether it would be retrievable or I'd have to bin it. I went in search. It looked quite innocent sitting there on the coffee table all bright and shiny. No visible scars at all. Good job it was plastic and not patent leather. I moved in slowly and gently lifted it. But it wouldn't lift. I lifted harder. It rose up with the small, lightweight coffee table still attached. Oh God. Stuck. I prized the two apart then wiped the surface and put a candelabra over the damaged varnish.

I carried the bag carefully to the kitchen, where I placed it on the draining board. I unzipped it. No odour whatsoever. I peered inside. No food, because I hadn't eaten anything, just a silvery shine across everything as though some sort of crazed snail orgy had taken place. Laying at the bottom was about £7.50 in change. Most of the coins had turned green. I spurted a laugh and then wondered what the fuck the booze had done to my stomach.

Filling up the bowl with warm, soapy water, I tipped out the coins and submerged the bag. The bag was easy to clean but I was going to need the scourer to attack the coins. Scrubbing hard, the green staining would not budge so I decided I would just dry the coins off and keep them for parking meters.

In the afternoon Callie turned up, to catch up on 'last night'. Upon arrival, she went to the kitchen, to make tea.

"Gaynor," she called. "What are all these coins doing lined up on kitchen roll... and why are they green? What's happened to them?"

"Don't ask," I said, then proceeded to tell her the whole story.

"Hilarious, so, you were totally trashed, wish I'd been there. Congratulations on another first, Gayn's!" she said, clinking her tea mug against mine.

KOSO KISSES

Eleven a.m. My phone rang and I stupidly picked it up without checking who it was.

"Hello."

"Hi, it's Max."

I didn't respond.

"Gaynor?"

I paused.

"Hi," I responded, very flatly.

He could tell by the tone of my voice that I wasn't happy. He seemed to be in a rush.

"I'm really sorry I haven't been in touch but I've had a bloody awful week, I was in Birmingham for three days then had meetings around the south west, I've hardly eaten and I'm bloody knackered…" he took another breath. "…and the thing is, I need to talk to you, face to face, I don't want to talk on the telephone, I need to see you…"

"Okay…" give him a chance to explain, I thought.

"I'll be in town on Tuesday afternoon. Can I come around then?"

"Okay," I said, wondering what he meant, by 'face to face.'

He changed his tone. "Are you okay?"

"No, not really."

He speeded up again. "Look, we'll talk on Tuesday… gotta go. Bye."

"Bye."

I put the mobile down and fell on the bed. What an exhausting (even though I'd hardly said anything), frustrating and annoying conversation that was. Face to face? Why couldn't he just talk on the phone? I was, in the least interested, as to what he was going to say to me on Tuesday.

No sooner had Bunty gone, than she returned back to London. Callie had a smoke with us then went around to see her new bloke.

Me, Bunty and Amy were getting ready to go to a new club, to meet up with some new gentlemen, Bunty had met at the Groucho Club, after her audition. We were off to a place called The Wellington, in Knightsbridge.

"Do you think it'll be really posh?" asked Amy, lifting and checking her breasts in the mirror.

"Bound to be, darling," said Bunty, in her BBC voice.

We put on our 'posh' gear. I was wearing a low, black, knee-length lacy dress with pretty short-ribbon'd sleeves AND the most expensive shoes I have ever bought. Pointy, black, beaded, kitten healed, £150. My hair and make-up were working and I was feeling confident and gorgeous.

We arrived at The Wellington and followed in behind a couple of celebs and made our way to the balcony. Below, was a large room filled with glamorous people, all of whom appeared to be drinking Champagne.

"Okay, girls," I said, turning to the others. "The real stars have arrived."

"Where?" asked Amy, eagerly.

"Us silly!" said Bunty, pinching Amy's bum.

Heads up, chests out, we elegantly made our way down the stairs. Other partygoers stepped back as we made our way on to the floor.

Bunty searched the room with her eyes. "There they are!" she said, pointing at her two new gentlemen friends who were sitting at one of only three tables in the whole room.

We've got a table! Excellent, I thought, as we made our way over. I do so hate standing.

Bunty introduced me and Amy then one of the gentlemen signalled to the waiter to bring over three more chairs.

Bunty kept her two gentlemen friends entertained, while me and Amy sat looking at everybody else.

Celebes and rich totty were everywhere and they started to look rather dull after a while and worse of all, there wasn't anywhere to dance.

People were trying, in small places, but it just wasn't happening. The atmosphere was nowhere near as good as 10room.

With Bunty preoccupied by her new friends and them preoccupied with her, after an hour, I leant and whispered in Amy's ear. "Fancy fucking off to 10room?" I whispered.

"Yessss!' she hissed, enthusiastically. "You must have read my mind."

We said our goodbyes with no protest at all from Bunty and cabbed it over to 10room. We parked ourselves at a table as a waiter came over.

"What can I get for you this evening, ladies?"

"I'll have a diet coke please."

"A diet coke!" quipped Amy, shocked. Then she remembered Thursday evening and laughed.

"I'll have a double shot, 'Twist my melon', please."

I got up from my seat, to dance on my own while Amy waited for her shots. While on the dance floor, I watched various men shuffling towards her, then walking away. She really was gorgeous with her wide eyes, tumbling blond hair and fab boobs. She oozed sex appeal. She had four invitations to dance in a matter of minutes. If I hadn't seen it with my own eyes, I wouldn't have believed it. They were like bees around a honey pot. She turned them all down, so I went and sat back next to her.

"No good, babe?" I asked, putting my arm around her waist to give her a hug.

"Nahh."

Within a matter of seconds, she was approached again. She looked at me with wide eyes, raised eyebrows and got up from her seat.

I was reminded of something I'd read about people raising their eyebrows. It happens the moment he or she sees someone or something they like. After reading this, I had caught myself unconsciously doing exactly this when a very attractive male caught my eye. I wonder if it's to do with making one's eyes bigger and wider, so as to take more in?

Amy danced with her gentleman for the next hour while I happily danced alone, in-between chatting to waiters and she decided she was going to take him back to her flat for 'coffee'.

Walking toward the bar to pay the bill, behind the counter I spotted the most gorgeous man who was already smiling at me. Couldn't understand why I hadn't seen him before. Maybe he was new. He was tall, dark, handsome, aged about thirty, with a fabulous white smile and twinkly, twinkly eyes. He... is... gorgeous, I thought. I gave him my bestest, twinkliest smile, in return. There was immediate attraction. We chatted away and shortly thereafter at the end of his shift, he ended up coming home with me. We were on my bed, quicker than you could say tickety-boo.

Was I becoming insatiable? Was I still trying to convince myself that I was indeed a very attractive, desirable woman? Was it because my life, with regards to men, had had such an impact on me that I was behaving so promiscuously? Or, was it about me, for the first time EVER, feeling that I was the one in control? I could do whatever I liked without having to answer to anyone. For me, I found there was something nice about being intimate with an attractive man with no strings attached. I felt like a promiscuous teenager in a grown-up body. Brilliant.

My new acquaintance had an eastern European name, one that I wasn't familiar with and couldn't remember or pronounce, so I just called him Twinkle.

He turned out to be twenty-six. He had come over from Kosovo when he was eighteen. He had been penniless and also didn't speak any English. Seven years down the line, he was putting himself through college (he wants to be an editor), has a flat and a computer, works all the hours God sends and speaks very, very good English. He was a lovely young man. He was articulate, intelligent, interesting, amusing and serious, but most of all, he was comfortable in himself. Quite something for someone so young.

Having spent the night, before he left, he turned to me and said, "Why did you invite me to come to your home?"

"What do you mean?" I responded.

"Well, I have seen you in 10room many, many times before. I see you dancing with the men. I even met you once... so why do you look at me now?"

I felt bad.

"Well... You never looked or smiled at me the way you did last night," I said, smiling.

He smiled back, grabbed my cheeks in his hands and planted a big wet 'puppy like' kiss on my forehead. "I love mature women," he said. "I wish I could spend the day with you… We could have such fun… but sadly, I have to go to my other job."

"Aren't you knackered?" I asked.

"No, not at all, I feel totally energised," he said, stretching out his arms like King Kong and beating his chest.

"I love sex, especially with older women they are so uncomplicated."

"Thanks for a lovely time," I said, as he climbed out of bed.

"The pleasure was all mine," he responded, falling to his knees and kissing my feet which were peeping out from under the duvet.

DIRTY BUMPER

Tuesday, 23rd July

One thirty p.m. Tuesday afternoon. message from Max.

Hi, babe. On my way. Be there in 30 mins x

Max arrived, we briefly hugged, mine was cold, then made our way to the terrace.

I didn't offer him a cup of tea, but just sat down on one of the chairs. He sat opposite.

"The thing is, Gaynor, I just can't give you anything. My life at the moment is my work and it takes up most of my time. I started a company a few years ago with two other guys and it's going really well. And I suppose what I'm trying to say, is at this time, and I'm not saying that this will be forever, we can only be friends."

"You already told me that, Max."

"Well, it's just that you sounded pissed off on the phone."

"I was, but only because you'd said you would call me, then didn't. I hate it when people say they'll do something and don't follow through. I bet you wouldn't do that to one of your clients."

"I know, it wasn't acceptable. And I AM sorry."

"So, why didn't you call?"

"I was with clients and couldn't sneak away."

"Couldn't sneak away? How did you go to the toilet?" I asked sarcastically.

I wondered whether his life really was that crazily busy. Maybe what he was trying to say was that he wanted to be 'just friends' because he really wouldn't be able to spend very much time with me due to his work. At least not for the time being, anyway. Maybe he really did like me and maybe he would like a 'relationship' but can't give it the time it deserves.

"At the moment, with me being all over the country with work, I could probably only meet up with you around once a week. Can we be friends? Would that be okay with you?"

"It's a possibility," I said, unenthusiastically.

"So, there's a possibility we could be friends then?"

"Maybe."

"That's all I wanted to hear," he said, getting up from his seat as though I had given him an outright 'Yes'.

"I've got something for you, in the car," he said, enthusiastically, leaving the balcony.

He disappeared, then reappeared, with a CD. "Tracks two and nine are for you," he said with a gentle smile.

"Let's play them now," I said, leading him into the living room.

I didn't know the artist. It was Darren Hayes. I put the CD on, track two. Max sat on one of the sofas and I chose one of the armchairs. The track started. I recognised it immediately but hadn't known who was the artist. The song was 'Insatiable'. It's a very sexy song with a 'late night' feel. And the lyrics... well... and the chorus! Talk about mixed messages. Is he mad?

"You can't give me this," I said, in a high-pitched voice. "Not after everything you've just said to me, about being 'just friends'. AND we don't even really know each other!"

"It's what I'm feeling inside, but I can't act on it at the moment," he said, looking down at the floor. "The thing is, you have really caught my eye and I'm incredibly attracted and drawn to you. I can't stop thinking about you."

Well, that was quite a declaration, I thought. He had quite a way with words. I went and sat next to him on the sofa. I didn't stop him wrapping his arms around me. My heart started beating quickly.

"I can feel your heart beating," he said.

"I can't do this," I said pulling away.

"Do what?"

"Lie close to you like this. It's not fair. I feel all mixed up."

"It's okay, just relax. I have to leave in thirty minutes. We are just having a cuddle."

"Do you cuddle all your friends?"

"No," he said, pulling me closer.

"Why did you bring me the CD?"

"Because when I was listening to 'Insatiable' on the radio in my car, I couldn't get you out of my mind."

Am I going mad? Never been so confused.

I threw myself backwards onto the cushions, exasperated.

Max laughed, then moved gently towards to me. I looked into his eyes and felt all shy again. As he went in for a kiss, I started giggling and spoiled the moment. There's that bloody little girl again.

"Sorry," I said, with my hand in front of my mouth.

Max laughed, waited a few seconds and then went in again. Again, I giggled.

"I'm really sorry, Max, you just make me really nervous. Just let me be quiet and still for a moment."

I lay with my eyes closed for about a minute. And then it just came out of me. "Okay, I'm ready now. You can kiss me."

"Oh, can I?" said Max, highly amused.

He lunged forward for his kiss and we followed up with thirty minutes of sexual activity. All self-control had gone out of the window. The best thing of all, was after Max had ejaculated, he just laid on my tummy and started giggling.

"I'm really sorry," he said. "But I find the whole thing really funny, it just makes me laugh."

"You're as bad as I am," I said, patting him on the back.

Giggling over, I lay on the bed and wondered if I had just been seduced? I think I had. I could have stopped it but hadn't. I had allowed it. Truth is, I had wanted him. It HAD been MY CHOICE at the end of the day.

I watched Max as he got dressed. He really was a 'terribly well-turned-out' man. Everything about him was crisp and clean. His tailor-made suit and black leather shoes were immaculate. He was about to put his jacket on when I noticed lipstick on his shirt.

"Ooops... I think there's lipstick on your shirt."

"Shit! Where?"

"On your left collar."

"Shit! Shit! Shit! Shit! SHIT!"

121

"Don't worry, come with me to the kitchen, I'll get it off for you," I said, taking him by the hand.

"I'm a bit odd about my clothes," he said.

"What do you mean?"

"Well… I don't usually let anyone near them. You're okay though," he said.

"Oh, well I'm glad I have the stamp of approval." I giggled.

I dabbled away at his shirt with Stain-Off.

"I'm bad with my car as well… My mates take the piss out of me… I make them wipe their feet…"

Oh God, I've fallen for Howard Hughes.

"Don't worry. I'll soon knock that out of you. Now turn around while I get the dog hair off the back of your suit."

"Dog hair!"

"Yes, dog hair."

It really is Howard fucking Hughes.

I felt like I was sorting out my kid for his first day at school. I wanted to ruffle his hair but it wasn't long enough, so I just kissed him on the cheek and sent him on his way.

We arranged to see each other on Friday night and he left the house looking as immaculate as when he had arrived. As I watched him approach his car, he bent down to check the shiny bumper. There must have been a small mark because he whipped out the silk hanky from his top pocket and wiped it.

"Dirty bumber, darling?" I yelled.

He laughed.

Definitely, Howard Hughes.

He texted me about fifteen mins after he left.

Hi, Darling. Great to see u again. Feel so much better now, hope you do too. See you soon x

There was something extremely odd about all these mixed messages. Or maybe he was just a bit odd. Time would tell.

TEXTS

Wednesday, 24th July

11.12 a.m. Text message from Max.

Hi, Sweetie. It was great to see you yesterday. Another mad day today. Lots of new contracts. Hope you are okay. PS. I won't say I'm sorry about our intimate encounter yesterday because I'm not but I will make it up to you someday X PPS. Are you free on Friday evening?

I waited until the afternoon then text him back.

Maybe.

I still felt confused but couldn't be bothered thinking about it.

JUST SHOOT ME

Friday, 26th July

Tired of waiting for a call from Max with regards to meeting up this evening, at 9.10 p.m, Callie and I jumped in, then out of a cab, at the steps of our beloved, 10room. At that very moment, a text came through. It was from Max.

Hi, baby. Where will you be around 10 p.m? Would really love to see you xxx

Hi, Max. I'm out with a friend.

Where?

10room

Great. I'll see you shortly xx

Does he think he's coming to my rescue or that I can't live without him? He REALLY is SO ODD.

Coats off, Callie and I ordered drinks then got up for a bop on the dance floor.

Suddenly, someone was in front of me. It was Mac. Bunty's tall, handsome, criminal lawyer.

"Hi, babe!" I said, throwing my arms around his neck. "How are you?"

"I'm great. How's Bunty?"

"She's fine. Gone back to the country again for a rest." Mac laughed.

"How's your love life?" he asked, with a cheeky smile.

"Actually, I've met a really interesting bloke. But he's a bit odd, Max, he's forty-three. Actually, I've got a bit of a secret crush on him."

"Crush? You sound like a sixteen-year -old. Isn't he a little old for you?"

"He's a grown-up!" I said all excitedly. "And he's coming here in about thirty minutes! Where's Chris?"

"He's elsewhere this evening. I was just heading off to Elysium but I think I'll stick around and meet this interesting, odd, new fella of yours."

"Yes do, he seems really nice, perhaps a little confused but I'd like you to meet him. Only thing is, he's about a foot shorter than you so please will you bend your knees when you meet him?"

I was serious but Mac just pushed me, playfully.

One of the waiters was planting a kiss on my cheek when I saw Max coming towards me. His eyes were fixed on me. And mine on him. The waiter's kiss fell into insignificance as I broke free. We threw our arms around each other and after we let go, he gave Callie a kiss and then I introduced him to Mac.

And Mac did bend his knees, bless him.

Max ordered more Champagne. I went back to dancing. He watched. After my performance, I sat close to him. Then Max took a call.

"Excuse me a sec," he said, then disappeared.

Ten minutes later, he returned.

"Where were you?"

"Paying the bill… I've got some mates outside but they can't get in. They're not members and there's too many of them for us to sign in. Will you come with us to The Atlantic Bar across the street?"

Before I had a chance to respond, Callie was up out of her seat, looking all eager. I imagined her, imagining a rugby team. I stood up.

"If you give me your cloakroom tickets I'll get your coats," said Max, enthusiastically."

It all happened so quickly, I just followed like a sheep.

Crossing the road to The Atlantic Bar, I started asking myself why Max had bought a 'rugby team' along with him when he'd said he wanted to see me… and then I wondered why was I following them when I had been perfectly happy in 10room. He'd chosen the lads over me. Mmmmmm…

Five minutes later, me, Callie, Max and the 'rugby team' were all seated at a large table with comfy chairs.

I whispered to Max. "Why have you got all these men with you?"

"They're from work… my mates…. We go out every Friday night."

"Why are we on a lad's night out, we shouldn't be here," I said, looking confused.

"Don't worry, the lads are cool. We'll go soon anyway."

Max smiled at me trying to be reassuring but I wasn't really buying it. Anyway, what about Callie? I wasn't going to leave her on her own with Max's work mates.

As he went to get the drinks, I took comfort from the fact that if Max was happy for me to meet all his workmates then at least he really, definitely, wasn't attached.

Max returned from the bar and plonked himself between me and Callie. I was preoccupied listening to 'What a great bloke' Max was, from all his work pals so Callie started chatting to him.

I was asking the lads about their new business and at the same time was trying to listen to Max and Callie's conversation. I could only pick up snippets because of the music but Callie seemed quite animated, sitting on the edge of her chair waving her arms around.

Suddenly, her voice rose above the rest. "YES! BUT ARE YOU STILL LIVING TOGETHER?"

She was obviously asking about Max's ex-wife. I felt she was being rather aggressive to him as he had already confirmed that he WASN'T living with his ex-wife, she had her own house, so I just left Max to follow through with a 'No, we're separated'. I turned toward them to listen and heard Max respond, with a "Yes."

I turned away immediately as I felt my face turning red and then I felt like throwing up. I was so furious, I couldn't even look at him. My brain went nuts. You fucking bastard! I thought. You lying fucking bastard! How could you lie like that? What the fuck are you playing at? Fucker! With my head still turned away from Max, I tried to listen more.

"I love my wife more than anything… we are best friends."

At that point I lifted my mobile from my bag and pretended I'd received a text.

I turned to Callie.

"It's Amy, she's in 10room, let's go and fetch her."

"Are you coming back?" said Max with his wide, puppy eyes.

"Sure," I said, grabbing my coat in one hand and Callie, in the other.

126

As we rushed out of the Atlantic Bar, Callie turned to me. "Gaynor! He's still married! And, he's still living with his wife! Bastard!"

"I know, I heard him tell you. I feel sick. I want to go home."

"What about Amy?"

"That was a lie, she's not in 10room. I just had to get out of there. I want to go home."

"WHAT AN ABSOLUTE BASTARD!" shrieked Callie.

"I know. How could he be so devious? What on earth is he playing at? It's bizarre that he told you the truth. He didn't tell me. He must have known you'd tell me. He is so odd."

"Something didn't feel right, Gaynor, that's why I really started grilling him."

"And what on earth is he doing, introducing me to his work mates when he's still living with his wife? Is he totally mad? I think he's totally lost the plot."

We found a cab and after turning my phone off in case he called, I really just sat in a state of shock for most of the way home. I couldn't find any words. I was so hurt, so devastated that he had blatantly lied to me. I felt used, betrayed and ultimately stupid for not seeing through him. All those mixed messages suddenly made sense. Worst of all, I had shagged a married man. I had never, or would ever, engage in any sort of sexual activity with a married man. I don't do that. I was horrified and absolutely seething.

A LIE, IS A LIE

Saturday, 27th July 10.10am.

After a fucking awful night's sleep, I woke up feeling more pre-menstrual than I do when I am. I immediately turned on my phone. Two messages from Max.

Message one, sent the previous evening, after we disappeared.

Are you coming back? X

Message two, sent this morning at 9.10 a.m.

I really need to talk to you, Gaynor. Can I come over on Monday sometime? I can fit around your schedule x

Fit around my schedule? You're supposed to be an incredibly busy man!

I turned my phone off again then went back to more disturbed sleep.

One p.m. Despite not wanting to do anything apart from curl up and die, I decide that I would force myself out that Saturday evening. I was determined that no fucking two timing bastard was going to ruin my weekend.

Ten thirty p.m. Amy and I decide to go to Elysium. We arrive looking gorgeous and looking for company. We were on a mission. We sipped our drinks for an hour and then decided we'd rather be in 10room, so off we trotted.

Eleven p.m. Various gentleman approach Amy, but none, me. I think I must be giving off bad vibes. Maybe I'm smiling through gritted teeth.

Eleven thirty p.m. I decide to text Hasan.

Hi Hasan. How are you? Where are you?

I got a message straight back.

China White. Where are you?

I'm in 10room. Do you want to meet up?

I waited twenty-five mins and then text him, again.

Too late. This window of opportunity just closed x

Wasn't keen enough. I did give him a very generous twenty-five mins in view of his lateness. And I wasn't in a patient kind of mood.

Twelve fifteen a.m. Spot Mac with a friend across the room. Thank God. A friendly face.

"Hi, Mac. How are you?"

"I'm good, this is Dennis."

"Hi, Dennis, nice to meet you. This is Amy."

We all sat down together and Mac ordered Champagne.

"So, how's it going with Max, Gaynor?"

"Do you have a gun?"

"Oh dear, what happened?"

"Fucking bastard's married!"

"Oh shit!"

"And if I find a gun, I might need a criminal lawyer."

"At your service," said Mac, giving me a gentle hug.

I changed the conversation and when the Champagne was finished, Amy and I politely declined an offer to join Mac and Dennis at Browns, and decide instead, to head home.

One thirty a.m. Bed. As soon as my head hit the pillow, Max was on my mind. I really just couldn't understand his bizarre behaviour. The somewhat brief events in our short time together kept going over and over in my head. The truth was, even though he had been unfaithful, which is totally unforgivable, and he had lied his balls off to me, I still felt like there was a good man in there, somewhere, but he was incredibly 'mixed up'.

THE EMAIL

Sunday, 28th July

Three p.m. Phone rings. It's Max. I let it go to answerphone. He doesn't leave a message.

Three thirty p.m. Phone rings again. Unknown number. I don't pick up, in case it's Max. No voice message.

Seven p.m. Text message from Max.

Gaynor, we need to talk. Please call me.

I don't call.

Eleven p.m. I have been thinking and thinking all day about Max and what'd gone on. I decide to write an email. I just can't let it go. Too many questions. And I want answers.

Dear Max,

Now that my anger and hurt have calmed, after consideration, I find myself asking, why, if you are still living and in love with your wife did you:

a. Pursue me?

b. Have sex with me?

c. Introduce me to your mates and work colleagues?

d. Give me CDs with sexy songs dedicated to me?

e. Ask for photos of me?

And also, why would you 'come clean' to Callie about your true situation but not to me?

I am hoping that what you have been trying to tell me but were somehow unable to get the words out, is that you are separated from your wife (emotionally anyway) and it's just the paperwork that need to be taken care of.

So, referring back to the conversation on the terrace, I take it that you are asking if we can be friends until you are 'free'. To do that you'll need to understand that our friendship can involve no kissing, sex, or intimacy of any kind. Just don't leave it too long or I will lose faith and give up. I also don't want to see you until you have sorted yourself and your life out. Even though you have stirred something inside me, I won't be able to hold onto it unless it's fed. For you to feed it you need to be free.

I'm giving you a 'second chance' because I still believe in you, Max. I'm hoping my intuition is right, in that, although you love your wife, you are not 'in love' with her any more. Maybe we can stay in touch by email? Alternatively, come find me when you have your wings.

X

Eleven thirty p.m. Email finished. Texted Max.

What is your email address?

THE ALTERCATION

Ten a.m. No email address received.

One fifteen p.m. Text from Max.

I'm just around the corner. I need to see you. Please.

I don't respond.

Four forty p.m. Phone rings. It's Max.

I pick up… but I can't find the generosity to say, hello.

"Are you there, Gaynor?" he asked, with gentle urgency.

"Yes."

"Are you okay?"

"No."

"I need to talk, to you."

"I want to send you an email," I said, devoid of any emotion.

Max's tone changed sharply as he unexpectedly, 'went into one'.

"That was a bloody horrible evening… I was going to get up and walk out when Callie started grilling me. We were supposed to be having fun… If I'd known that the evening was…"

"Hold it right there," I interrupted. "Before you say anything about Callie, you have to understand that we mean the world to each other and we 'look out for each other'. She felt instinctively something wasn't right when she was talking to you. She is a good person."

Max paused. "Okay, You're right. I'm glad what happened, happened. At least it's all out in the open now."

"Why did you lie to me, Max?"

"I didn't lie."

"You told me you were separated and that she had her own house."

"She does have her own house."

"But she's still living with you!"

"Yes, but we are having serious problems and I am very unhappy."

"So, you lied… and you are still married… Do you love her?"

"Yes, I love her very much. she has been a big part of my life but I'm not 'in love' with her any more."

"You made me break my most important rule, Max. You lied. I slept with you and you are still married. I don't do that. If I'd known you were still living together, I would never have slept with you. Do you have any idea how bad that made me feel? I felt used, betrayed and dreadfully hurt."

"I'm sorry, Gaynor. I never intended to sleep with you. You were so beautiful, so bright, so joyful. You were fresh air. I didn't mean for it to happen. It just happened."

"No, it didn't 'just happen'. You seduced me."

"…and you allowed me to."

"That's not the point! You are still married, Max, AND you are still living together! Having 'serious problems' does NOT mean you are separated."

"I'm sorry… but I did tell you we could only be friends right now."

"But you allowed us to become more than friends. We were intimate, we had sex!"

"I know and I'm sorry. I seriously thought about walking away after we slept together but I just couldn't."

"Well, that's nice to know, you thought about walking away after bedding me. Thanks, Max."

"I'm sorry. I didn't mean it like that. Everything just got out of hand…"

"So, what is it you want from me, Max?"

"I want us to be friends."

There was that fucking 'F' word again.

"So, you want to go from being lovers, to being friends?"

"If it's possible… until I'm free."

"I don't know if I can do that."

"I understand. I don't want to hurt you any more than I have done. Do you want to think about it?"

"Yes. I really DO need to think about it."

"That's fine, it's a good idea. I think we really need to chill out. And again, I'm truly sorry."

"Bye, Max."

"Bye."

I put the phone down and went to lay on the bed. I thought about all the things I hadn't said that the email had. Did he really understand how much he'd hurt me? I felt that Max didn't want to let go and was ultimately looking for more than a friendship from me, but the bottom line was he was still married. I didn't know whether a friendship would or could be possible. It didn't seem like a very clever idea under the circumstances. But it was hard. All those mixed messages. My head was telling me to stay clear but my heart was saying give him a chance.

***

Callie and Amy and came over, early evening, followed by Bunty, who had arrived back in town. I told them the whole story. Bunty wasn't having it at all and just kept looking up from her newspaper and shouting, "He's married!"

Callie thought he seemed like a nice bloke but was really pissed off that he had lied to me and kept saying, "It is NOT acceptable."

Amy just listened, with a sympathetic ear. She had taken my 'falling for Max', more seriously than Callie and Bunty. I'm not sure why. Maybe because she is younger.

After talking to them and listening to them, I still had no idea what I was going to do. I was determined to try and put him out of my head for a while. I felt like my brain was running after my heart, shouting, Stay away from him! And after all, ridiculously, insanely and madly, I had only actually, spent around ten hours with him.

ENOUGH

Tuesday, 30th July

Today, I worked out that I still didn't really know what Max's intentions were. He hadn't actually said he was going to leave his wife. All he'd said was that he was very unhappy. I didn't even know how long he'd been married for. In fact, I didn't really know very much at all. I felt like I was in limbo. I wanted more information, more details. I wanted to talk more. The agreed, 'chilling time', faded away during the day.

***

Wednesday, 31st July

I held off until 3pm and then texted him.
   Max, I need to talk more.
   I waited. and waited. And waited. Nothing.
   Went to bed feeling totally flat.

***

Thursday, 1st August

Woke up feeling like someone had died. Sat up in bed and started to cry. Then I started to sob. Through the tears I realised that something extraordinary was happening to me. I was crying. For many, many years, I had suppressed any tears. Whilst married, my husband had told me that I looked like a pig when I cried. My tears had never been taken seriously and were usually laughed at, so I ended up fighting against them, holding them in, every time I felt them rising up.

I stopped for a moment and thought, Well, good always comes out of bad, and at least the fucker has stirred so much up inside me that it had bought me to tears. I felt 'free' to cry for the first time, in so long, so I decided to carry on until I couldn't cry any more. It felt like a massive, massive release.

Four p.m. I decided I would call Max. He didn't pick up, so I left a voice message. "Max, it's me. I need to talk to you. I'm so confused. Please call me back."

He would have known from my voice that I was really upset. After a few minutes he called. He was unexpectedly angry. "Why are you calling me? I thought we were going to have a chilling out period. I feel like you're hounding me…"

His words, 'hounding me… hounding me… hounding me', echoed around my head. I felt so angry I thought I was going to explode. My throat closed up and I couldn't I speak. I was SO shocked. That was SO unfair and right below the belt. How dare he, after all his lies!

I found my voice. "You may feel like you're being hounded, Max," I said, fighting back the next batch of tears, "but you have been the one relentlessly perusing me. I need to know more about what's going on and I can't wait for two weeks, I have too many questions. I feel like I'm in limbo."

Max backed off. "I'm sorry about what happened. I've learnt a great lesson from all of this. Everything got out of control. It wasn't about the sex, I can get sex any time, I just couldn't walk away."

"Max, I just have one question I need you to answer. Do you intend to leave your wife?"

"I don't know."

Fuck. Hurt. Fuck.

He carried on. "And if I do, I don't know if I want to go straight into another relationship."

Ouch. Ouch. Fuck. Fuck.

He carried on again. "Everything is such a mess. I don't want to end up in a messy expensive divorce with an adultery case."

"Why didn't you tell me this before? Why weren't you honest with me?" I pleaded.

"Because I didn't know this was going to happen."

I could hear his voice breaking.

"I'm sorry, Gaynor, everything's such a mess… If you think we can be friends, call me."

I hung up before he did. I didn't know what the fuck 'friends' meant any more. Why on earth was he still trying to keep hold of a part of me? One thing was for sure, he was definitely having a mid-life crisis.

I rang Bunty, crying. "Bunty, I'm a mess…"

"What's happened, darling?"

"Max…"

"I'll be there, in fifteen minutes."

Bunty must have called Callie because they turned up together, to comfort me and after the tears, came the anger. I was raging. It had been such a total head fuck. The girls insisted we went out to drink and dance ourselves into oblivion.

The painful ten-hour affair was well and truly over.

DON

That evening...

We danced our way up the stairs and into 10room at ten thirty p.m., already having consumed two bottles of Champagne. The three of us were on our way-hey! We were shown to our favourite corner and were up on the floor in no time. Callie, me and Bunty, danced in and out of each other, me with my eyes open. It was a bit like a pissed maypole dance.

Sit down, more Champagne then, back up on our feet. We danced to a couple more tracks and then one of the lads who was sitting on the sofa beside us beckoned to me. Me, being an accommodating kind of person, danced my way over.

As I arrived, smiling from ear to ear, he jumped out of his seat and grabbed my hand. "I love the way you dance, the way you move... You ladies are having such a great time... it's great! My name's Don. Do you mind if I ask how old you are?"

"Forty-seven."

"WHAT!"

"Forty-seven. But don't tell management. I knocked ten years off on my application. I thought they might not let me join if they knew I was nearly fifty."

"I can't believe it. Look at the shape of you. You look about thirty-five. You're gorgeous! So sexy! you must work out."

"No, don't work out, I walk my dogs. But I think it's in the genes."

"Well, it's certainly in your jeans," he said, watching me roll my hips around.

I laughed. He laughed. Then we danced together. Apart.

Don was around the same height as me, fair hair, cropped, solid build, and a surprising thirty-nine years old. he didn't look it. He worked in the printing business.

He seemed like a really nice 'down to earth', 'tell it as it is', kind of bloke. I felt that what you saw, was what you got. There were definitely no secrets with this one. To any of my questions, the answers came flying out of his mouth without a second thought. He was very open about every aspect of his life.

Don ordered more Champagne for us all and toasted. "Life's too fucking short, not to be having fun!"

We all cheered.

"Don seems like a nice bloke," I said, turning to his friend.

"He's great. Salt of the earth. I've known him for years. He's one of my best mates. Are you really forty-seven?"

"Yes, I'm forty-seven. So, is he getting over his broken marriage, okay?"

"He is now. He was a right mess a year ago. He found his wife was having an affair. It was hard because he has two little girls."

"Yes, he told me."

"They are his life. He adores them."

"I know, you can tell by the way he talks about them. I think it's great."

Don, who was talking to Callie, suddenly turned to me. "God, I don't even know your name."

"Gaynor, 'Gayn's', for short."

"Hi, Gayn's, SO pleased to meet you. You're like breath of fresh air."

Get lost, Max.

Don asked me to dance again, which I did and then we sat and talked for a couple of hours.

Then I made a proposition. "Would you like to come home with me, no strings attached?"

"Are you kidding?"

His eyes lit up.

"No. I'm serious."

"Wow, I'd love to."

Bunty and Callie went off in a taxi, feeling I was safe, and I climbed into a cab with Don. We arrived home feeling dry from the alcohol. I went for water. As I came out of the kitchen, I saw Don in the bathroom using my electric toothbrush. He just grinned at me with a big, frothy, schoolboy mouth. I was amused by his total disregard for etiquette. I laughed. I couldn't be annoyed at him. After all, he was only using my brush so that he had fresh breath for me. Also, I was about to shag him, so what's a little saliva between friends.

After that, he stripped off then wandered around the flat totally starkers, with a 'semi' on for about five minutes. I was in bed waiting for him. He kept popping in and out of the bedroom, smiling at me. He looked so at home. He went for a shower. Of course, he didn't take a towel with him. Large, wet footprints on the bedroom carpet. Who gives a shit. His earlier words, re-entered my head. "Life's too fucking short not to be having fun!"

We shagged, in between laughing our heads off. It really was great fun and a great distraction, after Mr 'I can't make my mind up', and I forgot about him completely.

Two hours later, Don finally flaked out. Upon waking up, with the biggest smile, he asked if he could call me next time he was in town. We swapped mobile numbers.

I received a text message from him in the afternoon.

Gaynor, just gotta say u r so, so sexy. You've got more sex appeal and a better body than women half your age. You have really lifted my spirits. Thanks for a great night. U r such fun! And great shag! Don. x

I burst out laughing and texted him back.

You are a great shag too, Don. x

HASAN AND THE CANARY

Wednesday, 14th August

It was around nine thirty p.m. when Hasan rang my mobile.

"Hasan! How are you darling?" I said excitedly. It was always lovely to hear his voice.

"Gaynor! Gaynor! Something TERRIBLE has happened."

I could hear real panic in his voice.

"What's up? What's happened?"

My mind raced... Hasan. MOD. A missile must be heading for London!

"God, I'm in such trouble. Something terrible has happened."

Okay. Pause. Hasan was in trouble, not the rest of us, no missile.

"What is it? What's wrong?" I said, feeling very concerned for him.

"God, I don't know where to start really..."

"Start at the beginning. What's happened?"

"Well, a few weeks ago, I met a really nice girl and we became friends."

"Okay..."

"And... well... she was going on holiday to see her family in Italy and she asked me if I would look after her canary for a couple of weeks because her friend who was going to look after it had broken her leg so I said I would. How hard would it be to look after a canary?"

"What's happened?"

"Well, I started looking after it last Saturday and everything was fine. She asked me to pop into her flat in the mornings to take his cover off, change his cage, give him his seed and let him out to have a little fly around, then put him back and then come back in the evening again, just to give him a bit of company before his bed time and to put his cover over his cage before I left."

I was waiting for the words 'He's dead'.

"But what's happened?" I asked, trying to sound calm.

"Well, everything was fine but this morning when I went to sort him out."

He was dead, I thought.

"…he wouldn't fly back into his cage. I tried for about ten minutes to get him back in but he wasn't having it. I had to get to work so decided to shut the living room door and leave him to fly around freely for the day."

"Hasan, what's happened?" I asked, again.

"When I arrived eight o'clock this evening, he was gone. He had disappeared."

"He can't have disappeared, he must be behind the curtains or something. Did you leave any windows open?"

"No of course not… and I have looked absolutely everywhere. I've been checking the whole flat for about two hours in case he flew out of the living room door as I walked in. I just can't find him. She's going to kill me. She loved that bird SO much. She's going to hate me. What am I going to do? I just can't see him anywhere. I can't fucking believe it! I CAN'T FUCKING BELIEVE IT! WHY ALWAYS ME? WHY! WHY! WHY! She'll never forgive me. I only spoke to her yesterday and told her he was fine."

"Okay, calm down. First of all, he hasn't necessarily 'gone'. He might have just fallen asleep somewhere. He could be in any room in the flat."

"But I've looked everywhere. I've been calling him for over two hours."

"What's his name?" I asked, not really knowing what to say next.

"Sunny."

"Oh, that's sweet, because he's yellow."

"Oh God, Gaynor. What am I going to do?"

"Well look, firstly, stop panicking. He must be somewhere."

"Hang on, I'm just going to check the main hallway to the flats, he might have flown out there as I came in."

I waited for a couple of minutes.

"I can't see him anywhere, Gaynor, he's not in the hall."

"Look, go and make yourself a cup of coffee and try to calm down a bit. Have another good look around the flat. Is it big? How many bedrooms?"

"Just one, it's a small flat."

"That's good, so just go around again, very methodically, room to room, closing each door behind you when you've thoroughly searched each room."

"That's what I've been doing for the last two hours. He's not there."

"Well look again anyway, he might have changed position."

"Okay. I'll go now and have another look. I'll call you back."

"Okay, baby. Try to be positive."

"Okay, bye."

Feeling traumatized myself, I made myself a cup of tea and rolled a big joint.

I waited for his call back and prayed that Sunny would be found, alive and well.

Thirty minutes later the phone rang. Maybe he'd found him.

"Hello."

"Gaynor, he's not here... he's gone... he's just disappeared... What the fuck am I going to do?"

"Look, just cos you can't find him doesn't mean he's disappeared."

"What if he's stuck in something?"

I paused thinking of that as a new possibility.

"Have you checked in cupboards and any open drawers?"

"I've checked everywhere."

I paused again.

"What shall I do, Gaynor?"

"Erm... Well, there's nothing you can do right now. You've had a good look so why don't you go home and get some sleep then go back in the morning. You never know, maybe he will leave his hiding place and fly back to his cage. Let's be positive."

"I won't be able to sleep."

"Well, there's nothing else you can do right now."

I felt so sorry for him.

"Look, if he's not back in his cage in the morning, come and pick me up after work and I will come over to her flat with you and we can look for him together."

"Are you sure?" he said. I could feel him take some comfort, from my offer.

"Yes, of course, no problem."

"Okay, I'll go home then."

"Make sure you open up all the doors in the flat before you leave, just in case he is still in one of the other rooms."

"Okay."

"And ring me in the morning to let me know if he's returned."

"Okay… bye,and thanks."

"And try not to worry."

"Okay… bye."

"Bye, lovely."

Poor Hasan. I tried to think positively but had a really bad feeling that Sunny was trapped somewhere in the flat. How long can a bird last without water and seed? I really don't know. Poor little thing.

***

Thursday, 15th August

Nine a.m. Text from Hasan.

He hasn't returned to his cage and I still can't see him. Didn't sleep and feel sick. Will pick you up about 6 x

Oh shit. Not good. Sunny must be trapped. Or worse still, dead.

I text back.

Try not to worry. We will find him later. See you after work x x x

As the day went on, my fears for Sunny grew. If, God forbid, he was dead, then where was he dead? In a drawer? Under the sofa? Behind the fridge? We would have to find him. The shock of the lady owner would be horrendous if she found his dead little body in an unexpected place. And what if she didn't find him for months? All that might be left would

144

be a little pile of bones and a few yellow feathers. Yes, at all costs, we MUST find him.

Hasan arrived bang on six and we sped off to the flat. His olive skin was pale and his devastation was more than apparent.

"Don't worry, we'll find him, and we won't leave until we do."

"Thanks, Gaynor, thanks for coming with me."

We arrived at the house, entered, then Hasan tentatively opened the door to the flat. I watched for flapping, yellow wings. I closed the door behind us and quietly followed Hasan into the living room. My heart sank at the sight of the little empty cage.

"Right, let's start the search together, systematically, room by room, starting in here. Close the door, in case he's in here and flies out."

Hasan closed the door.

"Right. We are going to start in this corner and we are going to go through EVERYTHING. That means lifting the books off the shelves to check behind them, going through the drawers, emptying them, and then the cupboards. Check all the vases and pots, and any containers of any kind.

We meticulously searched the living room for forty-five minutes. Nothing.

"Okay, lets carefully look under the furniture. Do you have a torch?"

"I've got one in the car."

"Good. Go and get it."

"Okay."

Hasan rushed off while I thoroughly checked the curtains and window area.

"Here it is," he said, handing to me.

I got down on my knees, followed by Hasan.

"How do you turn it on?" I asked, handing it back to him.

He flicked a button then I shone the light into the one-inch space under the large leather sofa. Nothing.

We shuffled across to one of the chairs and shone again.

"I can see something at the back," I said, sheepishly. It was the size and sort of shape of a small bird.

"What is it?"

145

"I don't know, you'll have to lift the chair up for me to see properly, but don't drag the chair... just tilt it."

We got up and I leaned to look under the chair as he tipped it slowly forward.

We both saw it together. A crumpled tissue.

Five minutes later, there was nowhere else to look. We had covered the living room. Sunny wasn't there.

"Let's have a cup of coffee before we start another room," I said, trying to stay calm and collected.

"Okay."

Hasan went off to the kitchen while I plonked myself, on the sofa. I looked and looked around me. Yes, we had checked everywhere possible. Sunny must be in another room. He must have flown out of the living room as Hasan had walked in. There was no other explanation.

"Here's your coffee. What are we going to do Gaynor? Where the hell can he be?"

"Well, he's definitely not in here so he must have flown out as you walked in. They can be very fast. He must have flown over your head. He must still be in the flat. He must be in one of the other rooms."

Hasan's mobile rang.

"OH MY GOD! IT'S HER!"

"DON'T PICK UP. DON'T PICK UP."

Hasan put his phone back in his pocket.

We took our coffee with us and continued our search. First the kitchen, then the bathroom, then the bedroom. All rooms were completely ransacked, then reorganized, before we closed each of the doors. We had been in the flat looking for Sunny for three hours and twenty minutes. Nothing. Now I couldn't work it out. Where the hell, was he?

"Did you have the windows open at any time Hasan?"

"NO! I wouldn't have dared risking him escaping."

"Well, I'm flummoxed. I just can't imagine where he's gone. We've looked everywhere... thoroughly. I don't know what else to suggest."

Hasan started panicking again.

"What am I going to do? She's going to hate me! I've lost her beloved pet. She's had him for three years. I feel terrible. What if he's lying dead somewhere in the flat? What the fuck am I going to do? Why me? WHY ME! It's the fucking story of my life. NOTHING EVER GOES RIGHT."

I put my arm around him but he couldn't feel it. We walked back into the living room.

"Darling, it's not your fault that Sunny went AWOL. You did nothing wrong."

"I did! I didn't get him back in his cage before I went to work."

"Yes, but you tried, you did your best. did she leave a net for you to catch him in?" I said, trying to ease his guilt.

"No, no net. She just said to call him and he would come. He did. Until yesterday morning."

"Well, if he didn't come when you called him, it's not your fault. You couldn't stand here all day waiting for him to pick his moment. You had to go to work."

Hasan gave a deep sigh, taking a little solace from what I had said. It was the truth, after all.

"What shall I do? Should I buy a replacement? Would she know?"

He was serious, bless him.

"Well, maybe as a gesture, later down the line, but you can't buy one now. And yes, she would notice. Especially if she's had him for three years."

"But canaries all look the same, don't they?"

"Not to an owner. And he's probably got his own special little tweet and familiar habits."

"I need more coffee. Do you want one?"

"No, I'm okay," I said, as he sloped off to the kitchen.

I was reminded of a sweet story which echoed Hasan's 'innocence'.

A girlfriend of mine, Millie, had told me that as a six-year-old child, she'd had a guinea pig which she loved very much. The guinea pig was short haired, white with black spots. She had had him for about six months. One afternoon, after school, she went to her guinea pig's hutch to discover he had changed. He was just white. No spots. She carried the guinea pig into the kitchen to show her mum.

"Mummy, something has happened to Clover. He's white, his spots have gone and he's got bigger."

"Yes, darling, I know. I went to see him this morning and his spots had fallen off. They fell off during the night."

At this news, Millie turned and took the guinea pig back out to its hutch, only to return within a few seconds. "Where are the spots, Mummy? They're not in his hutch."

Her mother turned to pick up a small bowl and passed it to Millie. "They are here, darling. I collected them this morning."

Inside the white bowl were small, black, furry, randomly shaped little spots.

Millie was satisfied.

Millie's mum was to be congratulated on her creative and ingenious thinking. Death comes soon enough. Why ruin a six-year-old's day?

My thoughts returned to Hasan who was now sitting in a position I had become familiar with. Hunched over, elbows on knees, head in his hands with his eyes closed. I hugged him again. He didn't feel it.

"Come on, baby, let's go home. We can't do any more than we have done. No one would have spent more time and been more thorough than we have been. We gave it our absolute best" I said, stroking his arm.

I followed the depressed shadow to the door and into the car. We didn't speak on the way home but I sat and shared in Hasan's darkness. I hated not being able to help or comfort him.

I kissed him on the cheek as we pulled up. "Call me, baby, anytime... even in the night if you want to talk."

"Thanks, Gaynor. And thanks for giving me your time tonight."

"Anytime, lovely, anytime."

Hasan sped off, too quickly. His car sounded angry.

***

Friday, 16 August

Eight fifty a.m. Mobile rings. Hasan.

I prayed for a miracle.

"Hello."

"Gaynor, he's dead. I found him... and he's dead."

"Ohh fuck. I am SO sorry, dar…."

"I can't believe it!"

"Are you at the flat?"

"Yes, I called in this morning, just in case…"

"Where was he?"

"In the living room."

"But we searched the living room," I protested.

"You won't believe how I found him."

"How?" I said urgently, needing clarification.

"I was sitting on the sofa looking around and I suddenly 'lost it'. I kicked the pouffe so hard that it somersaulted and landed upside down. He was there."

"Where?"

"Trapped under one of the straps that holds the cover on the pouffe."

"But we looked under the pouffe last night…"

"Yes, but he is sort of inside the pouffe."

I sighed a sort of sigh of relief. "Well at least you've found him. Thank God."

"I'm holding him in my hand," said Hakan, choking up.

Tears filled my eyes.

"Oh, darling, it wasn't your fault. We never know how, we never know where, sometimes, it's just our time to go. It was Sunny's time."

"What shall I do with him?"

Good question.

"Let me think about that one. I'll get back to you."

'Okay. Well, I suppose I better go to work."

"Yes. Go to work and I'll speak to you later."

"Okay, bye."

"Bye, lovely."

Obviously, Hasan would have to tell his (not so potential) girlfriend the truth. Thing is, should he put the little bird in a box with some flowers until she returned home so that she could say goodbye to him or would little Sunny start to decompose, in which case, should Hasan bury him in a little tin somewhere, under a tree, perhaps?

Another thought occurred to me… but was it too weird? Put him in the freezer then just before she returns, defrost him, blow dry his feathers and lay him out caringly in a box with fresh flowers or even just lie him on his back at the bottom of his cage, as though he had just 'passed away' during the night? I asked myself, what I would prefer. I couldn't decide. I would discuss it with Hasan.

Hasan called at three p.m.

"How are you doing, darling?"

"I'm in the pet shop."

"What are you doing in there?"

"Well, I've got Sunny with me and I'm trying to find one that looks the same… the man in the shop is helping me."

"Hasan, leave the shop NOW! Stop what you are thinking. It won't work."

"No, it's okay, I'm not trying to fool her. I will tell her what happened. I just don't want her to come home to an empty cage."

A thought flashed through my mind. We could put the little box with Sunny and the flowers in, inside his cage. At least it seemed dignified. Apart from the freezing.

"Hasan, DON'T buy another canary. You have to allow your friend to grieve for this one first."

"But it might help…"

"No, it feels like 'This one's dead, but don't worry. Here's another one'. I can see that you might think a new canary would help but believe me, it's not a good idea. Maybe later… in a few weeks or something."

"Okay. You're probably right. I'm leaving the shop now. I'll just have to face the music. Shall I tell her if she calls?"

"No. No point in ruining her holiday."

"Okay. I'll wait until she gets back."

"Do you speak, every day?" I asked.

"No, every few days."

"Well try to avoid her calls and just text her, that everything is fine. I am sure she would understand that you wouldn't want to take the joy out of the time she was spending with her family."

"Okay."

"Where is Sunny now?"

"In my pocket."

"No, I mean is he in anything?"

"Yes, he's in my pocket."

"I mean is he in a box or a bag or something?"

"No, he's just my pocket."

Typical bloke.

I discussed my thoughts with Hasan regarding what we should do with Sunny. Feeling it was appropriate, I suggested a pretty little box in which we would lay Sunny, on cotton-wool and then surround him with small fresh flowers. We would put the little box in the cage with the lid on in case she didn't want to see him but could still take comfort from the fact that he was there and also make her decision on where Sunny should have his final resting place. I persuaded Hasan to go home, put Sunny carefully in a plastic bag and hide him in his mum's freezer until Tuesday, the day before his 'not so potential' girlfriend was due home.

***

Four p.m. Hasan called.

"Hi, Hasan. How are you doing?"

"Not looking forward to tomorrow. I was going to wait for her at her flat but she texted me and asked me to pick her up from the airport."

Knowing that she would be able to detect something was wrong the moment she saw Hasan, and to prevent her crying all the way home, I made a suggestion. "Text her and tell her your car has broken down but you have arranged a taxi to collect her. Tell her that a taxi driver will be standing with a card with her name on it as she comes through customs, and tell her it's paid for. Then tell her you'll meet her at her flat."

"Good idea," responded, Hasan, showing some relief at my suggestion.

"What time does she get in tomorrow?"

"Lands at 2.40 in the afternoon."

"Okay. Now, Hasan, have you got a nice little box to put Sunny in?"

"I've got a Nike shoe box."

Typical bloke.

"That'll be too big to fit in the cage," I said, trying to be sensitive.

"Oh. Okay."

We paused. He spoke.

"Gaynor?"

"Yes?"

"Will you help me prepare him?"

I sighed, inwardly.

"Okay. Are you at work?"

"Yes."

"After work, go and fetch him from the freezer and then come straight over here."

"Okay. Thanks, Gaynor. I have to work late tonight so can't get over to you until about eleven, is that okay?"

"No problem."

I sighed inwardly again… at the lateness.

"See you later. And bring him in the Nike box. Don't just put him in your pocket."

"Okay. Thanks. See you later."

By the time Hasan had pulled up outside, I had all the funeral service arranged. A pretty little blue box with small silver stars on, tissue paper, cotton wool and various small wild flowers which I had stolen from next door's garden.

The buzzer went and up he came through the door, with the Nike box in his hand. I hugged him, then lead him to the kitchen table where he placed the box. I slowly, respectfully, lifted the lid. One very small frozen canary in a large empty box. Poor wee thing, I thought, as I gently lifted the icy little creature out. As I turned Sunny over, through the ice, I could see his tiny little beak and two closed eyes. I felt really sad then reminded myself, as I often do after death, that the spirit of Sunny was long gone. He was now in canary heaven and I was just holding the shell that had once housed him.

Not being able to find anything to say, I lifted his little body from the box and placed him gently on some tissue paper.

"That's a nice box," said Hasan, picking up the little box I had bought. I like little stars… And nice flowers too. Thanks, Gaynor, you are so kind."

"No problem. Now, we are going to have to gently blow dry him with the hair dryer until he's defrosted.

"The hair dryer?"

152

"Yes, the hair dryer. We can thaw him out and fluff up his feathers," I said, praying it would work.

Looking at the frozen creature, I wondered whether it was going to be possible to return it to something resembling a pretty, little, yellow canary. I turned my back for one second and Hasan, in his eagerness to make everything all right, switched the hair dryer on. I span around to see the deceased fly across the work surface and into the sink.

"No! That's far too high. Let me do it," I said, putting Sunny back on the tissue paper and turning the hair dryer to its lowest setting.

"Fix us a drink please, Hasan."

"Vodka?" he said, producing a large bottle of Smirnoff from inside his coat pocket.

"Oh. Well, I don't usually drink spirits but Champagne seems a little insensitive so vodka will be fine with some orange-juice. It's in the fridge."

I started gentle, warm, blow drying from a distance, As the minutes passed, the surface ice started to melt away slowly revealing what looked like a newly hatched canary. He was all limp and wet. Not too bad so far, I thought.

Hasan stepped toward me with a very large vodka and orange. "Here you are, Gaynor. He's not looking too bad is he. He's thawing out nicely."

Thawing out nicely? Typical bloke.

"I need to fluff his feathers up. I don't know if they will… I'll just keep blow drying him for a while," I said, slowly turning Sunny over.

"Okay," said Hasan. "Would you like me to get you a chair?"

"Yes, please."

Hasan fetched two chairs from the living room. We sat down, me, still gently blow drying. We didn't talk, just sat patiently waiting for some feathers to start showing themselves.

"Maybe I should dry him off a bit with a towel?" said Hasan, trying to be of assistance.

"No, let's just keep blow drying," I said, thinking the poor little thing might disintegrate in his manly hands.

153

It seemed like forever, but slowly, tufts of feathers started drying out and shimmering in the warm breeze.

"It seems to be working," I said, as I slowly and very gently turned Sunny over again.

"Yes. It's working really well."

Sunny continued to fluff up and started returning to his original form. He was becoming a little yellow canary again.

A few more minutes passed.

"I think he's done," said Hasan, touching Sunny gently, with one finger.

I turned off the hair dryer and turned to Hasan. "He's done on the outside, but he's probably still frozen on the inside. We'll have to blow dry him slowly for at least another half hour."

"Well let's stop for a couple of minutes, let him cool down and then we can feel if he's still hard in the middle."

I didn't argue but I knew Sunny needed more time. I didn't want the girlfriend opening up the box to a dead, wet canary in a puddle.

Hasan carefully spread the feathers and pushed Sunny's tummy with one finger. Sunny slid, rigidly, three inches across the work top.

"No, he's still frozen in the middle, he needs longer."

I turned the hair dryer back on.

Half an hour later as midnight struck, Sunny looked as good as new, apart from 'sleeping'. I gently picked him up and looked under his wings. He was well and truly 'dried out' and his tummy felt soft and warm. I prepared the box and placed his little body inside.

"That looks really lovely, Gaynor. Thank you so much."

"No problem," I said, putting in the last of the little flowers.

I put the lid on and carefully handed the box to Hasan. "Don't let it get knocked about, and keep it in the fridge overnight Take it out about an hour and a half before she gets home, and check inside the box to make sure everything's thoughtfully in place, before you place it in the cage."

I changed my tone, as I looked into his worried eyes. "Oh, darling, I hope it's not too traumatic. Call me after if you need to talk. Good luck. I'll be thinking of you."

"Thanks again, Gaynor. I'll let you know what happens. Bye."

"Bye, darling. Take care."

PERFECT FLAT MATE WANTED

Sunday, 18th August

Because I had been spending and lending money as though I had a never-ending pot of gold, I decided I would get a flat mate to help out with the bills. I was ready to 'share' after my ten wonderful months of living alone. But. And a very big but, it had to be absolutely the right person. I was not going to compromise. And of course, there would have to be rules. I would keep the living room solely for my use along with the sunny terrace off my bedroom. We would share the kitchen. The new flat mate would have his/her own huge ensuite bedroom where he/she could have his/her own 'sitting area' to entertain friends.

Because I was lucky enough to be in the fancy part of West Hampstead and because I had a beautiful warm, loving, lavish, comfy flat and because the room I was letting was huge and because I was only five mins walk from the tube, I decided I would charge a whopping £800 per month. It was a rent a good professional could afford.

I got my computer out and searched the LOOT website, under 'Lettings'.

I wrote and submitted my ad. Payment by card… transaction complete. The ad would run in Tuesday's issue. Apart from all the basics about the flat, I included my most important thing, MUST LIKE DOGS!

***

Monday, 19th August

In anticipation of a speedy and satisfactory response to my ad, I spent all afternoon typing out an 'Agreement' which had everything in it that my potential new flat mate would have to agree to and then sign.

***

Tuesday, 20th August

Feeling a little disappointed that by lunchtime no one had called, I
popped up the shops to buy a copy of LOOT just to make sure my ad was
in there. It was. I went back home and extended my ad to run for another
five days. I told myself to be patient but at the same time, decided that if
after a week I still hadn't had any interest then I would drop the price to
£700.

My mobile rang around four p.m. I picked it up. It read
'UNKNOWN NUMBER'. Excellent.

"Hello," I said, in my most charming, up-beat, voice.

"Hello… I'm calling about the room"

It was a male.

"Oh! Hi!"

"Is it still available?"

"Yes…"

"Can I come over and see it now?"

"Er… sure… no problem. Have you got a pen? I'll give you the
address."

"Yes, go ahead…"

"What's your name?" I asked, before he hung up.

"Greg Lockly. What's yours?"

"Gaynor. Gaynor Moore," I said, following suit.

"See you in thirty mins, depending on traffic. Can I park?"

"Ring when you are outside and I'll pop down with a permit."

"Great. See you shortly."

He sounds a bit desperate, I thought, hanging up the phone. Maybe
he's just split up with his wife and needs somewhere quickly. Either that
or he's a city trader. IF he's a city trader and runs at full speed all the
time, I won't be able to handle him. He'll drive me mad.

I was looking out the window when a blue Porsche pulled up, a few
houses down. Was it him? My phone rang. Yes, it was. I grabbed a permit
and ran downstairs.

A good-looking smartly dressed middle-aged man with silver hair stepped out of the car and held his hand out to me. I smiled. I didn't know whether he wanted the permit or to shake hands. I did both things simultaneously.

"Gaynor. Nice to meet you. I've only got ten minutes."

Could at least smile, I thought.

"Hi, Greg," I said, in my most relaxed voice. "Follow me."

I walked off as he displayed the permit and locked his car.

I turned to smile at him again. He didn't smile back.

God, he's far too serious, I thought, as he followed me through the front door. Then I thought again, Or maybe his wife has just left him and he just doesn't have the inclination to smile.

We came through the door and Daisy and Flo rushed up to greet him. He ignored them TOTALLY. He's not a dog lover, I thought. Reluctantly, I showed him the room followed by the rest of my beautiful flat.

"Nice… Nice… Nice…" were his only words as he quickly darted in and out of the various rooms. "I'll take it," he said, very sure of himself.

No, you won't, I thought. Then smiled at him again.

"I also have two other people coming to see it this evening," I said, lying.

"Oh. Okay. Call me later if I can have it. Have to dash. Thanks."

He was out the door in a flash.

Even though he was eager, and obviously well off, he wasn't right. I felt for him but I didn't want him living with me. He was just too damn 'urgent'. He had also ignored Daisy and Flo even though they had greeted him eagerly with wagging tails. No. Can't help you. Sorry. Good luck.

I hoped for another call and it came almost immediately.

Still reeling from the last chap, I picked up the phone to another 'UNKNOWN NUMBER'.

"Hello," I said, far too urgently.

"I'm calling about the ad in LOOT, is the room still available?" a lady responded, in what I think was a mild French accent.

She sounded quite abrupt. Even a little pissed off.

158

"Yes, it's still available but I am seeing two people this evening who are also interested."

"Can I come to see the room now? I am in West Hampstead and could be there in five minutes."

Very pushy, these people with money in their pockets.

"Can I just ask you a few questions first?" I asked politely.

"Yes. Go ahead. What do you want to know?"

"How old you are, what you do for a living and…"

She interrupted before I had finished. "I'm twenty-four, and work for a large city bank."

I might as well see her. She might be less sharp in real life.

"Okay, I'll give you the address. Are you driving?"

"No, I'm walking."

"Ok. See you in a few minutes."

I looked out the window and waited for her to come down the street. Then she came. Bolt upright, walking fast and extremely confidently. High heels, suit, hair pulled back in a tight, tidy pony tail and carrying a briefcase. She looked like a powerful business woman. As she got closer, I noticed she was smaller than her stance suggested. A small powerful business woman. Scary. She didn't look like much of a dog lover, either.

As she approached the house, she looked up at me as I waved through the window with a welcome smile. She nodded politely, then I pushed the buzzer for her to come in.

"First floor," I shouted down the stairwell.

She didn't respond but quickly marched up the stairs to the flat.

I held out my hand. "I'm Gaynor."

She was very polished. Immaculately dressed, her extremely well applied red lipstick stood out against her pale skin and jet-black hair.

"Brenda," she said, taking my hand with her perfectly manicured paw and shaking it firmly.

Brenda? That's not very French I thought… Maybe her mother was English?

"This way, Brenda." I led her straight to the room.

As I opened the door to the room and held out my arm to show her in, she walked straight past me and then to my utter amazement, ran one of her fingers along the top of the radiator then checked it for dust. You're definitely not moving in! I thought, How bloody rude!

She turned to me. "Do you have a cleaner?"

I paused briefly. I do, but I'm not telling you that.

"No. No cleaner."

"Well, I would need a cleaner," she said, studying the room even more closely. "And I would want the walls a different colour. Also, you need to take away the furniture as I have my own."

What is it with these people who think they're in charge? I thought, then wandered off to let the dogs out of the living room so they could meet Brenda.

They bounded over to her with great excitement then in unison, jumped up, unfortunately scratching her legs with their eager paws.

"DOWN!" she shouted, as though she had known them for years. Daisy and Flo immediately sat down on the spot.

"OH MY GOD! THEY'VE LADDERED MY TIGHTS!"

"Oh sorry... Dogs will be dogs. It says in the ad that I have dogs. Haven't you got a spare pair of tights in your briefcase?" I asked, sarcastically.

"Thankfully, I do."

Of course, she did. I knew she would have a spare pair with her at ALL times.

I walked over to her and handed her a lint roller. "Dog hairs," I said. "They get everywhere."

She raised her eyebrows at me, took the roller and marched into the ensuite bathroom, sharply closing the door behind her. A couple of minutes passed.

"Can you take the dogs away so they don't ladder my new tights?"

"No problem," I said, taking them back to the living room.

She left the flat knowing that I wouldn't be calling her cute, little, uptight ass.

God, what is happening to people? The two experiences I had just been through were quite overwhelming. Shocking even. I got myself a drink. Where are all the NICE people, the gentle people, the artists, designers, musicians and actors of this world? If I was going to share my flat, I realised it was going to have to be with a creative spirit. Someone like me. And on reflection, I decided, my new flatmate would need to be male.

Brenda had managed to single-handedly wipe out any prospects for a potential female flat mate.

At seven p.m. the phone rang again. 'UNKNOWN NUMBER'.

"Hello."

"Hello."

It was female.

"I saw your ad in LOOT. Is the room still available?"

"No sorry, it's gone. Someone took it this morning," I lied, sticking with my plan to find a male.

"Okay. Thanks. Bye," she responded sweetly.

I felt guilty.

"Bye. Good luck in finding somewhere."

I turned my phone off until tomorrow.

✳✳✳

Wednesday, 21st August

I turned my phone on at lunchtime. No missed calls.

I turned my phone off again at midnight.

I lay down in bed and wondered how hard it was going to be to find the right person.

I decided I would ask lots of questions to any interested creative males that called so as not to waste any more of my time, or theirs.

***

Thursday, 22nd August

It was lunchtime. No calls yesterday and none so far today. I popped out to get another copy of LOOT, just to make sure the ad was still running. It was.

On the way back from the newsagents my mobile rang. 'UNKNOWN NUMBER'.

"Hello," I said, optimistically.

"Hi!"

It was male. And he sounded cheery. Hurrah.

"I am calling about the room. Is it still available?"

"Yes, it is," I cheerily responded.

"Oh good. I just have one question for you."

"Fire away," I said, still being cheery.

"Would you consider taking a couple?"

My heart sank. I couldn't possibly have a couple. I didn't want to be out-numbered in my own home, no matter how nice they might be.

"Oh, I'm sorry. I'm really just looking for one person."

"Okay, I understand. Thanks anyway. Bye."

"Bye. Good luck in your search."

"Cheers!"

We hung up.

Shame he wasn't single I thought. He sounded nice.

No more enquiries for the rest of the day.

***

Friday, 23rd August

Seven thirty p.m. Phone rings. 'UNKNOWN NUMBER'.

"Hello."

"Er... Hello..."

He was male.

"I'm looking for somewhere to live in West Hampstead and just saw your ad in LOOT. Er... Is the room still available?"

He was softly spoken and sounded slightly nervous.

"Yes, the room is still available," I responded politely and sensitively.

"Oh! Good! I am in West Hampstead now. Would it be okay if I popped around to take a look?"

"Do you mind if I ask you a few questions first? I don't want to waste your time."

"No, sure, that's fine. Er... What would you like to know?"

"Is the room just for you?"

"Yes."

"How old are you, and what do you do?"

"I'm twentty-seven, and I'm a designer, computer animation."

Excellent.

"Oh, cool! What's your name?"

"Ben."

"Hi, Ben! I'm Gaynor," I said, enthusiastically.

His voice lifted.

"Hi, Gaynor! Nice to meet you!"

We paused. Then Ben spoke first. "Would you like to ask me any more questions, Gaynor?"

"No. That's all for now. You're welcome to pop over and take a look at the room."

"Oh thanks. That would be great. Where are you? Can you give me directions from the tube? I'm in the pub and coming by foot."

"No problem. Turn left out of the tube and walk down the hill. Take the third on your left. That's my street. Compayne Gardens. Walk down the street and cross over Priory Road. I am in the row of houses on the right, that follows.

"Hang on... I'm just writing this down. Combain Gardens. How do you spell it?"

'C-o-m-p-a-y-n-e, Compayne Gardens."

"Got it. Out of the tube, third turning on the left, down Compayne Gardens, cross over Priory Road and carry on.

"Just look for the blue star lights."

"Okay. Blue stars. Excellent. See you shortly."

"Cool."

I was peeping on to the street from behind the curtains. He was casually walking along, looking at the houses. He caught sight of the blue neon stars hanging in my kitchen window and stopped outside the gate. He was smiling. Hurrah! He was smiling to himself. I revealed myself by knocking on the window and waving. He waved back... like an old friend. Now let's see what he's like in real life.

He rang the buzzer and I picked up the 'entry' phone. "Hi, Ben. When I press the buzzer, push the door open and come up to the first floor."

I waited for him to climb the stairs before opening my front door. I was looking through the spy hole at him so timed it perfectly.

I scanned him very quickly. He was tall, about 6'4", slim, short dark hair and had a lovely, gentle face. He was casually dressed in jeans and a bomber jacket with an 'art-bag' hanging over one shoulder. His body language was well placed. He was standing about four feet from the door. He was giving me plenty of space.

"Hello, Gaynor," he said, with a gentle smile.

I reached out to shake his hand. He wiped his hand across his jeans and responded with a firm, yet gentle handshake.

"Hi, Ben. Come in..."

"Thanks for seeing me so quickly, hope I'm not interrupting anything," he said, peering through the glass doors to the living room.

Daisy and Flo spotted him, through the glass and started barking excitedly.

"Ahh... Your dogs. Can I say hello to them?" he asked, sounding genuinely pleased to see them.

"Yes, of course," I said, throwing open the living room doors.

Ben bent down as they ran over to greet him. "Ahh... They're really lovely," he said, making a fuss of them.

"What are they called?"

"This one's Daisy and this one's Flo," I said, proudly.

"Hello, Daisy! Hello, Flo!" He stroked their heads then stood back up.

"Your flat is stunning," he said, looking around the room.

"Thanks," I said, appreciatively. He's the one, I thought, contentedly.

"I was beginning to lose hope... I've seen five flats this afternoon and they've all been shit. I was going to go home but decided to go to the pub for a pint and to take one last look in LOOT. I spotted your ad at the end of the 'Rooms to let' section so dialled your number on the off chance that you might be in... and the room might still be available."

164

"Well, I was and it is. Must be your lucky day, Ben! Would you like to see the room?"

"I'd love to," he said, following me into the hall. I opened the door. Ben's mouth fell open. "It's huge! It's fantastic!"

"Here's the ensuite bathroom," I said pointing to it. "The shower is very powerful… and if you look over here…," I walked to the windows, "there's a lovely view of the gardens."

"What a fabulous place! It's really amazing!"

Seeing that Ben loved the flat, and the dogs, I decided it was his.

"Come into the front room, Ben. I'll fix you a drink… Champagne okay?"

"Wow! Yes! Brilliant! Thanks!"

I returned to the living room where Ben was now sitting on the floor, stroking Daisy and Flo. I put his drink on the coffee table in front of him and decided to roll a joint. If he was going to be living with me, he needed to know I smoked occasionally. I wasn't going to smoke my hash in private so I needed to test the water. He didn't take any notice or ask any questions as I rolled. I lit up, took a big breath in, then passed it in his direction.

"Do you smoke, Ben?"

"Yes! Thanks very much, What a treat!"

Ben gave a broad smile as he took it from me. I hoped he didn't hang on to it beyond the polite stage. It would have put me off him. He took one large draw then passed it straight back to me.

"Thanks, Gaynor. And thanks for the drink. Most unexpected."

"My pleasure. Well, you seem like a really nice guy, so I'd like to offer you the room."

"Wow! Really? I feel honoured."

"Have you got anything you'd like to ask me about, Ben? Anything at all? I've actually written out all the rules for the flat but now I've met you, I think they can be relaxed a little."

"How much is it again?" asked Ben, taking a small sip from his drink.

"£800 per calendar month, including bills."

"OH MY GOD!" said Ben, quickly getting up off the floor and putting his hands over his face.

"What's wrong?" I shrieked, joining him in his upset.

"I am in the wrong house. I'm in the wrong fucking house. I shouldn't be here… I am SO sorry."

"What do you mean?" I asked, as Ben grabbed the copy of LOOT from his bag.

He raced through the pages to 'Lettings'. "Here," he said, pointing to the ad above mine. "I read this ad… for £400 a month, then somehow lost my place on the page and called your number by mistake. Your ad is under the one I was looking at. I am SO sorry. I've wasted your time. I can't possibly pay that sort of money, as much as I would love to be able to. I really am SO sorry."

I was devastated at the news from my perfect flat mate. I tried not to show it so took a long slow drag on the joint while I searched for the words to respond. Ben was such a lovely bloke. I didn't want to make him feel worse than he already did.

"Oh, Ben. What a shame. You would have been perfect. You seem like a really lovely man!"

"A really stupid man," said Ben, hitting himself over the head, with his LOOT.

He continued. "I thought it was extremely cheap. The street… Your flat… The huge room… When I came through your door, I felt like I'd won the lottery. I couldn't believe my luck. I feel like a right twat. I'm really sorry for fucking up and wasting your time, Gaynor."

"Don't worry… Mistakes happen," I said, getting up and then giving him a hug.

"I'd better go then."

"Don't be daft, sit down and finish your drink."

"Are you sure?"

"Of course, relax."

Ben sat back on the floor, shaking his head to himself.

"So where are you living at the moment, Ben?" I asked, changing the subject.

"Brighton."

"Brighton!"

"Yes, but I've been offered a job in Soho so I want to move up here. All my friends came up a few years ago but I stayed in Brighton. I liked my job but I'm ready for a change now. Time to move to London… and most of my old pals are in the Kilburn/West Hampstead area."

"Have you got to go back to Brighton tonight? If you can't face it, you can sleep in the room which had your name on it," I said, making a genuine gesture.

"God, that's really nice of you to offer but I'm staying with my sister tonight. She's just down the hill in Belsize Road. Thanks anyway."

"Well give me your number then when you find a place we can meet up for a drink. It would be nice to see you again."

"Cool, that would be great," said Ben, reading out his number while I entered it, into my phone.

"What's your number, Gaynor?"

"You'll find it in LOOT!" I said, laughing, as I hit him over the head with his copy.

"God, what is wrong with me tonight?" he said, shaking his head again.

We tried to be cheery but neither of us could really recover from the upsetting mistake of the evening. As the conversation slowly fizzled out, Ben got up to leave.

"Thanks again for the drink and smoke, Gaynor. It was lovely to meet you. I'll call you when I've found somewhere to live."

"Cool. Good luck in your search. I hope you find somewhere nice," I said, as I kissed and hugged him out the door.

"Bye, Gaynor."

"Bye, Ben. Take care."

I closed the door, then went to lie on the sofa. I closed my eyes and took a deep breath. It was Saturday tomorrow and my ad would run out on Sunday. I opened my eyes again then dragged myself over to my computer to book another seven days.

I tried not to think about Ben when I climbed into bed. It was useless. I had lost my perfect flat mate. I was thoroughly pissed off and what's more, I would probably have to weave my way through a lot more wankers before I came across another Ben.

***

Saturday, 24th August

Received three phone calls. One potential flat mate. A trumpet player from an established orchestra. Brian.

He came around at five. Daisy and Flo rushed to greet him as he came through the door. I decided not to shut them in the living room any more while I was showing the flat.

"Hello, dogs," he said, stepping back from their advances. With not even a pat, they quickly lost interest and returned to their beds. Brian was about forty years old. He seemed polite and pleasant enough. But he wasn't a dog lover. And he certainly wasn't a 'Ben'. I too, lost interest so quickly showed him around. He loved the flat.

"Would I be able to practice my trumpet in my room?" he asked, casually, even though he knew he was making a BIG request.

"No, sorry. I don't think the people in the other flats would approve. I've already had a couple of complaints from downstairs about the music. The flats aren't sound-proofed. They never are in these conversions."

"Okay, I understand. I can always go over to my mate's to practice. He's got a detached house in Hampstead."

"That's good," I said. "By the way, I have three more people to see over the weekend before I make up my mind who to offer the room to."

"Oh sorry. I didn't realise you had more people to see. Well, if I don't hear from you by Sunday evening, I'll take it as a 'No'. Would you like to take my number?"

No.

"Yes, please… in fact why don't you send it to my phone. You have my number"

"Okay, will do. Hope to hear back from you during the weekend then. Bye for now."

"Bye, Brian."

THE FLYING VASE

That evening...

I was lying on my bed feeling grumpy and depressed when Hasan popped into my mind. I hadn't heard from him since the canary incident. I had decided to not chase him up to find out what had happened. It was obviously going to be an awful and painful time for him so I just left him to his own space.

I looked at my phone and thought about calling him. It HAD been a week after all. But then, on reflection, I decided it wouldn't be such a good idea. There was a slim chance Hasan might be out somewhere, with Sunny's mum.

Fuck it. I picked up my mobile and called him. It went straight through to answerphone, I hung up.

A moment later he called back. "Gaynor! Hi! Sorry I missed your call. How are you?" he asked, cheerfully.

"I'm okay. How are you?" I responded, caringly.

How come he was so up-beat? I thought he would be suffering somewhere, in some lonely, miserable, dark corner of the planet.

"I'm fine."

Thanks for letting me know.

"And there was me being all concerned over you. What happened about Sunny?"

"She hates me. She said she would never forgive me."

"Did you put Sunny in the cage before she got back, and did he still look okay?"

"Yes, he looked beautiful, all thanks to you but it made no difference. She broke down and told me to get out. I haven't seen or heard from her since. She was really upset and really pissed off with me. She wouldn't let me explain, even though I was in tears myself. And she got me on the back of the head with a vase as I turned to walk out. I had a huge bump."

Thank God he didn't see me smile. I wasn't being wicked. The image of a vase bouncing off Hasan's head, just seemed so funny. And so typical.

"Oh… That was a bit mean," I said, trying to show more care and comfort.

"Well, it's over now. Thank God. What are you doing later, Gaynor? Do you fancy some company?" chirped Hasan, with great enthusiasm.

"Nothing… and I've had a shitty week. Do you want to come over and cheer me up?"

"Yes. Great. My turn to give you some love and support. I'll be over at eight thirty. Shall I go to the off-licence, en route?"

"Yes. Bring Champagne. AND DON'T BE LATE!"

"I won't," he said confidently.

He turned up at nine forty-five, and lifted something from the boot of his car.

I shouted down to him from the window. "You're an hour and fifteen minutes late, and you promised to be here at eight thirty. I'm not letting you in!"

He held up three bottles of Champagne, to show me. "Sorry! I had to do something for my mum."

"I don't care. You broke your promise, and you didn't call. I'm not letting you in." I laughed, then pushed the buzzer for Hasan to gain entry.

After hugs, he was on his knees, making a fuss of Daisy and Flo again. He looked up at me.

"Tell you what, Gaynor, I am never, ever, ever, going to offer to look after someone's pet again. It's too much of a responsibility. I was totally traumatized after Sunny died. I'm still trying to get over it, now."

A COMPROMISE

Sunday, 25th August

I sat around all day waiting for the phone to ring. Not one call to see the flat. The ad would be running again tomorrow for another whole week. I thought that maybe I should have dropped the price to £700. I decided that artists tended to have smaller wallets than city folk. Oh well. Too late now. Or was it? Actually, it probably wasn't. Surely it must be possible to change the amount to £700 for Wednesday's issue. I decided I would ring LOOT in the morning to see if they could change the ad for me.

***

Monday, 26th August

Rang LOOT and the ad was changed. No problem. The new price should bring in a wider range of punters. I felt more optimistic.

Two interested parties today. No good. Both, female. I wondered again about sharing with a girlie. DON'T COMPROMISE was my brain's response. No. I was right. I would much rather share with a nice steady chap. I thought about Ben again. And again. And again. I tossed things over in my mind. What would I rather have? £800 and a wanker or £400 and Ben? Ben of course but £400 was just too low. The new ad was offering the room for £700. I wondered if there was any possibility that Ben would meet me halfway and pay £600 per month for the room. For the sake of £100, I would rather do without it and have Ben move in.

I decided to give him a call. He picked up immediately. "Hi, Gaynor! How ya doing?"

"I'm fine thanks, Ben. Have you found anywhere to live yet?"

"No, still looking. £400 doesn't get you much in London. I've seen some single rooms smaller than your ensuite bathroom!"

"Well, I have been thinking about things and wondered whether you could afford to meet me halfway if I dropped the price and let you have the room £600 a month?"

He went silent.

"The thing is, I can't afford to let you have it for any less. I need help to pay my mortgage. I have had people round who have wanted to take the room but they've mainly been from another planet. And, you and I seemed to get on so well together. I would love you to have the room, if you can afford it."

"Blimey, Gaynor, that is a very generous offer to make. Are you sure you can afford to knock £200 off the rent every month?"

"Yes, absolutely sure. It's a small price to pay for my sanity and peace of mind."

"It's really is very kind of you to think of me but I'm really not sure I can afford it."

"All bills would be included." I said, grasping at straws.

"All bills? What about council tax?"

"That's included," I said, kicking myself under the table at my desperation.

"Do you want to come over after work to see the room again? And to have another little chat? I won't hold you hostage if you really don't want to take it."

"Are you sure you've thought this through, Gaynor?"

"Yes, it's all I have been doing, thinking things through."

"Okay, I'll come after work. I'm still staying with my sister so will be with you at about seven thirty. Is that okay for you?"

"Yes, that's fine."

"I can't make any promises yet, though, Gaynor."

"It's okay. I understand. I don't have any expectations. It would be nice to see you anyway."

"Okay. Great. See you at seven thirty."

"Great. See you then."

I hung up then put all thoughts of interviewing more aliens to the back of my mind. If the phone rings today with 'UNKNOWN NUMBER' displayed, I will direct the call to my answering service.

No one called but I didn't care. It was nearly seven thirty and Ben would be arriving, any minute. The buzzer went and I pressed it to let him in. He ran up the stairs and I gave him a broad smile and a big hug.

"Ahh. Are you all right, Gaynor?" he said, stroking my back caringly.

"Yes, I'm fine. Come in, I'll fix you a drink."

"Great!"

The dogs bounded over and jumped up at him. "Ahh! Hello, Daisy! Hello, Flo! How are you today?" The girls woofed at him as though understanding. Now that's someone who likes dogs, I thought.

"Here you go, Ben," I said, passing him a large drink.

"Thanks, Gaynor."

"Sit down," I insisted, as he collapsed his knees to sit cross-legged on the floor.

He held his glass up to mine. We clinked and said a chirpy "Cheers!" in unison.

I felt Ben was waiting for me to start up the conversation so I spoke first. "So, Ben. What do you think?"

"I think you're really sweet. I'm very flattered that you would drop your price for me… Er… You said that you had written out the terms and conditions. Do you mind if I take a look through them?"

"They don't really apply to you. They were quite rigid. I need to re-write them."

"Okay, then tell me what you would expect from me, as your tenant?"

"Not a tenant! A flat mate! Well, there are the basics like paying the rent on time every month, and being considerate."

"Okay… and what else?"

"Can't really think of anything else," I said, searching my brain.

"Well, it doesn't really feel like a 'flat share'. This is your home, and I can see you love it from the joy you have spread from room to room with all the fairy lights and pictures and pots."

"And…?" I responded.

"Well… What if I break something?"

"Like what? If you broke a window, I would expect you to pay for it."

"What about plates or glasses? Or say, one of your pots?"

"You keep your hands off my pots," I said, laughing at my own innuendo.

Ben laughed and responded. "Well, I suppose you're right. I don't need to go anywhere near your pots. I'll just keep my hands in my pockets."

We both laughed.

"Look, Ben, the pots never come off the shelves. I don't even dust them. I promise one won't throw itself under your feet if you arrive home drunk from the pub one night."

Ben laughed again.

"What about glasses and plates? I'm sure you have nice quality stuff."

"I get all my glasses and china from Ikea. I'm ALWAYS breaking 'food vessels'. Also, I kick over at least three cups of coffee a week because I put them on the floor. Despite understanding the bonus of putting all drinking vessels on the table, something inside me convinces me that my cup or glass will be totally safe on the floor. The red rug you are sitting on is specifically placed to catch and hide any spillages. And, it's had many hundreds over the years. Look, Ben, I am not a 'precious' person. I know that everything around me is 'borrowed'. I am just the keeper of it until such time that it is passed on or gets accidentally broken. You can't take it with you when you die. It's just 'stuff'."

"That's a very refreshing attitude you have."

"I wasn't always like this. I was extremely 'anal' up until a couple of years ago. Everywhere had to be immaculate, before I could go to bed. The worst thing was that I had four silk cushions on the sofa which I had to align and position exactly before leaving the living room. The cushions had to be standing up on a pointed corner as in a 'diamond shape' but without the pointed bit 'buckling'. Sometimes I was there for ages. I was totally fucking barking mad. I was very 'anal'."

Ben's head fell backward, as he burst out laughing. "You are fucking hilarious, Gaynor. And how old did you say you were?"

174

"I'll be forty-eight next month."

"Jesus! I thought you were about thirty-eight! You look amazing for your age!"

Ben spoke taking on a slightly more serious tone. "So, what about girlfriends?"

"I'm straight," I said, laughing.

Ben pushed my knee then I carried on.

"Why? How many have you got?"

"Just the one. She lives in Greece at the moment but wants to move to the UK."

I wondered where he was heading.

"She is coming over next month to look for a flat."

Phew.

"Would she be able to stay with me for two weeks while she finds somewhere? She doesn't know anyone in London."

"Yes, of course, no problem, two weeks is fine."

"She's a lovely girl, you'll really like her," he said, reaching into his wallet and lifting out a photograph of them both.

"Oh… she looks really sweet," I said, because she did.

"Her name's Angela. She would love you."

I studied the photograph more closely. She looked tiny next to Ben. Very pretty and very innocent looking, with her half, non-confident smile. I could feel her fragility.

"How tall is she?"

"She's quite small, about 5ft. But don't let that fool you. She has the heart of an angel but the courage of a lion."

More than meets the eye then.

"Well, Gaynor, if you don't mind Angie staying for two weeks and if you won't go nuts if I break something, then I'd love to move in with you. I can just about afford £600 if all the bills are included."

I jumped across the floor and threw my arms around Ben's neck. "Hoooray! I've got my perfect flat mate. Thanks, Ben. I'm delighted."

He patted my back as I squeezed him hard.

"You're delighted," he responded, pulling away from me so as to look me in the face. "You've just blown me out of the water. My ship has landed. Ben Woodhouse has arrived. Bring it on. My friends are going to be SO jealous." He laughed, and at the same time, did that 'hip', 'flicky' thing with his fingers.

We got pissed, stoned and arranged a moving in date. Saturday, 1st September.

Hurrah! Hurrah! and double hurrah!

BIRTHDAY RIDE

Ben had moved in and everything was 'tickety-boo'. Tonight, I would be taking a group of friends out, including my lovely new flat mate, Ben, along with one of his buddies, Mark. I invited him so my girlfriends could meet him and confirm he was an excellent choice. We would be having pop (and dinner) because I had a double celebration. Great new flat mate and tomorrow, it was my birthday.

Ben was messing around with the computer in his room in the afternoon when I flung the door open. "Fancy coming shopping, Ben?"

"Why? Where are you going?"

"Just up the road... West Hampstead, I'm going to buy a bicycle, I've been thinking about it for some time. I used to love my bike, as a kid, so I thought I'd buy myself one as a birthday present. Thought you could give me your expertise."

"Don't know about that, I'm not an expert but yeah, I'll come with you. Do you want to go now?"

"Excellent! In about ten minutes."

I suddenly felt all excited at the prospect. Except, I was concerned about traffic. I imagined I'd have to keep on the pavements, and then I'd probably get caught, and told off by a policeman. Oh well. I would just have to take it slowly and practice around the local streets.

We arrived at the bike shop. I wanted a metallic blue one, like my old one. Colour was far more important to me than performance.

I looked around at all manner of bikes hanging from the walls and many standing on the ground. Blimey. Biking had become a lot more expensive than I'd imagined. I think the one my parents had bought me as a teenager was about £17. State of the art too. Some of the bikes I was looking at were hundreds and hundreds of pounds.

"Can I help you?" said the young, 'bike' enthusiast.

"I was thinking of buying a bike, and I haven't ridden one for about thirty years."

The shop assistant paused for thought.

"I wanted to spend about £150 and I'd like it to be metallic blue."

"We don't have any metallic blue at the moment but there's this nice black one," he said, stepping to the right and pointing to one of the bikes on the ground.

I felt disappointed, as I stepped toward it to try it on.

"That's a nice bike," said Ben, enthusiastically, "and it's in the sale, only £189, fifty quid off."

I climbed over the bar and tried to raise my bum up high enough, to sit on the seat. "I can't get on it. It's too high," I whinged, on tippy toes.

"Don't worry, I can lower the seat," said the assistant, enthusiastically, as he pulled a lever, dropping the seat by about 4."

I climbed on. It was like sitting on a broom handle. All my tender girlie bits were being crushed against the underside my pelvic bone.

"Bloody hell! The seat's a bit small," I said, stepping off. "This definitely isn't a girl's bike. And my bum's far too big for it."

I peered behind me at the thin piece of tight black rubber that called itself 'a seat'.

"You can choose a different saddle if you like," said the assistant pointing to the back wall. Ben tried the bike out for size and comfort while I went to inspect the large display of seats. All were shrink-wrapped to show off size and shape to the maximum. I sized them up. I lifted my first choice, the biggest saddle on show, off its peg. Being practical, I then squatted, bent my legs and whipped the saddle up between my legs with one hand so I could pretend to sit on it. I positioned myself, then pushed my ample duvet bum in and out of the plastic sandwiched seat. It was far from ideal. It didn't feel very big or supportive at all. I kept squishing. It didn't occur to me that my behaviour may have looked somewhat amusing, until I noticed Ben, laughing.

"Gaynor, you're so funny."

"Just being practical, Ben," I responded, in a matronly voice.

"How is it?" said Ben, trying not to laugh.

"It's small."

"Oh," said Ben.

"But I think it's the biggest they've got."

I double-checked the display.

"Can you put it on the bike for me please," I said, handing it to the assistant.

"I'll be able to nip up to the shops for you, Gaynor," said Ben, while perched on the bike and lifting the front handlebars as though he was going to do a wheelie.

"I'll be there and back in five mins."

That was true. At least it didn't look too girly for Ben to ride.

He climbed off, as the assistant removed the broom handle so as to position the new, wider version seat. I sat on it.

"How does that feel?" asked the shop assistant, feeling positive of an imminent sale.

I shuffled and squished.

Then I couldn't resist.

"Ben, does my bum look big in this?"

He laughed, and so did the shop assistant.

Determined to have my birthday present immediately and instead of having to boringly search for another one, I opted for the black 'boy looking' bike. Paid for, Ben rode it home while I walked alongside.

Eight p.m. Me, Ben and Mark were sipping Champagne when Callie and Amy arrived to join us at The Globe restaurant.

After introducing my new flat mate and his friend to the girls, I turned to Callie. "Callie, I've got a new bike."

"Who? Ben?" she responded, laughing.

I elbowed her in the ribs then we all proceeded to have a jolly old time.

COME OUT, WITH YOUR HANDS UP

Thursday, 12th Sept.

My forty-eight birthday had been enjoyed by all and now the celebration was over, I decided to take the plunge (which I had been thinking about for some months) and be very adventurous and 'modern' thinking and join a website dating service. The main reason being although the young men I had spent various nights with had been wonderful and glorious and great fun, I was now feeling that it would be nice to find someone of a similar age group to spend some time with, someone between forty and fifty.

I joined a site, wrote my profile, attached a photo then went to bed. My profile and photo now had to be checked for indecency or obscenities, before approval.

***

Wednesday evening, I went back to my computer to see if my profile was up and running. Not only was it up and running, I had had thirty-seven emails from different gentlemen all telling me a little about themselves and asking me if I'd like to 'instant message' with them.

I didn't know how 'instant messaging' worked but sat and read the profiles of the chaps who had taken the time to write to me. I also looked at their photos. Now, since leaving my husband and coming to my senses, I have come to realise that looks aren't everything.

BUT there has to be something in a photo that for me, anyway, pulls me in and makes me interested. Could be the eyes, could be the smile. Maybe even the aura. Anyone who had attached a photo of themselves wearing sunglasses, I dismissed. Anyone who was standing ten metres from the camera so you couldn't see their face, I dismissed. And anyone who sent a photo of their car instead of themselves, I dismissed. That left me with twelve. Along with a smiley, friendly photo, their initial messages to me also needed to 'bring something'... a little charm, politeness, wit and information.

Three were left by the time I had read, and re-read the introductory messages from the potential 'web' daters. 1) A policeman from Manchester, Andy, who had a wide, glorious smile and nice aura. 2) A documentary maker from Hertfordshire, Paul, who was very handsome with lovely warm eyes. 3) An artist from London, Bryn, who had an excellent sense of humour.

I decided not to do 'instant messaging', with the three front runners because I was still a little overwhelmed by the whole internet dating thing. I also wanted to feel as though I was the one who was in control. Instead, we could send various emails backward and forward between each other. Then I changed my mind. I decided to start 'instant messaging' immediately to see how the conversation and communication went, when in 'instant' mode. Andy first, followed by Alan and then Bryn. All three chaps were very different but all were interesting and great to 'instant chat' with.

That out of the way, each of them then gave me *their* phone number so that I could call anonymously, in order to have a brief chat. It would also give me a chance to hear how well they communicated on the phone. A couple of things here, first of all, no matter how good the 'instant messaging' had been, if any of the three chaps had a spoken in a voice akin to Minnie Mouse then I wouldn't be meeting up with them. I'm sure they would have the thought the same if I sounded like Minnie Mouse. Also, I know that only 20% of communication is through the spoken word. The rest, is pretty much made up of body language so it wouldn't be until each of my three dates were standing in front of me, that I would be able to get the whole picture.

Luckily, there were no Minnies. They all had nice voices, so I put three dates in my diary for three consecutive weekends. Andy, the policeman was the first to be booked in, Saturday, 23rd Sept.

Dating sites make it very clear that you should meet your first time 'dater' in a public place and not to give them any details like your home address etc. so I followed instructions.

Because Andy was catching a train down from Manchester, he asked me, rather cheekily, or maybe it wasn't cheeky, in view of his effort to come down to London, whether he could stay over at my place, on Saturday evening.

I told him if he bought his ID and photos of him in his uniform, standing by police car, then it would be okay. He could have the sofa. Plus, Ben had agreed to be in the flat upon our arrival so he could also check Andy out before he went out for the evening.

Because it was only Andy's second visit to London, I was very accommodating and went to meet him at Euston Station. We were in contact by mobile as the five thirty train pulled in and I told him to look out for a blonde in a blue coat standing by the gate. It seemed like hundreds of people stepped off that train and I didn't have a clue what Andy was wearing. I stood there as the people rushed past me. So many men. It seemed like forever. Then, as the crowd thinned, in the distance I saw a man waving so I waved back. He's a bit small for a policeman, I thought, as he got closer and wasn't smiling. He walked straight past me. Ooops, wrong man, then a tap on my shoulder.

"Hello, Gaynor."

I turned around to be greeted by a huge smile.

"Hello, how did you get past me?"

"I'm a policeman," he said laughing.

I smiled back at him and then he threw his arms around me and lifted me off my feet.

"You didn't see me because I used my badge to cut through over there," he said, indicating a different platform exit with his head then gently stood me back on my feet. "It's lovely to meet you, here's my ID to put your mind at ease," he said producing the evidence from his inside pocket.

It looked pretty authentic... not that I'd have a clue if it wasn't.

"You might have made that," I said, giggling.

"Don't worry, I've got photos too," he said lifting up a hold-all.

"Sorry to be a pain, but can I see them now?" I asked sweetly. "I just want to make sure you're not a mad axe-murderer."

"Of course, you can," he said, unzipping his bag and pulling out a pile of photos out of him in his uniform. "I think it's really good that you are so careful."

"Thanks," I said, taking the photos from his hand, feeling all sensible and grown-up.

"Okay, I believe you," I said, flicking through the mugshots. "Follow me," I said grabbing his arm and leading him off to the taxi rank.

As we queued for a cab, all 6'6" of him stood confidently behind me with his arms placed gently around my shoulders. He was very at ease. Oddly, I felt comfortable and very protected wrapped in his arms even though we had only just met. Maybe it was because he was a policeman.

After a little conversation, a little flattery and lots of smiling we arrived at my flat.

I threw open the front door and shouted to Ben. "Ben! It's a raid! Hide the drugs!"

Ben came bouncing out of his room to greet us, followed by Daisy and Flo.

"This is my policeman, Andy. Andy, this is Ben, my flat mate."

"Oh, I didn't know you had a flat mate. Hope you don't mind me staying over, Ben," he said, shaking Ben's hand.

"It's okay, Ben. He is a real policeman. I've seen his credentials," I said, reassuringly.

"Cool," said Ben, smiling nervously at my antics.

Andy pulled out his ID badge again just to confirm and to put Ben's mind at rest.

"I'm off out now then, Gaynor. Have a nice evening. Nice to meet you, Andy. See you later," said Ben, grabbing his jacket and giving me a hug. The front door closed.

"Lovely dogs," said Andy, kneeling down to give them a good firm rub behind the ears. "I'd love to have one but it wouldn't be fair with my job. They'd be on their own too much," he said, allowing Daisy to lick his face.

***

Wednesday, 13th September

Andy left at ten a.m. because he was working in the evening. No sooner had the front door closed than there was a tap on my bedroom door. "Gaynor?"

"Yes, I'm awake. Come in, Ben."

He was smiling eagerly and sat on my bed. "How did it go?"

There was no easy way of saying it, so I just told it, as it was.

"Ben... have just spent the last fourteen hours with that policeman's head between my legs."

Ben fell backward onto the bed, laughing.

"Are you serious?"

"I'm serious. He did. I hardly saw him. He even slept down there!"

Ben howled.

"I couldn't believe it. I couldn't tear him away... even for food. It really was quite extraordinary. I was starving so after going, knickerless, to the loo, I grabbed a bag of crisp from the kitchen. I opened the bag up and offered them to him as I sat back down on the sofa but he wasn't interested. Even though I was starving, I politely put the crisps down and then, wait for it, he got back, between my legs and said, 'It's okay, you go ahead and eat your crisps'."

Ben now had his knees bent and was holding his tummy.

"So, I sat, trying to eat my crisps quietly and subtly while he carried on. He was in a world of his own. He was totally lost in pussy world. There's more. After I'd finished the crisps, he lifted his head and said, 'Oh, there's a box of chocolates in my bag for you, would you like them now?' I said, 'Oooo, yes please', and still kneeling, he reached into his bag, pulled them out to give to me, then carried on! I ate them. He didn't mind at all. It was really odd, him down there eating and me up here, eating."

I couldn't help smiling.

"Why didn't you tell him to stop?"

"Because he seemed so happy. And so grateful. And sooo at home."

"Bloody hilarious!" said Ben, lifting himself up again to a sitting position.

"But was he nice? Did you like him? Will you see him again?"

I didn't see him last night, Ben. So no, probably not. He seemed sweet but it wasn't really my idea of an ideal evening."

Ben laughed again.

"What would you think, Ben, if you went on a date with a girl and she spent fourteen hours attached to your knob?"

"I'd think I was the luckiest man alive," he said, laughing again.

I slapped him.

"No, not really. It's a bit much… especially on a first date," he said, more sympathetically while smiling from ear to ear.

"First date. It's too much full stop," I said, slapping him again.

Still chuckling away to himself, Ben gave me a comforting fatherly hug and then stood up. "Would you like a cup of tea?"

"Love one… and some toast… with marmalade… and an ice pack."

Laughing all the way to the kitchen, Ben returned five minutes later with my order.

"Here you are, Pussy Galore," he said, in a Sean Connery, Scottish accent. He put the tray on my lap, still laughing.

I looked down. Tea, toast with marmalade and a bag of ice cubes.

I giggled.

"Thank you 007. Professional job, well executed."

AGEIST V HEIGHTIST

Tonight, would be my second internet date. This time with documentary maker, Paul. Thankfully, he lived in Wood Green so wouldn't need a bed for the night. We decided to meet at West Hampstead tube station at eight p.m. He told me to look out for the guy with a daffodil in his mouth. He should be easy to spot, I thought, even without the daffodil. From his photo, he was extremely good looking and would easily stand out in a crowd.

Bang on eight o'clock I spotted a man coming up the steps towards the barriers with a daffodil in his mouth. I giggled. I recognised his handsome face immediately. But wait. As he arrived at the top of the steps, I realised I had been conned. He definitely wasn't 5'8"! He was 5'4" tops! I felt extremely disappointed. Not at his height but the fact that he had lied about it. It meant he was insecure about himself. I rose above it and greeted him with a smile and a peck on the cheek. I had to bend because I had 3" heels on, making me about 5'10."

He came straight out with it. "Firstly, Gaynor, I'm sorry for lying about my height."

"Why did you?"

"Because if I had told you I was 5'4" you wouldn't have met up with me."

"I would," I said, wondering if I would have.

"No, Gaynor, you wouldn't. Not a single lady responded to my emails when I stated my height on my profile. That was over a three-month period. As soon as I added 4" I had loads of interest. I don't have a problem with my height, other people do."

Actually, I thought, he does have a point.

Height aside. Apart from his good looks, he had proportionately nice broad shoulders and was very fit looking.

"Anyway, Gaynor, on your profile you said you had lied about your age. You said you were thirty-eight. You look thirty-eight but how old are you?"

"Sixty-two."

He laughed.

"I've got a good surgeon."

"No, but really?"

"Forty-eight… but only just."

"So, why did you lie?"

"Because, you are right. Just as some people are heightist, some people are ageist."

"Right then… So, I added 4" on, and you took ten years off. I think that makes us pretty equal," he smiled confidently at me.

I liked Paul's reasoning. I also liked his confidence and the fact the he had challenged me.

"I have no problem with your height. My first boyfriend was the same height as you and I was with him for seven years," I said, smiling again and bending to give him another peck on the cheek.

"What size feet have you got?" I asked looking down.

"Six. Why?"

"So am I. We could swap shoes," I said playfully, even though I'm an eight.

"Don't worry. I'll walk on the pavement and you can walk in the curb," he said, grabbing my hand and taking charge. I smiled as I stepped into the gutter then realized how ridiculous we would look so I took off my shoes and walked bare-footed.

I didn't want to go into the local wine bar shoeless so asked Paul if he would like to come back to the flat. I knew he wouldn't be able to overpower me simply because of his size so I felt quite safe. He happily agreed and grabbed a bottle of champas on route.

***

Sunday, 1st October

I was woken up by a slight rustling in the corner of the bedroom. I opened one eye and peeped over the top of the duvet to see Paul pulling his trousers up. I quickly closed my eyes again and pretended to be asleep. Despite the excellent banter and him being great in bed, I couldn't really see 'us' going anywhere. It would never feel right, being with a man who had smaller feet than me. I imagined his mini-me size brogues sitting next to my Shrek size eight trainers.

He kissed the sleepy me on the cheek upon leaving and whispered in my ear, "Thanks for a fab evening, Gaynor. I'll call you."

PS. I would like to take this opportunity to expel any myths you may have heard regarding men with small feet. In this case, it most definitely wasn't true. It was the total opposite in fact.

THE VOICE AND LADIES' THINGS

Friday, 8th November

Bryn and I had been trying to meet up for several weeks but we had ended up blowing each other out for various reasons. Tonight was the night. Because I had communicated with him so much and because he seemed like a really nice man, I had invited him to the flat. He was due to arrive at eight p.m. I was looking forward to sitting and listening to his marvellous voice which had a wonderful tone. He sounded so 'well rounded' on the phone and had a great sense of humour. He was also an 'artist' amongst other things. Something close to my heart. It would be good to spend some time with a creative, kindred spirit. Some of his texts and emails had been quite superb with regards to 'creative writing' and seemed to be very much from the heart. He seemed very genuine. I decided to meet him wearing a hat, which covered my eyes and holding a glass of Champagne in one hand and a joint in the other. I would hand the goodies over to him upon answering the door.

The knock at the door came bang on eight p.m. and I opened it holding out the gifts with a huge smile.

I couldn't see Bryn's face because of my hat but I could see his black shoes, then his blue jeans and then I saw some string hanging down. As I tilted my head back, I spotted a bunch of beautiful purple tulips wrapped in brown paper with string.

"Aahh, that's nice," I said, tipping my head completely back so I could see his face. He was beaming.

"What a greeting. It's lovely to finally meet you, Gaynor," he said, passing the tulips and holding a bottle of Champagne. I took the tulips, handing him his glass and the spliff.

"Come in," I said, after a brief hug.

He smelled lovely.

"Yes, finally… Sorry I had to keep cancelling."

"Me too. It's been a heavy month."

Daisy and Flo did their usual jumping up to greet. "Lovely dogs. Which one's Daisy and which one's Flo?"

"Daisy is white and gold, like a daisy and Flo is the black and white one."

"Like a Flo," said Bryn, amusing me.

"Got a light?" he said, holding up the spliff.

"I don't usually smoke but hey, how can I refuse your wonderful gesture."

I lit him up and pointed to a seat.

"It's quite strong so take it easy, especially if you're not used to smoking."

"Will do," he said, taking one large drag then handing it back to me.

"Stick this in the fridge, Gaynor," he said, lifting Champagne from his black leather bag.

"Is that your over-night bag?" I said, hoping he would laugh and say 'of course not'.

"Well, you never know," he said, smiling.

He must have seen my eyebrows raise slightly and subtly in disapproval.

"Only joking, I went for a run at lunchtime, it's my running kit. I need it for the weekend."

I smiled approvingly.

"Thanks for the lovely tulips, excuse me a sec, while I put them in a vase."

Bryn was a well-built man, some ten years younger than me, with denim blue eyes, hidden behind finely framed gold specs. He was about 5'10" and his dark suit jacket showed off his lovely big, broad shoulders which were just right for hanging off. His shirt was a mixture of pink, blue and purple stripes and was tucked into blue jeans. He had a bit of a beer belly or maybe it was a food belly, not sure which. He was the size and shape of the sort of chap that makes a girl feel safe and protected. I wondered whether he HAD been for a run. He didn't really look like a runner. But his voice. Oh, his wonderful voice… It was the sort of voice you could listen to forever, and never get bored of. All in all, I was pleased to finally be meeting up with him. I had enjoyed listening to his dulcet tones every time he had called.

I returned to the living room with the vase'd tulips.

"So, you're Welsh then? Why haven't you got a Welsh accent?"

"Because we moved about a bit when I was growing up."

"My dad's Welsh," I said, proudly.

"Really? Which part?"

"Mountain Ash, Glamorgan. We used to go there a lot when I was a kid and stay with my cousins, the Davies."

"Davies! That's my surname!"

"Crikey! We might be distant cousins."

"Don't worry about it, there are millions of Davies in the phone book, no one will ever find out."

I giggled, missing my mouth with the Champagne and spilling it straight down my cleavage.

"Weak wrists?" quipped Bryn, passing me a hanky from his jacket pocket.

"Only when I'm trying to impress," I said, dabbing the top of my boobs with the blue silk.

I passed the joint to him and he took another large drag.

I leapt from my seat lunging at his shirt with a flicking motion.

"Hot rocks, hot rocks!"

Bryn leant forward and started choking on the smoke in the mayhem.

"What are… cough… hot rocks?"

"Little bits of red-hot hash that I didn't crumble up properly."

He looked down and spotted a small burn hole in his shirt. He tried to speak while still choking. "FUCK!" Cough. "New on today." Cough, cough, cough, cough.

"SHIT! I am SO sorry!"

"Don't worry." Cough, cough. "It's not your fault." Cough, cough. "I should have had an ashtray under it." Cough.

"I should have rolled it more carefully… can't tell you how many items of clothing I have with little burn holes down the front. Sorry, Bryn." "The trouble with choking on a joint is that it goes straight to your head," I said, as Bryn's coughing became more intermittent.

"You're not wrong there," he said swaying to the side with his eyes rolling. "I'm off my bollocks."

I started giggling.

"Oh, I am SO sorry, Bryn."

"Stop apologising and get me a top up," he said, passing me his empty glass.

"Would you like some water?"

"Absolutely not. If I'm going to die now, I'd rather do it on Champagne."

Bryn put the joint in the ash tray, while I went to get a refill. I returned to see Bryn patting his sweating brow with the sodden silk hanky. "Are you okay?"

"Yes, just a bit warm, and I'm VERY, very, stoned."

"Just sit back and relax," I instructed, "I just need to make a quick phone call."

"Paramedics?"

I giggled and left the room. I didn't really need to make a phone call but I thought it would be a good excuse to leave Bryn on his own for a few minutes, so he could recover. I decided to go for a pee.

Upon pulling my knickers down I spotted a small reddish-brown circle on my panty liner. That's early, not due for another week, I thought, sitting myself on the toilet. I peeled the sticky-back panty liner from my knickers and stuck it on the tiled wall while I unwrapped a tampon.

"Gaynor! Someone's at the door," I heard Bryn calling, down the hallway.

"Can you get it please," I said, quickly inserting a tampon and pulling up my knickers. I quickly washed my hands.

"It's your neighbour."

"Coming…"

It was the old lady from upstairs. Mrs Tweener.

"Sorry to bother you, Gaynor, but did the postman leave anything for me today? I'm expecting an urgent package but had to go to my sister's today and I left the house before the postman came. It should have arrived yesterday because it was first class. It's coming from America and my daughter has been tracking it on the internet and she

192

said it should have come yesterday. It didn't come yesterday because I stayed in all day waiting for it. It's from my sister, the one who lives in Florida. She posted it last week by special mail. It's got to be signed for so the postman wouldn't leave it outside."

"Hello, Mrs Tweener, no, nothing arrived for you today. I have been here all day and no one has rung my buzzer."

"They can't have called then because they would have put a card through the letterbox to say they'd called but they didn't. Maybe it will come tomorrow. Will you look out for a delivery van for me?"

"Yes, of course, no problem."

"Thank you, Gaynor, I hope it hasn't gone to the wrong address."

Mrs Tweener did an about turn and disappeared back upstairs, mumbling as she went.

Ah bless her, I thought, closing the front door and returning to the living room.

"Have you recovered?"

"Yes thanks," said Bryn, adjusting himself. "Have you made your call?"

"She's not picking up... I'll try a bit later."

"Lovely flat, Gaynor. Your creativity shines through. Do you keep your fairy lights up all year round?"

"Absolutely. I love fairy lights. They are just so twinkly... and cheery... and magicy."

"Maybe I should put some up in my flat?"

"Maybe you should. They make me feel happy." "Happy-lights."

"Yes, happy lights."

Pregnant pause.

"I was wondering if you would like to go out for something to eat?"

"Ummm..."

"Or, we could get a takeaway?"

"Yes, takeaway. I'll get the menus," I said, rushing off to the kitchen.

"Indian, Chinese, Pizza... take your pick."

"What do you fancy?"

"I'm not really hungry so you can choose whatever you like."

"I can't eat on my own."

"Course you can, what do you fancy?"

"Okay, let's have a look," he responded, taking the menus eagerly from my hand.

Bryn ordered an Indian and pushed me into an onion bhaji which I knew I wouldn't eat.

"Are you a full- time artist, Bryn? Do you make a living from it?"

"No, although it is my passion and first love. I work at The Royal Free Hospital in Hampstead during the week."

"Oh, what as?"

"In the IT department."

Wish he'd said 'Doctor'.

Losing all interest in internet technology, I returned to art.

"So, what do you like to paint?"

"Portraits."

"Are you good?"

"I don't know. I can't judge. I do know I'm a harsh critic of myself. I don't paint to exhibit. I just do it because I enjoy it."

"I am more an illustrator than a painter, well I used to be, before I discovered advertising. I loved working on ideas so changed lanes and became an 'Advertising Creative'. Had ten wonderful years at it... And won lots of awards."

We swapped stories until the Indian arrived. I carried the brown paper bag into the kitchen while Bryn went to the bathroom. I lifted out the numerous plastic containers, took the lids off and lifted a plate from the cupboard.

"Bryn... Come and help yourself."

"Comiiiing," he sang back to me.

As he filled his plate, I went off for another pee.

I felt quite merry as I plonked myself down on the toilet seat. And then. "OH MY GOD! OH MY GOD! OH MY GOD!"

I spotted my panty-liner still stuck to the bathroom wall tile.

OH... MY... GOD! I DON'T BELIEVE IT! HOW FUCKING EMBARRASING! I sort of went into mild shock.

"WHATEVER MUST HE THINK?"

I jumped up and stood in front of the toilet where he would have been standing if he'd had a pee. YES, HE WOULD DEFINITELY HAVE SEEN IT!

But maybe he didn't have a pee, maybe he just washed his hands? I turned to face the sink. I looked into the bathroom mirror to see if he would have spotted it. My face was bright red. I was so embarrassed. I turned back to the toilet to look for evidence that he had peed. And there it was. A tiny splash back. I lifted up the seat. Yes, he had definitely peed. And if he peed, he'd have seen it. I felt sick. I sat back on the toilet and stared at the evil, soiled panty-liner before wrapping it in toilet tissue and then throwing it in the bin. He must think I'm disgusting. I wonder whether he would notice that the bin is out of reach while sitting on the toilet, hence me sticking it temporarily to the wall. It was Mrs Tweener's fault. I was interrupted. I took a few deep breaths. Now. How should I move forward from this point in the knowledge that Bryn had seen my soiled panty-liner stuck to the tiles. Only one thing to do. Totally ignore it. Pretend it hadn't happened. Shit. Hope it hadn't put him off his tikka masala. God, he must think I'm a right one. God! Hope he doesn't think I did it on purpose to test his 'shock response'. Jesus, I've never been so embarrassed. FUCKING FUCK, FUCK, FUCK!

I waited for my skin to return to its normal colour then returned to the kitchen with a broad smile. I was looking for some sort of clue from him but he just looked at me, smiled, then carried his mountain of food through to the living room. FUCK, FUCK, FUCK, HE DEFINITELY SAW IT. I KNOW HE DID.

"More Champagne, Bryn?"

"Yes please, get the one I put in the fridge, it should be cold by now."

"Will do." I held the cold bottle against my head and took another deep breath followed by a long, slow, deflated sigh. I was so mortified.

"Here we go, it's lovely and cold," I said popping the cork and pouring.

"This is really delicious, Gaynor. Great Indian! Where's your onion bhaji?"

"I'll have it in a bit."

I let Bryn do most of the talking for the next couple of hours. I believe I really was in shock at what had happened. I couldn't get rid of the image of what he had most certainly seen. My joy that evening had been killed by a 'Carefree' panty-liner' and I don't think I will ever recover. I did, however, my best to be up-beat and accommodating.

I went from sitting, to laying on the sofa. I felt incredibly tired. I believe that happens after a bad shock. Bryn, however seemed to have just taken it in his stride. As I listened to him talk, I realized I would be extremely lucky if I ever listened to a voice with such satisfaction again. There was just something about it that was so incredibly comforting. When he talked, I felt like I was being wrapped in a soft, warm blanket.

I could hardly keep my eyes open, and by eleven, I started yawning secretly, behind my hand.

"Are you tired, Gaynor?"

"Yes, sorry, exhausted. Had a heavy week. Sorry."

Bryn got up from his chair. "Well, I'll be going for an early morning run so I better be off. Thanks for a lovely evening, really enjoyed myself. Would you like to meet up again?"

"Yes, that would be lovely," I said, climbing to my feet. "How far do you run?"

"About ten miles."

"Ten miles! Blimey! You must be fit."

"I do my best."

I imagined his strong, large frame pounding the pavement.

"Bye then."

"Bye. See you soon."

We hugged each other goodnight.

Fucking panty-liner.

SWING LOW

Saturday, 23rd November

It had been two weeks and Bryn, was coming around for our 'second' date. The panty-liner hadn't been mentioned so was 'dead and buried', well, as much as it could be, I knew I would remember the incident in the bathroom for the rest of my life. Anyway, one thing was for sure, I'd never stick another one on the wall.

Now, out of shock, I was looking forward to having a lovely, happy, 'carefree' evening.

It all started so well. His voice, the funny stories, the wonderful creativeness, then my lovely little bubble burst. BANG.

"Have you ever considered 'swinging'?"

"What? From a tree?"

"No, seriously, you know... Swinging!"

"No, I haven't! It's not my sort of thing at all. I'm not one for judging people, if they are all consenting adults but it's definitely not for me. I'm far too selfish to share. I want to be concentrating on one man and I want his whole attention. It all looks so messy, all those arms and legs knocking into each other trying to find an accommodating position. And it just doesn't seem sexy somehow. And definitely, not intimate. I like to hear a man breathing. I want to know whose legs are entwined with mine... Why, are you a 'swinger'?"

"I'd like to, but haven't had the chance. You have to go in couples."

Oh, bloody hell. He wants me to go swinging with him.

"Good luck in finding somebody. Have you been looking long?"

"No, only a few months. I've thought about it in the past but decided to see if I could find someone to come with me."

I responded, sarcastically. "Maybe you should have put it on your internet profile."

"Well, I don't want people to think that's all I'm interested in."

"Well, I suppose you HAVE waited until our second date, to bring it up," I responded sarcastically. Again. Couldn't help myself.

"Oh, don't be like that."

"Well, if you are on the lookout for a swinging partner you are in the wrong place. I am not in the least bit interested."

"That's fair enough. You just seemed like the sort of free-spirited lady that would be up for most things."

"WHAT DO YOU MEAN?" The sort of lady that would be up for most things! I do not know how that could possibly equate with having a free spirit."

"Sorry. Didn't mean to offend you."

"Well to be honest, you have." I sighed, disillusioned.

Weird isn't it. You just never know what is going to knock you for six. Definitely hadn't seen that one coming. One thing though. I didn't feel so bad about the panty-liner now. What's a soiled panty-liner compared with all those jumbling, tumbling grown-ups writhing in white, red and brown excretions. Swinging... Orgies... Hieronymus Bosch... It all seemed the same to me.

Despite feeling like a bird with a broken wing, I put 'swinging' behind me and the conversation soon picked up and turned to far more interesting things. Me. I decided to get my art school folio from under the bed and show Bryn what a talented illustrator I had been before turning to advertising.

Now if there's one thing I do know, it's that I am a very talented illustrator. The detail in my work is quite extraordinary. I took several pictures from the folio and passed them to Bryn. Each of the pictures had taken weeks. He went through them fairly quickly, looking for only a few seconds at each picture. And then he didn't say a bloody thing. I felt hurt and confused. In thirty years of showing my 'jaw dropping' work to many, many people, my 'art' had always been met with astonishment, amazement, and awe.

Maybe he was speechless at my 'wonderful' work? No, his body language was far too 'flat'. He rested the pictures on the arm of the chair. I waited. He still didn't say anything.

Well that soon wiped the smile off my face.

He spoke. "Well... I can see they are very well executed."

I could feel him struggling for words.

"But it's not really the sort of 'art', I like."

"Bit like me... And swinging," I responded.

I quickly lifted the pictures from the arm of the chair putting them straight back in the folio and then shut the lid. I then pushed the large, black folio out of sight by hiding it under the table. I wanted to join it. Realising that this would not be feasible, I decided instead, to open up a restricted debate about Art.

I could hear the slightly sarcastic side of me coming out as I spoke. "So, what sort of 'ART' do *YOU* like, Bryn?"

Before he had a chance to answer, I jumped in. "Are you one of these people who feels that one stroke of paint on a canvas can be called a masterpiece?"

I anticipated his response... 'Yes'.

"Actually, yes, I am."

"Well, I think that concept is a load of intellectual bollocks. For me, one stroke can NEVER be a masterpiece. It is just an idea. In the same way that one note on a piano can never be a masterpiece. It's one note. Yes, it's musical but no musical talent is required to tap one key on a piano, anyone can do it, even a one-year-old.

"So, Bryn, do you think one note on a piano can be called a masterpiece?"

He totally ignored my question. I didn't care because I knew I WAS RIGHT.

"Let me get you a top-up," he said, grabbing my half-filled glass.

I gave a retaliatory smile.

Returning from the kitchen he handed me my drink, while peering at me over the top of his specs. He reminded me of one of the 'elite' artists from my art school days. You know, the ones that paint in oils as opposed to the ones like me who just did 'graphics and illustration'. I did go to one of the 'oil painting' classes once but the tutor plastered a big bold blue brush stroke over the beautiful green apple I had just finished painting. He tore the palette from my hand and squeezed half a tube of blue paint on it then attacked my work, shouting 'TOO TIGHT! TOO TIGHT! WHERE'S THE COLOUR! WHERE'S THE COLOUR?' I felt humiliated and devastated. My eyes filled with tears, I left the class and never went back. In my world apples were green. Or red. Or yellow. They were never blue. Elitist wanker.

Bryn turned to me. "What are you thinking about?"

"Elitist colour-blind wankers and blue apples, why, what are you thinking about?"

"Sex… and taste."

My mouth fell open with a gasp of utter shock at his unanticipated answer. My mind did somersaults as I searched for some kind of response.

Before I found any words, he spoke again. "Let me show you how artistic my tongue is."

"I most certainly will not!"

"Come on, Gaynor, let me show you some of my 'art'."

"You are absolutely outrageous," I said, trying not to laugh at his totally unbelievable audacity.

"I take that as a 'yes'," he said, lifting himself from the chair and placing his drink on the table.

As he moved toward me, I grabbed a cushion and placed it between my legs, giggling. I watched the big man fall to his knees as he gently opened my legs and started kissing the parts around the edge of the cushion. Am I being seduced again? Yes, I believe I am. What am I going to do, knee him in the balls or check out his art. I lifted the cushion to cover my face to see if he could create a masterpiece with one stroke of his tongue on MY canvas. No, he couldn't. My point was proved and confirmed in its entirety.

In the weeks leading up to Christmas, Bryn made lots of masterpieces. I didn't make any. Not just because I was being gloriously lazy but also because I had a wonderful, true excuse. My jaw was out of alignment so I couldn't open my mouth very wide.

Going to the dentist was a bloody nightmare. And also, the bottom line is, I'm not really into willy sucking. Just because HE wanted to go down there, it didn't mean I had to. It wasn't a deal. Andy and the law had proved that beyond a reasonable doubt.

After all the initial 'shocks', I discovered that Bryn, was in fact a really nice 'easy-going' kind of fella to have around and I was enjoying spending time with him. But. But, but, but, but, but I knew there would not be a future for 'us' because there were far too many things he still wanted to experience in life which were way outside my spectrum. I also knew that I would feel that I, alone, would never be enough.

So, we kept our relationship more as a 'friends' having sex, type of thing. Which was fine by me. I think.

DEMISE OF THE GREY FAIRY

Friday, 20th December

It was a week before Christmas and after a bath, I decided to trim my lady's fluff. I put on my reading glasses then suddenly gasped with shock. I spotted not one but a group of grey pubes. WHAT! Grey pubes? What! I'd had no idea whatsoever that one day my pubes would turn grey. No one had ever told me nor had I ever read about it anywhere. In a common-sense sort of way, yes it made sense, but I was not at all happy. I felt betrayed. What was the point of dying my head hair, if, when I dropped my knickers, I exposed grey hair. I grabbed the magnification mirror and threw myself backwards onto the bed to take a closer look. Oh my GOD! Not just a small group but the whole area was woven with fine silver hairs. I was absolutely mortified. How dare these unwelcome, untimely pubes interfere with me being a first time, belated, teenager. Didn't they realise I was in my prime.

I laid there wondering how I had reached the age of forty-eight without any knowledge at all of pubic hair turning grey.

Well, now the dastardly deed was discovered I considered the options. Of which there were only two. Dye it. Do they make pubic hair dye? or alternatively, have it off. I was not delighted with either prospect. And in both instances, the upkeep was going to be most inconvenient and time consuming.

Now, I know, for lots of the younger generations of females that there was a whole new angle on the way they presented their pleasure ground. For many, this meant having a narrow 'strip' made from pubes, as opposed to my generation's 'traditional triangle'. The new, small, narrow 'strip' even has its own name. I think it's called a 'Mexican' or could it be a 'Brazilian'. Not sure… maybe it was a 'Hitler'? The thing is, my silver streak goes right down the middle, so neither of the above would be able to work as a disguise.

Having it ALL off, seemed so severe. It felt like I would be taking away my/her comfort blanket. Could I destroy the nest that had nursed the golden egg for so many years? And at forty-eight? Should she be so exposed? So brazen?

I thought about pubic hair dye. I even invented a little plastic tray in my head that was combined with a comb so the comb would sit at the base of the pubes while I painted on the dye. Somehow it didn't feel feasible. Also, it might be impossible to do the roots. Not that any man would notice, if he was that close, he wouldn't be able to focus.

I reconsidered to the idea of having it all off.

Three hours later I returned from the chemist with hair removing cream for sensitive areas. I had ruled out waxing because it seemed so barbarically brutal and I didn't want to send 'her' into shock. Shaving was also out of the question. I didn't have the courage, precision or skill to get into all those tricky areas with a sharp razor blade.

I had used hair removing cream periodically on my legs and it was totally pain free. Just smear it on. Wait eight minutes then shower it off. Simple. The hair just falls away. Removing the pubes should be relatively straightforward.

Being organised, I got a small bowl of warm water, cotton wool balls, box of tissues and a cushion with a towel to sit on top along with the 5xmagnification mirror. With three pillows under my head, I wiggled my bottom on the covered cushion and placed everything else around me in an accessible position. I tried to balance the large mirror between my knees. Well, that wasn't going to work, I couldn't open my legs wide enough. Because I did not have the courage to attempt the job without a mirror I decided to get back up and make a contraption to keep the mirror in place. I attached the mirror to a large plastic box using strong, black duct tape. Good. It was secure. I lay back in a comfortable position and directed the mirror at the right angle. Sorted. I looked at my massive 5x magnified vagina. It looked like it belonged to an elephant. Because I also needed to see the area around my vagina, I got up again and re-taped the mirror on 'normal' reflection, 1x1 with no magnification. What a palaver.

Finally. Everything ready to go.

I had read the instructions thoroughly and made a mental note to avoid the cream coming into contact with particularly sensitive areas, including all three apertures. I decided not to use the spatula and rubber gloves provided but instead, to use my finger for a more precise application. Leave on for no longer than eight minutes.

Now.

Where to start.

Mobile rings.

Fuck off.

I decided I would start at the back, near my bottom and work my way forward. Then I changed my mind. I would start with the triangle at the front. Taking my time and applying the cream in an artistic manner, I squeezed a series of big blobs onto my finger and covered my triangle from root to tip. Good. Satisfactory.

Now, gently and carefully, I spread the cream down either side of my Libby-Lala. Excellent. All especially sensitive areas, avoided.

Now the back bit. Access was going to be a bit trickier because of the nature of a 'closed' bottom with access only via the butt crack. I looked and wondered if I really needed to invade that area in view of the fact that I never let gentlemen near it. It was out of bounds. Nothing wrong with 'up the bum' but just not for me. Also, on opening said bum, it really wasn't very hairy. I thought about it. Oh, might as well. I prized open my bum cheeks with one hand and applied my creamed finger around my star. Good. Excellent. Application complete, I washed my fingers in the little bowl of warm water and laid back.

Everything was okay for about three minutes. Then my bum hole started feeling a bit stingy. Then it started to feel really stingy. Then it started to burn with stinginess. My bum hole was on fire. I tried to wipe it with a wet cotton wool ball but it just screamed in rage at me. I had no choice. I got off the bed and waddled with an invisible 'space-hopper' between my legs to the bathroom. Face-cloth, under very cold tap water, soaked, then straight to the rescue. I 'cold watered' my bottom for a couple of minutes until the pain subsided. I couldn't use the shower head because the spraying water might mess up the rest of the application which was still in a state of calm. I returned to my original position on the bed with the cold, blue, face-cloth still wedged and hanging out of my bottom.

Eight minutes were finally up so I waddled off to the bathroom. Grabbing the head of the shower and setting to warm, I stood, legs akimbo, intensively showering the whole creamed-up area. Looking down, I was amazed to see tufts of hair heading toward the plughole. It seemed to have come out so easily. And painlessly.

I touched between my legs and felt shocked at the smoothness of the soft skin. 'She' felt so innocent. It was like meeting up with an old, but very good friend, long forgotten about.

Showered down and towel dry, I returned again to the bedroom. First view, full frontal, naked 'V'.

Oh my god! I really wasn't sure about the new look. It seemed very 'out there'.

Oh dear, really REALLY, not sure especially not at my age. I laid back down on the bed and looked at her in the mirror. It was like looking at someone else's. Crikey! Well it's done now. No going back. The fluffy protection was well and truly destroyed and disappeared down the plughole. Just have to get on with it.

I grabbed some knickers from the drawer and put them on. Weird. The fabric was touching my new hairless skin. It felt like I was wearing knickers for the first time. The sensation of 'her' moving around in my knickers, was odd yet familiar. I was a bit spooked so felt compelled to share my experience, with someone.

I rang up Nancy, my niece.

"Hi, Aunty Gaynor."

"Hi, darling. Can you talk?"

"Yes, what's happened?"

"Why do you think something's happened?"

"The urgency in your voice."

"Well, it's not urgent but I've done something and I'm not sure about it."

"What have you done?"

"Well, I found some grey pubes."

"Grey what?"

"Grey pubic hair."

"I didn't know pubic hair went grey."

"Nor did I until this morning. I found quite a few and didn't know what to do so I 'Immac'd' them off."

"You what?" she said, laughing, "Shit, got a client calling me, I'll call you back."

Decided to ring Bunty. Went to answerphone.

Rang Callie. Went to answerphone.

Not having the patience to wait for Nancy's return call, I decided to ring Bryn because he was the closest thing to my pink paradise at this time. I wanted and needed some sort of instant reassurance. I felt oddly guilty about what I had done, like I had committed some sort of crime. Weird. Bryn would be easy to share with. He was a man of the world.

I spoke as soon as he picked up. "Hi. baby," I said, as though nothing was wrong.

"Hello, darling. Is everything okay? Are we still on for tomorrow night?"

"Yes, it's fine. Just needed to share something. Can you talk?"

"If it's quick."

I paused. And found I didn't have the courage to tell him. How would I say it? Where would I start?

"Oh, don't worry, darling. I'll see you tomorrow."

"Are you sure?"

"Yes, no worries. Bye, babe."

After putting the phone down, I realised, in my mania, I hadn't considered what reason I would give for choosing to 'go naked' because I certainly wasn't going to divulge to Bryn that my pubes were turning grey. Being ten years older than him was more than enough to be getting along with.

Three a.m. Couldn't sleep so texted Bryn because I knew he would be. At least then I wouldn't need to get into a conversation about it. As a back-up, after I had texted, I decided I would immediately turn my phone off. Send...

Don't ask me why but I decided to remove all my pubes x

Having finally off-loaded, I slowly unwound, around my naked vagina and fell asleep.

TINSEL TOWN

Saturday, 21ˢᵗ December

Woke up and the first thing I did was touch 'her'. It still felt like I had my hand down the wrong person's knickers. I patted her reassuringly then I remembered the text I had sent Bryn in the middle of the night. I turned my phone on. Four texts. Nancy, Bunty, Cally and Bryn. I opened Bryn's.

WOW! CAN'T WAIT! X X X X

'Wow? Can't wait?' typical man! But hang on, suddenly the spotlight was off me and shone on Bryn's delighted face. I burst out laughing at the irony. In an instant he made me feel sexy and also like an acceptable member of society again.

I thought for a couple of minutes then texted Bryn back.

Happy Christmas, darling. See you later.

He texted straight back.

Looking very much forward to seeing you too!

I giggled, extremely nervously, at the prospect.

Thinking, I started trying to give myself positive reasons for being 'pube' free. Most of us I am sure, at some time will have ended up with an inconvenient pubic hair in our mouth. The tongue's natural action is to search it out and get it removed as quickly as possible usually via a 'spitting' action.

And, we all know how we feel when we find a hair in our food. Positively repulsed. Having a mouth full of pubes, one cannot deny, must be rather like eating a shag-pile carpet. I felt blokes were more, lucky. Imagine if their willies were hairy all the way up to the top, blow-jobs would be out of the question. For most people it would be like sucking on a dog's tail. Well, maybe that's going a little too far. I mean, for ladies, there wasn't actually any hair on the really important bits, just around the edges.

Bryn tuned up bang on eight o'clock with the broadest of smiles. He peered over his glasses at me with wide eyes and amusingly raised eyebrows.

"Why are you looking at me like that?" I said, giggling and knowing exactly why.

I grabbed his hand and walked him into the living room to show him my splendid, magnificent Christmas tree. Eight feet tall, eight hundred fairy lights and a plethora of baubles and Christmas paraphernalia from around the world.

"WOW! What a tree. It's amazing. How long did it take you to decorate?"

"About twelve hours," I responded, knowing I had, as usual, done a positively marvellous job.

"I love decorating Christmas trees!" I said excitedly.

"Well, it really is fantastic. Well done darling."

He whipped his phone out and took a photo.

Feeling as though I had, at last, received some recognition for my 'art', I went to fetch drinks.

Returning to the living room with both hands full, Bryn reached down and stroked my inner thigh.

"Anything else you want to show me?"

"Yes," I said, putting down the drinks then took his wandering hand and led him into the hall. I threw open the bedroom door with a, "DA-DAAAA!"

His mouth fell open at the sight of a second tree.

"Wow! You really like Christmas, don't you."

I giggled with delight, then quickly closed the bedroom door and led Bryn back to the living room.

Having managed to divert attention away from my knickered area for a couple of hours, I realised that I was running out of ideas and then, I had another one. As Bryn disappeared into the bathroom, I quickly ran into the bedroom. When he returned to the living room and sat down, I asked him to close his eyes then stood in front of him.

"Okay, I'm ready. You can put your hand down my knickers."

"Just my hand?" he said, blindly feeling his way into my unzipped jeans.

I pulled the front of my knickers forward. "Keep your eyes closed."

"I am! I am!"

His hand gently entered the top of my knickers. "I thought you said you had shaved it all off."

"I have," I confirmed confidently.

He looked confused as he delved deeper. And then he started laughing.

Pushing me on to the chair he pulled my knickers down and buried his face in the soft, purple tinsel I had stuffed down the front of my pants.

MONEY

I have been in bed since Boxing Day with the most horrible fluey bug and every time I thought it was over, the bastard came back and knocked me down again. I'm still finding nose plugs in odd places around the bedroom. In fact, Daisy had collected a nice pile of them and placed them neatly in her basket. Nose plugs? Those things where you tear off a small piece of tissue, fold it carefully, roll it into a Swiss roll shape and shove it up a nostril to stop the constant dripping. I couldn't believe I had paid a tenner for a flu jab only a few weeks earlier. Anyway, it forced me to lay in bed and face the fact that I had no money left in the bank. I had been spending like crazy since leaving my husband. I had been burying my head in the sand for weeks and although I had put a whopping £300,000 deposit on my flat, there was still around £80,000 mortgage outstanding, and I had no cash to keep up with the payments. Ben's rent would only cover the bills.

I was owed around £30,000 by a few people who I had helped out when I was 'flushed' and they weren't paying me back along with £20,000 which I had lent to The Globe Bar. Threats of solicitors had got me nowhere. There was no dosh in the bank and I was up to my £16,000 limit on my credit cards. Money, money, money, money, money. Whenever I lay down and closed my eyes, '£' signs flung themselves around inside my head like bees trying to get out of a jar. That little symbol that looked so cute and bouncy when you had some, suddenly became the enemy. The colour had changed from gold to black. Daytimes weren't so bad but when nights came, I tossed and turned in my sweaty, money, flueyness. Weird anxious dreams. Awake, asleep, awake, asleep. The thought of losing my fabulous flat turned my stomach many times. Asleep. Awake. Asleep. Awake. And why weren't people paying me back what they had borrowed? If I hadn't lent them the

£30,000, it would be sitting in my bank account and I'd be just fine and dandy and not going through all this shit. Bastards. Awake. Awake. Awake. In three weeks, my mortgage was due. How the hell was I going to pay it?

I contemplated for hours and hours about the different possibilities. Borrowing was not an option. My family had little to spare and I would not ask to borrow money from friends, not knowing how or when I would be able to pay them back. Loan? Bank would not give me a loan without a steady income. Or maybe they would against the flat? But then again, ex-hubby's name is still on the mortgage and he would have to sign all the papers. Also, I didn't want him to know that I had been spend, spend, spending.

So. Options?

1. Car boot sale? Could do but I would probably at best, make a few pounds.

2. Auction off some of my pots? Could do but specialist sales take time and I can't wait, perhaps a good move to do it now for the months ahead though.

3. Get a job in Selfridges? Still wouldn't pay enough and what about the dogs? Can't and won't leave them all day.

4. Go freelance and try to get some design, illustration or advertising work. It would take forever.

5. Turn the small dining room into a room to let? £300 per month. Not enough.

6. Start a bed and breakfast? Don't be ridiculous.

7. Sell the living room furniture and let the living room for £500 per month. Too many people and I didn't want to give up my living room.

8. Sell my car? I didn't have one.

9. Escorting? Are you mad?

10. Buy a lottery ticket.

These things took a lot of time to think about and little time to disregard.

In between sleepless nights and runny-nose days, I was aware of one word that seemed to sit calmly at the back of my head, only showing itself at first in whispers. It was a scary word but it didn't come frighteningly. It drifted in and out of consciousness as the days went by, each time calling a little louder. Slowly but surely, the word finally placed itself at the front of my mind and settled in. Escorting.

I hear you, I said, let me think. I started searching around my head. I really, really, need to think this through.

1. What would best friends think?

Can't tell some of them. Think it would be too hard for them to deal with. Could probably tell Bryn, with his willingness to 'swing'. And also, maybe Ben. Hopefully, both would have sympathetic and supportive ears.

2. What about morals?

Never can quite work out where these start and finish in society. So many 'cross-overs' and sneaky things going on. Remember Cynthia Payne? Good money for dressing politicians up like babies in nappies, hitting men with twigs and brambles and such like. Anyway, I was going to be my own special type of escort.

3. What about safety?

Only meet clients at 5-star hotels and let my policeman friend, Andy, vice squad, know where I am at all times.

4. What will I charge?

Don't want to be doing this more than once a week/fortnight so will be high class totty catering to the wealthy, elderly gentleman for £350 an hour.

5. Do I really want to do this?

No, but I will, if I can save my home. And it would be totally, on my terms.

6. What now?

Take a deep breath, decide what I am prepared to do and then go find some wealthy gentleman. I started singing 'The Twelve Days of Christmas'.

"On the twelfth day of Christmas,
my true love sent to me,
TWELVE LORDS A LEAPING…

DISCLOSING

Saturday, 4th January

Having slept better last night, I woke up to glorious sunshine pouring through my bedroom window. Feeling more positive and somehow feeling all my problems were solved, I decided to tell Ben about my temporary career change. I stumbled into the kitchen in my yellow bunnikins nightshirt and hugged Ben with a smile.

"Morning, Gaynor," he said, squeezing me gently.

"Good morning, darling man," I responded chirpily.

"Want some tea?"

"Yes, please, sweetie, and we are going to have a toast!"

"A toast? What for?" said Ben, throwing the bag into the cup

"We're not going to lose the flat."

"How come? What happened?"

"I'm going to become an Escort!"

"What?" coughed Ben, with a laugh and raised eyebrows.

"Yes! I am going to become a gentleman's lady on MY terms, of course."

A look of disbelief, but not disapproving, followed by a fast-falling jaw then an open-mouthed laugh, Ben was knocked right off course for a couple of seconds.

"Are you serious?" he said, wide eyed with his mouth half open.

I responded in a Mae West 'Texan' style accent. "Yesiree, I'm gonna find me some fancy gentlemen with big hearts and even bigger wallets."

"Where?" said Ben quizzically.

"The internet."

Ben nodded knowingly and echoed my words slowly, "T h e i n t e r n e t ..."

I could feel his brain flipping over around behind those calm green eyes. He realised I was being serious so took it on board and passed me my tea.

I waited for some questions but Ben, sweet, sweet Ben, just smiled his Ben smile then returned to his world of fried eggs and waffles. There's got to be more to it than that I thought… probably be questions later over vodka and cranberry.

Taking my tea back to bed I decided I would text Bryn and tell him what I was going to do. I didn't have the courage to tell him face to face. At least a text would give him the all the space he might need to deal with the idea so I just came straight out with it.

I'm going to be an Escort xxx

No sooner was it sent that the phone rang. It was Bryn. "Fancy some company?" he said sweetly.

The softness and caring of his voice made my eyes fill with tears. I suddenly felt guilty and unsavoury.

Yes, please x

Okay, I'll be with you in twenty minutes x

Both Ben and Bryn knew I was out of money and both knew it was because of my ridiculous generosity, always insisting on paying for everything on nights out, plus all the money I had lent to friends and associates. Ben, especially, whom I had discussed my finances with, kept saying to me, 'Rein it in, Gaynor, you're paying for the whole world and its dog. You don't have an endless pot of money'. I had heard his words on many occasions but always just believed everything will turn out all right.

I laid on the bed thinking about Bryn's weirdly tolerant, disposition. Never phased, never spooked. Then I felt the need to jump out of bed and make myself look as fresh and clean, as I possibly could.

The buzzer rang, I checked myself in the mirror and opened the door. Bryn came bounding up the stairs two at a time. He smiled and put one arm around me. Something felt odd. I knew it was Bryn but it didn't 'feel' like Bryn. It felt like the size and shape of a much taller person… or was I just feeling smaller? He patted me reassuringly, took my hand and led me into the bedroom. "I knew you were having difficulties, babe, but I didn't realise things were this bad," he said, pulling me onto the bed. "Why didn't you say something?"

"Because I wouldn't face facts and I tried to believe it wasn't happening. I just believed, somehow, everything would be all right... and the money has just run out... it's all gone... it's ALL gone."

"Oh, babes," he sighed, pulling me down into a cuddling position.

"What about all the money you are owed?"

"No one is paying me back... and I'm not giving up my flat, I'm just not."

"You've obviously given this a lot of thought."

"Well, yes, I have, in as much as one can without having actually gone there."

Bryn gently stroked my hair. "I will always love you, Gaynor."

"And I will always love you," I said, holding him tightly, "and thank you for being cool."

"How much are you going to charge?"

"£350 an hour."

"You mean, I've got a high-class escort as a 'girlfriend' and I don't have to pay! Rock and roll!"

We both started laughing and then Bryn got serious.

"You'll have to be careful, babe, on every level."

"I know. I'll be safe, I won't take any risks and I've got a good friend who will look out for me."

"What? Who? Not a pimp?"

"No. The police."

"The police?"

"Yes, the police."

"Okay..."

"Where are you going to find clients?"

"The internet."

"Where will you meet up with them?"

"The Dorchester or The Ritz etc."

"Well, if you need me, I'll be here and it's only sex after all. If you're happy to do it and it helps save the flat then go for it. Tell you what, if I could make £350 an hour from shagging someone, I'd have given up work years ago and if I had a dick the size of my sexual appetite, I'd have been a porn star."

"I'm NOT going to be SHAGGING anyone!"

"What, £350 for a blow job?"

"Absolutely not."

"What do they get for their money then?"

"Dinner and great company."

Bryn, laughed.

"I suppose they'll have to pay for that then, as well."

I pushed my elbow into his ribs then he carried on. "It will be £350 for some pleasant conversation over dinner with a very attractive lady."

"And counselling... if they need it... I've got my degree don't forget."

"So, you're going to be a 'high-class counsellor'. You are so funny, Gaynor."

"I've thought it all through. I am going to advertise for the more elderly type of gentlemen, who are perhaps, a little lonely or just want to have a lovely evening out... for dinner... or drinks..."

"Mmmmm, it will be interesting to see how it works out."

I could see by Bryn's expression that he didn't think there would be much interest.

"Do you know, Bryn, when I met you at the door, you seemed sort of bigger... a lot bigger. Taller and wider."

"I can't believe you just said that. How bizarre. I thought you felt really small, really, really small. I was even looking down on you... how odd, we must have slipped into another dimension for a second... a parallel universe

I later told Ben, what services I would be offering my clients. He responded, "Are you sure that clients will be happy with just dinner and drinks?"

"Well, they're not getting anything else. I'll make that VERY clear in my profile."

ELDERLY GENTLEMEN

Sunday, 5th January

Settling down, with racing heart and a bacon butty, I wrote my ad.

Very attractive, warm, classy female looking for dinner dates or drinks with nice elderly gentlemen who appreciate good company, intelligent conversation and the finer things in life. Photo available.

I had no choice, but to look on the traditional type of escorting website because I was going to charge for my time. I think I'll design a website for men, just wanting to take ladies out to dinner, with no strings attached, except for the cash of course. I think an ideal name for the website would be 'Dinner Ladies'. Not sure it conjures up the right image, in view of some of Cynthia Payne's clients, grown men dressed as schoolboys, in short trousers and caps, but it is catchy and memorable and the press would probably mention what it was all about. Anyway, ad written, I posted it.

It didn't take long to create interest. I had fifteen credible responses. I read through the information that each gentleman had disclosed, and two, in particular, stood out. I also received about thirty photos of men's willies.

Of course, the first thing, the two 'possibilities' wanted to see, was what I looked like, so I dug out one of the snaps of me, in a posh black frock with white trim, classy black hat with white bow and black kitten-heel shoes, standing alongside the winning race horse at Ascot. I scanned it and sent it to their private email addresses, along with a price tag of £350 per hour. Within minutes, I received very well written responses, with charming compliments from both gentlemen, so I requested a photo of each of them, in return. Satisfied, I agreed, I would be happy to meet up, at one of my favoured hotels in town, so said, I would check my diary for available dates and get back to them, within the next couple of days. They both appeared to be extremely pleased and were looking forward to hearing from me.

Client number 1, I will name, 'Goldie'. He was a very wealthy, fine arts and antiques dealer, aged seventy-eight. The photo of him, on his enormous, luxurious, elegant living room, sitting on a sumptuous sofa with his hounds by his side, was the evidence.

Client number 2, I will name, 'Roger', as in the 'Jolly Roger' because he owned a superyacht. He was aged eighty-four. He also sent a photo of confirmation of himself, seated on his yacht, holding a glass of Champagne, surrounded by staff.

I emailed 'Goldie', with a date of Friday, 10th January. He asked me, if he could call me. I agreed.

"Good evening, Gaynor, how are you?"

"I'm very well thank you, how are you?"

"I'm good, thank you. I'm just recovering from a hip operation I had several weeks ago so I currently have a bit of a limp, but apart from that, I'm absolutely fine. I just wanted to say a quick hello and tell you I am looking forward to meeting and having dinner with you, on the evening of Friday, the 10th of January."

"Me too. I'm looking forward to it very much. Just so you recognize me, I will be wearing…"

"Don't worry, I have your image imprinted on my brain from the photograph, you have sent to me. I'll spot you coming through the entrance. I will wait in the lobby."

"Fantastic. See you on the 10th then."

"Good. I look forward to it, Bye for now."

"Bye."

Text to Bryn.

I have a date. Meeting at The Ritz for dinner on Friday! x

Text from Bryn.

Well done, babe. Call you later. x

"Ben. I have my first client." I shouted, as he walked through the door, from work.

"Oh, congratulations," he responded, as though I'd just passed my driving test.

"How do you feel about it?" he continued, with a positive, but slightly concerned, look.

"Fine! He's taking me to dinner, at The Ritz on Friday evening."

"How much?"

"£350 an hour"

"How much? £350 an hour! He must be a millionaire!"

"He is! And he seems really sweet. A real gentleman."

"Are you really sure he won't want more than dinner?"

"He might want dessert," I said, giggling, "and coffee to follow. No, really, it's all good. He's seventy-eight and recovering from a hip operation, bless him."

Ben burst out laughing, then I started giggling at Ben's amusement, of it all.

"Bloody hell! £350 an hour... that's a great price. And you are bound to be there, for a couple of hours at least."

"Top totty," I said.

"He'll love you," he said, throwing his arms around me, for a big hug.

I squeezed his arms, with my hands.

"Thank you for your support, Ben, fancy a vodka and cranberry?"

"Absolutely."

GOLDIE, THE RITZ AND THE REVELATION

Friday, 10th January

Lovely navy dress, not showing my cleavage, slightly above the knee, pretty three strand pearl necklace, fake, cream kitten-heeled shoes and navy handbag.

"Bye, Ben," I yelled through his bedroom door.

He came hurrying out.

"You look fab," he said, leaning forward to kiss me goodbye.

"Shit! I forgot perfume!"

I ran back and sprayed.

"I will keep my phone nearby, in case you need to call me."

"Bye, darling, thanks."

The taxi pulled up outside The Ritz. My heart was beating fast so I sat on a step outside, and mediated for a few minutes, to calm myself.

One of the smartly dressed doormen, walked toward me. "Are you all right, madam?"

'Yes, fine thank you, darling. Just getting some air. I'm just about to come in, I'm meeting a friend for dinner."

I smiled, stood up, then followed the doorman, as he held the door open for me

I didn't need to scan the lobby. I saw Goldie heading toward me, with a smile and a walking stick. First impressions. He looked younger, than his seventy-eight years, with his full head of neatly cropped, light grey hair. He was dressed immaculately. Dark suit, matching silk tie and hankie in the top pocket of his jacket. I was about to hold out my hand, to shake his, then I thought he might fall over, as he was a bit unsteady.

"Good evening, Gaynor, it's lovely to meet you."

"Good evening, Goldie, lovely to meet you too."

"Would you like to take my arm, and I'll walk with you, into the dining room?"

How lovely, I thought, as we walked, steadily, into the restaurant.

It was easy to understand why The Ritz Restaurant was considered to be one of the most beautiful dining rooms in the world. Marble columns, from floor to ceiling, wonderful, sparkling chandeliers, sumptuous drapes, huge displays of white roses and the most elegantly laid tables.

We were immediately approached, and greeted by the restaurant manager, who obviously knew Goldie well.

"Lovely to see you, again, sir."

Goldie nodded.

"Please, follow me."

We were led to a discreet table, in one corner of the room. I was pleased. I much preferred to be in a corner, with a wall behind me, rather than in the middle, surrounded by people.

Sitting down, I studied Goldie's face, a little more. He resembled, an older-version, of the renowned actor, Steve McQueen, who was at the top of his game in the sixties and seventies starring in many celebrated films such as The Thomas Crown Affair and Bullitt.

Looking at my face, he said, "Has anyone ever told you, you look a little like Helen Mirren?"

"Yes, funnily enough, quite a few people… Has anyone ever told you, you look like Steve McQueen?"

"Yes, in my younger days," he said, smiling.

"Well, the resemblance is still there," I said, smiling back.

While eating the incredible five-star cuisine, we talked, laughed and enjoyed each other's company, for a couple of hours, discussing art, music, theatre, a little politics and our shared love of dogs. He was a very charming man, but something about his teeth was rather odd. I could see they were his own and not dentures and they were white, but they were very wonky and uneven. I'm not being unkind, but they reminded me of old tombstones in graveyards, toppling in different directions. I just didn't get it. With SO much money, why hadn't he had them sorted. Good teeth were really, very important, as far as I was concerned. I kept thinking, Thank goodness I don't have to kiss him. I would have left much sooner, if I had been a different type of escort. Those teeth could have done some real damage.

With the meal coming to an end, Goldie invited me back to his flat, in Grosvenor Square, for coffee. I had already earned £700 and because I felt happy in his company, I agreed. Business is business and another £350 wouldn't go amiss.

I excused myself, to visit the ladies, to call my policeman friend, Andy.

"Hi, Andy."

"Hi! How are you? How's it going? I was waiting for you to call, just to check you were okay."

"Ahh, bless you. So far, so good, I am in The Ritz, having dinner with my elderly, gentleman friend. Everything, is as suspected. He is very wealthy and well known, as a regular, in the restaurant. He's sweet and interesting. The only thing is, he has the most terrible teeth."

Andy laughed. "Well, you can't have everything."

"I know, but having so much money, I don't understand why he hasn't had them fixed. Everything else about him, is immaculate. I don't know how the food he was eating, stayed in his mouth."

"Give him a break, he's seventy-eight. At least he's still got his own teeth."

"Yes, but if you saw them, I think even you would be surprised."

Andy laughed again.

"He's invited me back to his flat in Grosvenor Square, for a coffee, so I'm going to go. His chauffeur is coming to pick us up, in ten mins."

"Okay, well, be careful. Let me know the house or building number and which flat you are in."

"You're such a darling, thanks, Andy. I really appreciate you looking out for me."

"No problem, at all."

"Okay, bye for now, Andy."

"Bye."

We arrived, in Grosvenor Square, and with arms linked, we entered his building and walked toward the security desk. The guard, and Goldie, nodded at one another, then we took the lift, to the third floor.

"I have really enjoyed spending time with you this evening, Gaynor. You are a lovely woman and delightful company," he said, tapping three times on his flat door, with his walking stick.

The door was immediately opened, by whom I presumed to be, Goldie's butler.

We walked along a very wide hall, with fresh flowers sitting on elegant tables, then into a vast, stunning living room.

"Please, do take a seat, Gaynor."

"Thank you," I said, perching myself on the edge of a very large, sumptuous, velvet, cushioned chair. I sat elegantly, like Her Majesty, with one foot tucked behind the other.

"Would you like to meet the dogs, Gaynor?" he asked, heading back to the hall. He didn't need to wait for my reply because he knew, I would.

"Oh, yes please, I'd love to meet them," I responded, enthusiastically.

Seconds later, two, large Borzoi dogs walked elegantly into the room. I knew, they were waiting for a command from their master.

"Go and say hello to Gaynor," said Goldie, pointing toward me. They gently walked toward me and sat down. I couldn't resist them and fell to my knees, to say hello, and give them a stroke. As I rubbed behind their ears, they nestled into my hands. Goldie watched.

"I love them. They are beautiful," I said, meaning every word.

"They seem to love you, too," said Goldie, as one of the dogs rolled onto its back, for me to rub his tummy.

"I'll leave you to get acquainted, while I arrange coffee."

Goldie entered the room two minutes later, followed by his butler who was carrying a beautiful silver tray, along with silver coffee set and china cups. They were placed on a low, beautiful, gold rimmed, antique walnut, table.

"Thank you," I said, looking up and smiling at the butler. He didn't smile back, but responded with an agreeable, appreciating, nod.

I was still sitting on the floor, legs tucked neatly under, and to one side, stroking the dogs, as the coffee was poured.

"Glorious creatures. I'd have lots of them, if I had the space."

"Yes, they really are man's best friend," responded Goldie.

"And woman's," I said, wanting to make the point.

Not wanting to appear rude, I got back up, and perched myself back on the chair. "This room is quite wonderful," I said, looking around at all the paintings, objet d'art and antiques.

Spotting some photos in silver frames sitting on a large, grand piano, I walked toward the corner of the room, to get a closer look. Halfway there, I realized I might be being intrusive, so pretended to be captivated by a beautifully crafted bronze of his two dogs.

"This bronze is wonderful... and look at all your photos. I have lots of photos around my flat... are these of family and friends?" I asked, moving toward them.

Goldie, walked over, to join me. "Yes, and my dogs."

Goldie pointed out each family member, individually.

"Mother and father, twin sisters, nephews and nieces, children and grandchildren."

I acknowledged each of the handsome family members and then Goldie paused, and sighed. "And, this one, is of my brother, Freddy, who passed away when he was only ten."

"Oh, that is sooo sad," I said, seeing by his face, that the loss of his brother, was still, very much with him, even though, many years had passed.

"Yes, he was my older brother, by just a year and I adored him. He died in the dentist chair."

Those words hit me like a bullet in the back of the head, as I inadvertently took a quick intake of breath, with shock, and disbelief. In that second, Goldie's teeth flashed before me. It all made sense. The obvious fear, that any kind of trip to the dentist, would simply be too much, for him. Traumatic and sad.

"God, that's terrible... How awful..."

Goldie picked up Freddy's photo, and gently stroked his face, with his fingers.

I couldn't stop my eyes, welling up with tears.

When Goldie saw my tears, he stroked my face too. Fighting back more tears because of his tender, gentle action, I took a deep breath.

"Oh, Goldie, life can be so incredibly hard at times. I am truly sorry for your loss and at such a tender age."

Goldie nodded and we returned to sitting. I felt a bit traumatized, after Goldie's revelation and found it hard to return to any sort of lively, or normal, conversation.

Goldie could see how much his story had affected me, and shortly thereafter I said I felt it was time for me to go home. With well-meaning hugs, and exchanging kisses, on cheeks, each of us thanked the other, for a lovely evening, and then I was safely chauffeur driven back to my flat, with £1,500 in my pocket, whilst feeling very guilty about being mean, about his teeth. There was always a reason for everything, but I certainly didn't see that one coming. C'est la vie.

PIGEONS AND FIREMEN

Ben was waiting in the kitchen for me, when I went to get tea. "Morning, darling."

"Morning, Gayn's. How did it go?"

"Perfectly fine… all good."

"Great," said Ben, asking nothing more.

With Goldie's lost brother still front of mind, I decided I would pick myself up, and take Daisy and Flo to Regents Park for a lovely walk, and also to feed the pigeons. It was sunny, but chilly, so we were all wearing our warm coats.

Upon arrival, lots of people were in the park, many feeding the swans, ducks and other feathered friends in the boating lake. Over the little bridge, I kept walking until I found a bench, away from the lake and all the people, where I could see lots of pigeons sitting in a tree. Sitting on the bench, I lifted the large bag of seeds from my carrier bag, while Daisy and Flo ran into a little wooded area, to explore.

Tearing open the bag, I took a handful of seeds and threw them a few metres from my feet. Immediately, a flock of around thirty pigeons, landed by the seeds and started hungrily pecking away at them. When the seeds were all eaten, I threw another handful. This time, a little nearer to my feet. The pigeons pecked away, happily, moving closer. Upon throwing the third handful, I spotted, out of the corner of my eye, a park warden, walking slowly toward me.

"Sorry, madam, please don't feed the pigeons."

"What do you mean, don't feed the pigeons?"

"We try not to encourage them."

"What are you talking about? There are loads of people, all over the park, feeding the birds."

"Yes, but pigeons are vermin."

I took another handful of seeds, and threw them, onto the grass. The warden looked at me, disapprovingly. I responded, with a very cross glare, and the following words. "Do you know, that British pigeons were domesticated, during World War 1 and World War 2? They saved over 50,000 lives of service men and women? They were even presented, with a medal, for their services."

"Well, no, I didn't know that, actually, but it is still against the rules."

"Did any swans or ducks save lives during the wars? No! I don't think they did."

"I'm not concerned about the ducks or swans, only the pigeons."

His response sent me over-the-top, so I started singing, at the top of my voice, 'Feed the birds', as sung by Julie Andrews, in the film 'Mary Poppins'.

Because it was one of my favourite 'Mary Poppins' songs, I had sung it many times, often to children at bedtime, so I knew all the words.

Nothing, was going to stop me. As I sang, Daisy and Flo, hearing me, ran back and started barking at the park warden, as though they knew he was annoying me. I sang louder, over the barking.

He slowly turned, defeated and walked away. I continued to sing until I had completed the whole song, lasting for around four minutes. Warden gone, Daisy and Flo ran back to the carry on exploring, while I carried on feeding the pigeons.

Maybe, later, the warden might consider, that maybe his father, grandfather or great-grandfather were saved by pigeons.

After my triumphant time in the park, we walked back home via Avenue Road, St Johns Wood. I saw a fire engine in the distance, heading down the road toward us. No 'bee-baa, bee-baa', no siren, so not an emergency. I've always loved firemen. They are all absolute heroes. So, being in a rebellious mood, not against firemen, but other silly people in uniform, like park wardens, I stood by the side of the road, and as the fire engine grew closer, I lifted my blouse and bra, and flashed my boobs at the red engine. It was simply an act of appreciation and to make the firemen laugh. It worked. They responded waving and laughing and gave a short, appreciative, noisy 'WHOO-OOP' via the siren. I walked the rest of the way home with a smile on my face. I had put the park warden down and lifted the firemen up.

ROGER

Two weeks had passed, since my dinner date with Goldie, and I was off to meet Roger, eighty-four, at the Savoy.

Dressed smartly again, I jumped out of the cab and entered the Savoy lobby. Roger told me he would meet me in the bar, so after being led there, by one of the concierges, I scanned the bar for an elderly gentleman, sitting on his own. There was only one and he was busy on his phone. I didn't want to approach, in case it wasn't him, but then he looked up, saw me, and stood up, smiling.

"Gaynor! Lovely to see you!" he said, as though we were old friends.

"Hello, Roger, how are you?"

I decided, not to say, Nice to meet you, in case someone thought I might be an escort, so gave him a quick kiss, on his cheek. Elderly man, pretty, much younger lady, at least the greeting could have been perceived as father and daughter.

Because he was seated on a sofa, by a low table, with no chairs available, I had no choice but to sit next to him. Well, that is what a daughter would do, when meeting up with her father, so that was fine.

Roger, like Goldie, was also smartly dressed. Suit, tie, not one that I would have chosen, and shiny black shoes. His face was very suntanned and weathered. It confirmed, that he must spend a lot of time on his luxury yacht. He was bald, with a bright white, perhaps, a little too white, smile.

He must have had a fair bit to drink before I had arrived, because I could smell it on him, but he wasn't in any way, drunk. I wasn't feeling terribly hungry and nor was Roger, so we decided, rather than go to the dining room, we would order some snacks, to eat at our table.

Over an hour and a half, I consumed a whole bottle of Champagne, while Roger knocked back, glass after glass of whisky. I felt a little merry, but well in control, but couldn't work out why Roger wasn't drunk. Just as I started to get a bit worried about him paying for my company, he invited me back to his flat, which was on the same street as the Savoy, for coffee. I agreed, but first excused myself, to go and call Andy, to let him know where I was, and where I was heading. I told him, I'd text Roger's full address, upon arrival.

Roger's flat was a short stroll from the Savoy and it was only during our walk, that I noticed Roger was beginning to be a little unsteady, so, thoughtfully, I linked arms with him, so he didn't fall over. It was what any thoughtful daughter would do for her father.

Into the building, up to the penthouse. He opened the door to his apartment himself, and we entered a massive, minimalist, but very stylish room, with huge windows which overlooked the bright lights of the London landscape, against a backdrop of a dark, starry sky.

Roger poured himself another whisky and then offered to make my coffee.

"Would you like to watch something while I make your coffee, Gaynor?"

I didn't respond and was immediately suspicious. Blue movie?

"What did you have in mind?"

Before I had a chance to respond, he picked up the remote and pressed a button. "The Rat Pack, live at Carnegie Hall, New York... Do you like The Rat Pack?"

"I love The Rat Pack," I responded, feeling extremely relieved.

I sat in front of the massive screen, on one of the comfy sofas that were sitting either side of a large, low, glass table.

Roger headed off slowly, toward the kitchen, as though he were on a gently swaying, boat. He returned, still with his whisky in one hand and my coffee in the other. As he got closer, he tripped, catching his foot on the edge of a rug, and went flying toward the glass table. I don't think I have ever moved so quickly, in all my life. I felt like a rugby player, as I leapt toward him, grabbing his head in a headlock then tackling him to the floor, to stop him from smashing his head through the glass.

We were both lying on the floor, me, with his head still in my hands, when he started giggling. "Ooops, that was a bit close," he said, rolling over and picking himself up then plonking himself on the sofa.

My dress was up, showing my knickers, so I quickly pulled it back down, then retrieved the empty cup of coffee and glass of whisky, which had rolled across the floor.

"Sure was. VERY close. That could have been a very nasty accident!" I said, grabbing handfuls of tissues, to mop up the mess.

"Don't worry. I've escaped death many times. Should have been dead many years ago… and don't worry about the rug, the maid will take care of it in the morning, she's used to my spillages. Would you like to play a game?"

"What game?" I enquired, knowing that even 'Snakes and Ladders' wouldn't be possible, with the state he was in.

"The cream, game?"

"What cream, game?" I asked, again, suspiciously.

Roger put his hand under the sofa and pulled out a large sheet of plastic, about two metres square, then, stumbling, spread it out on the floor in front of the TV screen.

"I just need to fetch the cream," he said, swaying to, then back from the kitchen, with a very large jug of cream.

"You're not thinking of eating me, are you?" I said, trying to make a joke, and at the same time, lifting my phone from my bag, ready to call Andy.

"Good God, No! I'm not Hannibal Lecter," he responded, placing the jug of cream on the table, then plonking himself back on his sofa.

"Well, that's good!" I said, wondering what on earth, he was considering.

Roger lifted a big wad of notes from inside his jacket pocket. I had spent two hours with him, so he owed me £700.

"There's £2,000 here," he said, placing it on the table.

Oh God. What does he want?

"Will you allow me to pour cream on your legs and feet?"

Cynthia Payne, immediately sprang to mind, again. Then Jackson Pollock.

"And then, what?" I asked.

"Nothing else. Just remove your shoes and tights and lie on the plastic. You can keep your knickers covered with the hem of your dress."

"And what else would you be doing, while pouring the cream?"

Very suspicious.

"Nothing else, just slowly, pouring."

I sat there, a bit stumped.

"I'm not going to masturbate or anything like that, I'm too old for all that nonsense. I just want you to allow me, to slowly pour cream on your legs and feet."

Definitely, one of Cynthia Payne's old clients, I thought.

"Can I roll a joint and think about it, Roger?"

"A joint! I haven't had a spliff for years. Smoked it all the time in the sixties. Will you roll one for me, too?"

"Of course, with pleasure," I responded, thinking how 'hip' he was, for a very elderly gentleman.

Roger sat quietly, tapping his foot out of time, to The Rat Pack, while I built two, very large, joints. Having completed the task, I threw one of the joints to him. It went flying over his shoulder, so I got up, retrieved it and handed it to him, along with a lighter. His hand couldn't find the end of the joint, so I lit it for him and passed it over, then I lit mine.

"Thanks, Gaynor. You're a sweetheart."

"No problem, enjoy."

He took a massive drag on it, taking the smoke deep into his lungs.

"Careful, it's quite strong," I said, feeling slightly concerned, for him.

"It's okay. I'm used to it. Used to smoke all the time."

"How long is it since you last had a joint?"

"About twenty years."

He took another very deep drag and closed his eyes. On the third large intake, the smoke made its own way out. His eyes rolled, then closed. He was totally and utterly smashed, high as a kite. He slowly rolled over to one side, and his head fell onto the seat of the sofa.

I sat motionless, for a couple of minutes, just watching him, to make sure he was still breathing.

"Roger... Roger..." I sang, quietly.

No response.

"Roger... Roger... Are you with us?" I asked, at normal volume.

Nothing.

"ROGEEEER!" I called, quite loudly.

No. Nothing. Not even a flicker.

After fifteen minutes, he was in a deep, deep, sleep, snoring away, like an old dog. I got up and went over to him, carefully removed the joint from his hand, then removed his shoes, and gently lifted his feet up, on to the sofa. I spotted a blanket over one of the chairs, so carefully placed it over him, then sat back in my seat. I looked at Roger. I looked at the £2,000. I looked at Roger. I looked at the £2,000. I looked at Roger. He was still, deeply asleep.

Then, I had an idea. I picked up the jug of cream, and slowly, finely, trickled it, over the area, where my legs and feet would have been, had I been lying on the plastic sheet. I think I would probably have gone through with his fantasy for the extra £1,300, so didn't feel too guilty. I gently smeared the cream to try to make it 'look right' then smeared and wiped cream on tissues and left them in situ, along with my tights, which I had discarded to make it look like I had wiped myself down. I was very pleased with my work. It looked very convincing.

I sat back down again, just to check he was still okay. He was, so I grabbed my coat and bag, picked up the £2,000 and tiptoed out of his flat.

As soon as the main door to the building closed, behind me, I hailed and jumped in a cab. Was I feeling guilty? Yes, a bit but he's a big boy and is responsible for his own actions. I comforted myself with the thought that I HAD stopped him flying face first, into the glass coffee table. He could have ended up with deep cuts and lots of stitches. I might even have saved his life, in which case, £2,000 was a small price to pay. I no longer felt guilty. More like a heroine.

PAYBACK

Sunday, 26th January

I woke up the next morning, still feeling a little guilty. It had been a very unexpected, easy £2,000 to make. I stretched and then rubbed my eyes and ran my hands down my face.

What is that?' I re-felt the left-hand side of my chin. What the fuck is THAT? OH MY GOD, OH MY GOD! IT'S A FUCKING WHISKER! I pushed it with my finger. It wasn't a soft whisker. It was a fucking bristle. Horrified, I grabbed the mirror, to confirm the nightmare. Yes, there it was. A hard, light grey bristle, about a millimetre, in length. As if grey pubes hadn't been enough to contend with. This is my 'payback' for partaking in immoral activity... but was it immoral? I didn't do anything really naughty... or maybe I did... the cream... could I be prosecuted for fraud? Maybe there were hidden cameras in his room. The whisker was definitely 'pay-back'. I felt a higher force was telling me not to go down the 'escort' path. It's a precarious game and things could easily go wrong. It's also, potentially, a dangerous game and some old gentlemen might want a lot more for their money. Have to change course. My escorting was over. At the very least, I wouldn't end up with a beard. Now, where are my tweezers... or should I say, pliers?

Later that day, I received a text from Roger.

Hi, Gaynor. Thanks for last night. I haven't had so much fun for years. Would you like to meet up again?

Bless him. He didn't remember a thing but he knew something had happened due to the empty jug and the evidence left on the plastic sheet.

Hi there, Roger. I had a great time too. It was lovely to meet you and thank you so much for a fun evening. I have, however, at this time, decided not to engage in escorting any more, but to take a different path. Good luck and best wishes for the future. Gaynor x

Sail away Jolly Roger, sail away.

UNACCEPTABLE

Saturday, 1ˢᵗ February

Bryn arrived in the evening with a warm, accepting smile and a bottle of bubbly.

"Hi, darling, how are you, how was it, last weekend with Roger... what did you get up to?"

Suddenly I felt as though I didn't want to discuss any part of the date I'd had with Roger even though nothing had actually happened. I felt like Bryn was being intrusive. I was not allowed, or supposed to ask him, about his extra-curricular activity, so why should I share mine with him.

"Actually, I don't really want to talk about it."

Bryn looked really surprised then sort of 'frowned'.

"I thought you were going to tell me all about it this evening."

"Well, I was, but now I've changed my mind. Woman's prerogative."

Bryn's expression softened, then he put his arms around me. "It's okay, darling, I understand."

As I felt the warmth of his embrace, I thought actually, you don't understand.

Why did he always have to be so goddamn accommodating? I loved him. Hated him. Loved him. Hated him. I had been thinking about my exploits and was actually quite upset and even a little angry that he had so readily accepted that I was prepared to be a 'classy' escort. If he really cared for me, wouldn't he have contested? On the other hand, I suppose he couldn't really. He was his own man doing his own thing and the choices I had made were my own. Still hurt though.

We spent the rest of the evening relaxing and watching movies, on the sofa. There was no mention of sex and he did not make any kind of move on me. Around half ten, he took himself off to my bed, inviting me but I decided to stay and watch TV.

"I'll come in a bit," I said, convincingly. Truth is, I didn't want to share my bed with him, even platonically.

Half an hour later, a text message came through, only thing was, it wasn't my phone that was receiving it. It was Bryn's. He had left his phone, unknowingly and unbeknown to me, on the sofa. He was probably now fast asleep so I lifted it from the sofa and placed it on the coffee table. Then it received a second message.

I sat, staring at his phone. I knew I shouldn't. I knew it was unacceptable. I knew it would probably, actually, completely, totally 'fuck him off', but I just couldn't help myself. I grabbed the phone, unlocked it and read the first text. It was from someone called Tricia.

Hi, baby. Are you still up? Do you fancy coming over?

I felt sick. And then I felt spiteful.

No, he's not still up. He's in my bed fast asleep.

I waited not more than twenty seconds and got a reply.

Who the hell are you?

I immediately responded.

I'm his girlfriend. Who the hell are you?

Twenty seconds.

Girlfriend? Do you know your boyfriend is sleeping around?

I thought about my reply.

Yes, of course. We have an open relationship.

Twenty seconds.

You must be fucking mad. You can tell him Tricia says fuck off, and don't ever call her again.

I responded.

Okay, Tricia. Bye.

Then, I immediately felt guilty about what I had just done. Ohhhh SHIT! SHIT, SHIT, SHIT, SHIT, SHIT! He's going to go crazy. He'll be furious. Probably won't ever want to see me again.

I sat, looking at Bryn's phone for around fifteen minutes, thinking of how I might explain my actions. I had invaded his privacy, in an appalling, disgraceful, shameful way. Absolutely unforgiveable. There was only one way out. I decided to act on it. I picked up his phone, deleted all of the messages Tricia and I had exchanged, deleted her number and then blocked her. Hopefully, she would delete and block Bryn too. Then I turned off his phone, fetched a duvet and pillow and decided to stay on the sofa, for the rest of the night.

CAUGHT OUT

8.20 p.m. My phone rang. It was Bryn. I froze for a second then decided to pick up and act innocent.

"Hi, darling, how are you?"

"HOW AM I? WHAT THE FUCK DID YOU DO? I'VE JUST HAD A DRINK THROWN IN MY FACE!"

I hung up. Oh shit! OH SHIT!

He rang again. I diverted him, straight to answerphone. After a couple of minutes, 'voice mail received' appeared on my phone.

I played it.

WHAT THE HELL DO YOU THINK YOU'RE DOING TOUCHING MY PHONE! AND WORSE STILL RESPONDING TO A PERSONAL, PRIVATE MESSAGE. YOU HAD NO RIGHT. WHAT YOU DID IS TOTALLY INEXCUSABLE. IT WAS AN INVASION OF MY PRIVACY AND I AM ABSOLUTELY FURIOUS WITH YOU!

With his fury raging in my ear, I just went into another dimension. I starting nodding my head from side to side, then started mouthing BLA, BLA, BLA..... BLA, BLA, BLA... BLA, BLA, BLA', back at him. I knew I had done wrong but I wasn't going to sit there, letting him lay into me. I had no idea Bryn could be SO angry. He was usually so placid. It didn't even sound like him.

While he continued ranting and raving, I stopped his voice mail, and immediately deleted it. Then, I blocked him. I had beaten myself up all week, as it was, with regards to my misconduct and I simply couldn't be dealing with such uncontrollable anger.

After recovering from the voice mail, I started smiling. The thought of Bryn innocently enjoying a quiet pint after a hard day's work at The Royal Free then having 'Tricia' walking up to him and throwing a drink in his face must have been an enormous shock. Then, it dawned on me. Bryn hadn't mentioned his relationship with me to Tricia, so why had I been feeling so guilty. All I had done, was to tell the truth, even though it wasn't my position to do so. Perhaps the manner in which I had told her, had been somewhat 'harsh', but knowledge is everything. She had obviously known nothing of his extra-curricular activities, so he deserved what he got. Wet. On reflection, I believe I did her a big service, by divulging what he was up to. By her reaction, it appeared that she believed he was only seeing her. I now felt pleased with what I had done and I hoped, after getting over the shock, Tricia would be pleased too.

FLUFFY COMES HOME

It had been ten weeks since I 'creamed away' my pubes. I wished I hadn't removed them, on refection. The early regrowth had initially felt like stubble, then when the hair was as long as whiskers, they would 'push through' the front of my knickers, even the cotton ones. It was also, a very 'itchy' experience, with me secretly trying to have a discrete quick scratch, at every available opportunity.

I thought about men with hairy chests. Personally, I rather liked it. I felt those hairs were very masculine and a compliment to the soft silky chest of a female. I like hairy arms and legs on men too. So soft, it reminded me of a new furry toy, snuggly and comforting.

With male baldness, I felt quite different. I loved bald men. That love started, when I was in early my twenties. I remember getting the 'hots' for Telly Savalas, Aka Kojak. I loved his face and the shape of his head, his fabulous deep voice and the way he moved, always casual and unfazed and, of course, the never-ending, round, red lollipop, that sat inside his cheek, which he occasionally took out and licked or sucked on. The second thing was, if men are bravely bald, it sends out a signal, that that man is confident. Thirdly, a bald head allows the features on the face to stand out more, especially the eyes.

Back to fluffy. As the weeks had passed, the itchy whiskers stopped fighting with the front of my knickers and stayed where there should be, inside. As the hairs became longer and softer, I would often pat her, in encouragement. Everything, eventually returned to where and how it should be and I literally felt the way I used to, back to normal. The golden egg was back in her soft, warm, comfortable nest.

PROFILES

Tuesday, 4th March

It had been a month since my altercation with Bryn and neither of us had attempted to contact each other.

Being so short of ready cash, I hadn't been out partying for a few weeks but had, instead, decided to redecorate my living room during the day and browse the internet dating apps, in the evenings. My understanding of men, in general, grew with every communication I'd had. I was very wary and often ended up 'grilling' potential dates, or 'counselling' non-potential dates.

My profile, read as follows:

Intelligent, warm, loving, honest female, age thirty-eight, looking for intelligent, interesting honest man with a kind heart.
Animal lover, especially dogs, I have two.
Highly creative, including illustration, design and advertising.
Enjoy writing, visiting places of interest, great movies, crooners and similar music, also some classical and some 'pop'.
Prefer Champagne and chips rather than dinner in a restaurant.
Love dancing, at good London clubs, and occasional visits to the theatre, especially Les Mis.
Friends describe me as honest, warm and funny with a magnetic personality.
Please contact if you feel you might be the kind of gentleman I am looking for.
Recent photo attached.
PS. I lied about my age.

From all the men that I had communicated with, there was one that stood out significantly. He was called Bruce. This was his response to my profile.

Love your profile, especially the age bit!
Age fifty-one years, an ex-barrister who prefers making money with a social conscience, earn more money than I know how to spend. Interested in charities.
Educated, intelligent, witty, guitar playing, avid reading, man about town.
Also, animal lover, and enjoy walking my dogs in the countryside.
Good teeth and full head of hair.
Recent photo attached.
Would love to meet you. Please get back to me, if you are interested.
Regards, Bruce Billington.
PS. I lied about my hair.

Bruce's photo showed he was totally bald. Sense of humour. Good. I was interested, so did get back to him and after swapping phone numbers and a brief conversation, we arranged to meet. Bruce would come to London.

BRUCE, AKA, BILL

Thursday, 13ᵗʰ March

Six thirty p.m. Directed Bruce in from East Finchley. It took about fifteen minutes. I appreciated that Bruce didn't know his way around town and could have easily got lost. Worse still, stressed.

I leant out of the window as the long, strong, shiny black, convertible Jag pulled up outside the door. I caught sight of a big man in a soft pink shirt just before the bat wing wrapped itself over the car and settled into position. A hand waved through the glass. Although we couldn't see each other, I was beaming with anticipation so turned and raced down the stairs with a Resident's Parking Permit.

As I reached the gate, the low, stylish snazzy door opened and a large, strong, man stepped out. Still beaming, I looked into the face of the man with very broad shoulders. A soft face, a kind face and very blue eyes. A nervous smile greeted me, as I put my arms around his neck. I hugged warmly, as he patted me on the back like an old dog, who he was once friends with, but hadn't seen for a long time.

"Hi, Bruce. Great to meet you."

"Hello, Gaynor, call me Bill as in my surname, Billington. No one ever calls me Bruce."

"Hello, Bill."

He opened the boot. "I couldn't fit two guitars in the boot... sorry."

"That's okay," I said, thinking Ben might be a little disappointed, as he was looking forward to meeting Bill and having a little jam with him. I lifted out a small suitcase leaving the guitar and huge, heavy box briefcase, for Bill.

"I'll take that," said Bill, with no hands free.

"No, you won't," I said, wandering off with it.

Bill followed me upstairs.

"It's really good of you to put me up, Gaynor..."

"No problem. It's a pleasure."

I found it quite odd, that the man who had driven all the way down from Manchester, was thanking me for a potential sociable evening and a night on the couch.

I showed Bill into the living room and told him to make himself comfortable. Taking his jacket and placing it across the back of a chair, I looked at the big man from behind.

"Please sit down and relax, Bill. Can I get you a glass of wine?"

"Actually, I'd love a cup of coffee," he said, perching himself on the edge of a large, open armchair. I was glad he sat on the edge. It showed, to me, someone who was polite.

"I'm really sorry, Gaynor, but I'm really nervous."

His broad, Mancunian accent, was lovely.

"That's good," I said, "so am I."

"Where's Ben?" I was surprised that he enquired about Ben, so quickly.

"In his bedroom."

"What's he doing in there?" he asked, quizzically.

"He is allowing us a bit of time, to say hi."

"Don't be daft... Get him in here."

Trying not to focus on the fact that he had called me daft, but realising his sentiment was lovely, I smiled and asked if he was sure.

"Of course, bring him in."

Delighted that Bill was keen to meet Ben and realising his presence would put us both more at ease, I walked gracefully out of the room and dashed to Ben's door. Knocking hard and quickly and not giving him time to respond, I threw the door open and fell in.

"Bill wants to meet you, now! Come and have some wine."

"Who's Bill?"

Oh, sorry, Bruce... but he's known as Bill."

"What, already?" said Ben, getting up from his seat.

"Yes, come on."

I waved Ben through to meet Bill, who was already standing with his hand outstretched, ready to greet him. Hands shaken, greetings spoken, I left them to it for a moment and went to get wine and coffee, then I turned around and came back, because I had forgotten to ask Bill how he wanted his coffee.

"White, two sugars, please."

I repeated the words, until said items, were safely in the cup, knowing that in the past I had asked people the same question and not listened to their answer, so had had to ask again.

"Cheers everyone." I said, encouraging the glasses and coffee cup to chink. We sat down, then I realised me and Ben were sitting together, on the sofa opposite Bill. I thought he might feel interrogation was about to start, so I sat between the both of them, cross legged on the floor.

We exchanged pleasantries for a few minutes and I studied Bill as we spoke. He was a big guy, big chest, big arms and big thighs. Maybe, I thought, he is one man whose lap I can sit on, without being told to get off because I was too heavy. Through his accent, I listened to the tone of Bill's voice. It was deep, but not too deep, and soft, but not too soft.

"I have some photos," he said, reaching for his briefcase.

"Great! I love piccies!" I responded, enthusiastically, but rather surprised at his fast, willingness to share.

His large hand lifted out about twenty pictures, in all shapes and sizes, some battered at the corners. As Bill sorted them out, I moved closer, to get a better look. First photo, the largest of them all. A family picture of mum, dad, brothers, sisters and other relatives, circa 1972. Swirly green carpets and Del Boy curtains, brown and yellow, in colour. A family. A lovely, happy, working-class family, that resembled my own. He pointed everyone out.

"I was good looking, then," he said, pointing at himself.

I looked at the young man, who had become the man before me. Standing behind the seated elders, arms folded, back straight, fit looking, slim, square shoulders, sleeveless vest, moustache, and curly, auburn hair. I wondered if he had felt he was going to be successful, back then. More photos of family and friends followed, along with one, of his two dogs, greyhounds, Blue and Bella.

"Who looks after your dogs, when you are away, Bill?"

"My neighbour. She loves them. She has a dog, too, they are all friends."

Having passed the photos to Ben, I sat back and thought what a lovely thing that was to do, to bring pictures of one's life, to new people. It was a gesture that was all embracing. It said, come into my private world, I want to share it with you.

I grabbed Bill by the hand, pulling him up from his seat. "Come and see my wall of joy... It's in the hall."

Bill stood in the hallway, facing the wall of smiling faces. About two hundred, altogether. I started pointing out family members and friends.

"What a great idea. What did you call it? Wall of Joy?"

"Yes, it's my wall of joy. I did it at Christmas, when I had flu for a couple of weeks. Let's go and sit down again," I said, not wanting, to bore him.

I followed Bill back into the living room. Must say, I really did like the shape of the man.

"Sorry about the guitar, Ben."

"Don't worry... let's have a look at yours though."

Bill got up from his chair and lifted a six-string guitar from its case. Perching himself back on the edge of the seat, he positioned it, like a professional, and began to play. I watched the large, strong fingers, dance across the cords, with eloquent dexterity. Gentle giant, I thought. He was very, very good.

Clapping at the end and congratulating Bill on his playing, he took no acknowledgement, but went straight into another piece. Clapping at the end of that one, he got up and passed the guitar to Ben. Ben played for us, also, very well. The guitar went backwards and forwards and then I encouraged Bill to sing something. Instead, he played a very tender and beautiful piece, which I did not recognize, but loved immediately. Quite short, it finished before I wanted it to.

"That was really lovely, Bill. What is it?" I asked.

He turned to me. "I wrote it for you, Gaynor. I write a lot of music."

I felt my throat give a large swallow and looked at Bill's face. He looked at mine, and smiled. For a split second, before he averted his glance, something in me was touched. It is hard to describe the feeling I had, but, the nearest thing to it, I can explain, is like a low voltage ache with an endless supply of small sparks. I felt sick and excited all at once. Feeling uncomfortable, I asked myself how I could possibly be having feelings of such magnitude, for a man I had only spent half an hour with. A question in my head, then challenged me. Had Bill really written a song, just for me? Then the cynic in me wondered if he had played that song to many women, telling them all, he had written it specifically for 'them',

"Did you really write it for me, Bill?"

He glanced at me, nodded his head, then glanced away, all the while playing the next number. I got up and went for more drinks, wondering whether it was true.

As I poured more Champagne and made more coffee, I decided to try to be positive and take Bill, at his word. If it was true, it was the first time someone had written a song for me. And such a tender song. I had liked it so much. It was something I had always liked the idea of, who wouldn't! How lovely, I thought. It was a big gesture for someone to make, considering we had only been in communication for a couple of weeks. By the time I had finished pouring the Champagne, I had sorted it out in my head. The song that had come from the man, WAS written for me. I returned to the living room and requested 'Gaynor's' song, again. I smiled all the way through. I couldn't help it. I felt very special.

After the silence at the end of the final note, Bill offered to take us all out for a Japanese. "Do you like Japanese, Gaynor?" asked, Bill.

I wasn't going to be polite for the sake of it. "No, nor Chinese. Sorry."

"Have you tried Japanese?"

"No. But I'm not a big foody person. Some people live to eat and some people eat to live. I'm the latter."

"Don't knock it until you've tried it, Gaynor, you might love it."

Bill looked slightly disappointed but, to be honest, I wasn't in the mood to go out.

Thinking firstly of me, Ben waited for my response. I took control. "How about, we order an Indian? There's a really good curry house up the road."

"That'll suit me," said Bill.

"And me," said Ben.

I sang in my head, Bill and Ben, Bill and Ben, flowerpot men, flowerpot men.

"What do you fancy, Bill?" asked Ben, passing over the menu.

"No need to see the menu, Chicken Tikka Jalfrezi, please, Ben."

Food delivered and eaten, apart from mine, because I didn't feel hungry, the guitar came out again, for a few more songs, then was placed back in its case.

"Would you like to see some of my illustrations, Bill?" I asked, leaving him no choice, as I marched off to my bedroom.

"Love to."

I opened my folio, in my bedroom, and lifted out twelve of my best pieces. Returning, I placed them in a pile on Bill's lap. He looked at the first one carefully.

"This is really good, Gaynor," he enthused.

"Thanks."

"They're all really good."

"Thanks."

What a different reaction, compared to Bryn, I thought.

Bill went through my illustrations lifting out three. "I love this," he said, holding one up, with his left hand... "and I love this," he held it up, with his right hand. "But THIS, is my favourite," he said, putting down the others and holding it with two hands. His choice was a black and white, very detailed illustration of a row of four, old, tightly packed Victorian houses and arching through, and behind the windows of the houses, was a rainbow. That was the only colour on the picture. I sat on the arm of Bill's chair as he spoke, and looked down at the artwork completed some thirty years ago.

"What I like about this picture," said Bill, "is that the rainbow, is like the gaiety and colour of life, that goes on, behind those old, brick, 'samey' Victorian exteriors. I used to live in a house like that... and our front door was different, like this one, and Mrs Woodhouse used to live next door... here." He then pointed to the fourth house. "And my mate, Ronnie, used to live here. It was a great street and this is a great picture."

"It's yours," I said.

"I can't!"

"Yes, you can. It's yours. I'll have it framed for you."

"Oh, Gaynor, are you sure?"

"Yes, it's for you. I want you to have it. You understand the idea behind it. Those houses were in a street in Watford where my art college used to be. On cold winter evenings I used to walk by those houses and look in through the windows, and I would see warm lighting, people sitting watching TV, people eating, people laughing, children playing, dogs lying by the fire and it was REAL. It is what is going on, on the inside that counts. Also... you wrote a song for me, so I am gifting you, in return."

"Well, thank you very much, Gaynor. I don't know what to say, I'm very touched."

I took the pictures away, except for Bill's, and on returning, he told me he was really tired and asked if he could go to bed.

My response was immediate. "Yes of course you can."

"I've been up, since five a.m."

'Follow me."

I showed Bill into my bedroom. I had made an executive decision. "I'm going to sleep in the front room, Dill."

"No. I'm going to sleep in the front room," responded Bill, heading out of the door.

I grabbed him. "No. Don't argue. You're sleeping in here. I'm not very tired, anyway, so I'm going to watch TV for a bit. Would you like a glass of water?"

"Yes, please."

I returned with the water and placed it on the bedside table. He was already undressed and in my bed. I could see his magnificent, hairy chest, exposing itself, from the waist up. I wanted to run my fingers through it but restrained myself.

"It's very rare, that I have walked into someone's home and it has felt like home. Yours does."

"Yes, I love making homes. I make them wherever I go. Home is important to me."

"I can see that," said Bill, "and what a lovely home you have."

"Thank you, Bill," I said, knowing that a string of fairy lights, make all the difference.

Bill yawned, so I turned to leave the bedroom. He then managed to gently grab my hand. "Kiss goodnight?"

I leant to kiss him on the cheek but he turned his face towards me and caught my lips. I felt uncomfortable for a second but, as I stayed there, holding my breath, Bill's kisses were so tender across my lips, that I stayed for a couple of minutes. I then, gently broke free, and moved away, wishing him goodnight.

"Thanks again, for everything, Gaynor," he said, as I disappeared into the hall.

"You are most welcome, Bill. Night, night. Sleep well."

I closed the door behind me and then congratulated myself, on keeping my knickers on.

On returning back to the living room, Ben had gone off to bed so I climbed under the spare duvet. I couldn't stop wondering about Bill, and needed some distraction, so turned on the TV to watch 'Late night Trisha', until I finally fell asleep.

***

It was about eight a.m. when I heard Daisy and Flo trotting off, up the hall, to say good morning. I knew it was Bill. Too early for the rest of us. I stuck my head around the door and could hear noises coming from the bathroom. Quickly grabbing my dressing gown, I checked myself in the mirror and then jumped into my empty, but still warm sofa-bed. Five minutes later, suited and booted, Bill stuck his head around the living room door. "Morning," he said, with a smile.

"Morning, Bill. How did you sleep?"

"Like a baby! Your bed is SO comfortable. It really was so sweet of you. It's the first time someone has given up their bed, for me."

Bill's mobile rang.

"Have to take this... Business... Sorry..."

"No problem. Go ahead."

Bill chatted away about business, while I propped myself up, on the sofa-bed.

"Sorry about that... Business..."

"It's no problem, Bill. Business is business."

"What are you going to do today, Gaynor?"

"Well, the first thing I am going to do, is make you some coffee."

"Haven't got time," he said.

"I'll make you a take-away. Give me two minutes."

White with two sugars. Excellent, I had remembered from the previous night.

Handing Bill his coffee, he thanked me again for my hospitality and said what a great time he had had.

"Me too, I had a lovely time," I said, hugging him.

He hugged me back, kissed me on the cheek, then pulled away, to look into my face. "I shall carry the vision of you, with me, all day."

Bill carried his suitcase and guitar down to the car. I followed him in my dressing gown, carrying the huge box briefcase. I thought about the world inside the box, and was glad there was still room for the family snap shots amongst the piles of paperwork. I waited with it, by the main door to the house, whilst Bill filled the boot. He came up to the step. "Thanks again, Gaynor. You really are, a lovely person. I can't wait until we meet up, again."

"Me, too, Bill. Have a good journey back."

I hugged him again and this time held on. I kissed his cheek then the big man walked away. I wish I could have spent the day with him.

"I'll call you later," he said, not turning, but with a wave.

"Bye, Bill. See you soon. I'm going to wave at you out of the window."

I dashed back up the stairs and ran into the living room, lifting the old, awkward, heavy sash window, with two hands. The bat wing was folding back on itself, ready for take-off. Bill looked up and waved again.

"Bye, Bill," I shouted, as he motored off, down the street. I followed him, until he was out of sight.

BACK TO MANCHESTER

Friday, 14th March

The journey that took Bill back to Manchester, should take about five hours. He called me every time he was stuck in a traffic jam. In one jam, he was stationary, in a tail back on the motorway, bursting for a pee. I told him the idea I'd had for a new product. The Traveloo. Two versions. One for the ladies and one for men. Realising that Bill was amused, but wanting to get toilets out if his mind, I told him about a board game I had invented.

"What's it called? I'll look out for it."

"It's called, 'If'. The game is designed and has been played but, I need to get it 'art work', ready. It's good fun, a family game, a game of 'chance' and the people who have played it, from old to young, absolutely love it. I wanted to design a game that was for EVERYONE, and have done so."

"Aren't all games for everyone?"

I explained further. "With Scrabble, you need to know how to spell. With Trivial Pursuit, you need good general knowledge. With Pictionary, you need to be able to draw. With Monopoly, you need luck but also, strategy. Risk is also a game of strategy, same goes for Cluedo."

"Wow, well you really seem to have thought it through. There's definitely a gap in the market for it."

"Yes, anyone can play it, without fear of feeling dumb or inadequate. I've also designed it to work in two ways, one way for kids and a different way for gown-ups. It is totally inclusive, suiting children up to grandparents."

"Why isn't it out there?"

"Story of my life. Great ideas. All finished up to a point of a 'finished working idea', then it goes in the drawer."

"Gaynor, I think your confidence is the thing that is holding you back. You should be flying high with the rest of them. Moving again… Call you later…"

"Bye, Bill. Hope you find a loo, soon."

I realised, too late, that it would probably have been best not to mention the loo again. I thought about what Bill had just said. I think he hit the nail on the head. Lack of confidence. As long as it was in the drawer, and no one had seen it, it was a possibility and not a rejection. The thing is, I absolutely knew the board game was a winner, people really loved it, so where, is the goblin coming from?

Bill finally arrived home, around eight p.m. that evening, having missed two business meetings.

"What a day! Twelve bloody hours to get from London to Manchester I've got a sore back, and a sore bum"

"How awful, what a nightmare for you, you must be exhausted," I said, knowing about long car journeys and sore bums.

"But it was worth it, just to come and meet you. Next time, I think I'll get the train. I'm absolutely knackered, so will wish you goodnight. I'll call you tomorrow. Big hug."

"Great, sleep well and speak tomorrow. Great big hug, back."

FLOWERS

After an interrupted night's sleep, I woke up and thought about Bill, then I got up and went to join Ben, in the living room.

"Mornin," said Ben, giving me a hug.

"Mornin... What do you think of Bill then?" I asked excitedly, throwing myself on to the sofa with a bounce and hoping for a really positive response.

"He's great! I really like him. Seems like a really good, down-to-earth bloke."

Ben continued.

"He's a great musician too. Singer-songwriter, and what a great voice. He might be quite a catch, Gaynor. How do you feel about him?"

"I'm in love... No, not really, not yet, anyway. I thought he was really lovely. I really like him and can't wait to see him again."

Ben then got up from his chair, went to the kitchen and returned with an absolutely stunning, bouquet of flowers, which he handed to me. Delighted, I opened the little silver envelope.

"They're from Bill," I said, beaming, and handed Ben the little card. It read:

Gaynor, you are quite simply, wonderful xxxxx

I immediately texted Bill.

Dear Bill, I am so touched by the stunning bouquet of flowers that have just arrived and want to say thank you. What a lovely, thoughtful gesture. I really appreciate it. Speak soon. With love, Gaynor x x x x x

The day went slowly and by ten p.m., I was feeling troubled. I hadn't heard from Bill. No text, no call, no email. The words that Max had said,

'I feel like you're hounding me', had been going through my head for most of the day, so I didn't want to call, for fear of appearing impatient. Instead, I preferred to wait, until Bill contacted me.

THIN AIR

Sunday, 16th March.

Morning, no contact.

Afternoon, no contact.

By Seven p.m., Sunday evening, I was feeling frustrated but, also concerned. I couldn't understand why Bill, hadn't, in the very least, sent me a message. I decided to message him.

Hi, Bill. Hope you have had a lovely, relaxing weekend and are well recovered, from your nightmare journey, back to Manchester. I took Daisy and Flo to Primrose Hill for a lovely walk in the sunshine this afternoon, then arrived back home to a lovely surprise, a late Sunday lunch, which Ben had made for us. He's a great cook. Much better than me! Enjoy your evening. With Love, Gaynor x x x x x

I hoped, and waited, for a response. By midnight, nothing. I just didn't get it. I began to think maybe something bad had happened to him. Car crash? Heart attack? Someone in his family had passed away? Then, I thought I was probably just being over dramatic. Maybe he just lost his phone? But if he had, why hadn't he emailed me? Maybe his phone and computer were in his car and his car was broken into, or even, stolen. Or maybe his home had been burgled so he had no way of contacting me? I considered every possible option as to his silence. My head was all over the place. I started to feel a bit sick. I decided to send an email. I didn't know what else I could do.

***

Monday, 17th March.

Today, came and went. No response to my email, no texts, no calls.

***

Tuesday, 18th March

I phoned Bill, twice. It went to the answer machine. I didn't leave a message.

***

Wednesday, 19th March

I sent another text.

Hi, Bill, it's Gaynor. Just wanted to make sure you are okay. Have been a bit worried about you because you haven't been in contact. Please let me know you are all right. With love, Gaynor xxxxx

No response.

***

Thursday, 20th March

Ben knocked on my 'half open', bedroom door and walked in.

"Just checking if you're okay. You've been a bit quiet for the last few days and you don't seem yourself. Has something happened? Is something wrong?"

I burst into tears.

"What's happened, Gaynor? What's wrong?" asked Ben, walking forward, to comfort me.

I tried to speak through the tears. "It's Bill. I haven't heard anything from him at all, since Saturday, after I sent him a message to thank him for the flowers. He's not responding to my texts, emails or calls. I've given him 'space' and only sent a couple of texts, in case he's busy with work, but I've heard nothing back. I don't get it. It's been six days. I'm really, so confused."

"That's weird," said Ben, gently, patting me. "I felt really good about him and am sure he was genuine. I wonder what's happened. I wonder why he hasn't contacted you…"

I talked Ben through all of the possible scenarios, I had considered.

He sat there, looking as confused and concerned as I was. There was nothing he could say, that was going to comfort me.

"Would you like me to make you a cup of tea?"

"Yes, please," I said, not really wanting one.

Ben returned a few minutes later, with tea and some chocolate digestives, on a plate.

"I don't know what to say, Gaynor. He was so keen on you. Something has happened but, I have absolutely no idea, what."

I spoke through my tears. "I don't want to think the worst, but I can't help thinking the worst, maybe he's dead."

Ben, who would often lead me when I was struggling, stayed silent and just stared out of the window.

"I think he's gone, Ben, and even if he's not dead, something has happened to him. He's gone. He's just disappeared into thin air."

HASAN TO THE RESCUE!

Tuesday, 1ˢᵗ April

It had been nearly three weeks since Bill, and my mind and body had been in a constant state of 'ache'. I knew questions would never be answered, so had no choice but to 'let it go'. I had suffered long enough. Not knowing what, where, why and when, had taken its toll on me and I had felt very depressed. Slowly, I began coming back, returning to the land of the living, through a sad, grey haze.

At five minutes past noon, I received an extremely welcomed text message, from Hasan.

Hi, Gaynor. How are you? I'm sending this message at 12.05 because it's April Fool's Day and I didn't want to jinx myself. I wondered if I could 'try' to take you out to dinner again, LOL. Are you free this Saturday?

I smiled, at his humour.

Hi, Hasan! Good to hear from you. I am free, all day Saturday, but instead of dinner, how about a walk in the park with the dogs in the afternoon? The weather forecast is good.

Please, agree.

That's a great idea. What time would suit you?

I suggested two p.m., knowing he would turn up at three p.m.

Great! Look forward to seeing you then x x x

Excellent, just what I needed.

See you then. Have a good day x x x

It had been around six months since I'd met up with Hasan. I didn't call him after the bird incident but, instead, left him to get over the trauma of the loss of Sunny, and to nurse his wounds. Apart from the canary, he had also lost his 'potential' new girlfriend, whom he appeared to like very much AND he'd received a vase over the back of his head, for trying to help someone out, with the very best of intentions. Bless him. Still can't help smiling.

RANTING, ON PRIMROSE HILL

Saturday, 5th April

Hasan pulled up outside at 3.20, in a smart black Audi. I recognized the make from the four circles on the grill. Nice and shiny, it looked brand new. I was looking forward to seeing my old friend very much and as he stepped out of the car, he spotted me from the window and gave a big smile and a wave.

"Stay there. I'm coming straight down."

Quickly putting Daisy and Flo's leads, on, I was about to lock up, then thought I should take a blanket for the dogs to sit on, on the back seat. Blanket in hand, I made my way downstairs and towards Hasan, who was walking toward me. We gave each other a warm hug and I added a 'squeeze' because I was so happy to see him. Time spent with Hasan was never boring, it was more like an adventure.

"Hi, Gaynor! How are you?"

"I'm great. How about you?"

"I'm good!"

"Lovely car, is it yours?"

"No, belongs to a friend. It's brand new."

"I've brought a blanket for the back seat, for the dogs to sit on."

"Good idea," he said, taking it from me and making sure the back seat was totally protected. Daisy and Flo jumped obligingly on to the back seat and immediately laid down. I jumped in the front and Hasan closed the door after me, like a chauffeur. The car smelt brand new and the luxurious interior with its leather seats was quite simply, fabulous.

"Shall I direct you?"

"No, it's okay, I looked at the map."

"And you can remember the way?"

"Yes, it's imprinted on my brain."

'Great."

As we pulled away, Hasan slipped a CD into the player. It was one of our all-time favourites, 'What's going on' by Marvin Gaye. Volume up, I sat and danced in my seat, while Hasan took us to Primrose Hill. It was only a five-minute ride, just enough time to play the track twice.

"We can park on this road at the top of the hill. Oh, it's a bit busy up here. Go down to the bottom and turn right, there's usually more space down there."

Daisy and Flo were sitting up in their seats as we pulled into one of the numerous available parking bays. They could smell the park. I let the dogs out of the car, while Hasan went to get a 'Pay and Display' two-hour parking ticket.

All sorted, we headed through the gate and into the glorious park.

"I'm going to take you to the top of the hill, it has a great view, right across London. Dogs off their leads, they chased each other, keeping one eye on us and the direction we were heading in.

"It's really good to see you, Hasan, what have you been up to?"

"Listening for radio signals from outer space, most recently."

"Listening to signals from outer space?"

I was fascinated.

"For the MOD?"

"Changed jobs. The National Space Centre."

"Wow! Where is it?"

"In Leicester."

"That's a long way to go for work."

"I only have to go once a week, I'm working from home."

"How exciting! Searching the universe for aliens!"

Hasan laughed.

"Tell me more."

"If I told you, I'd have to kill you," he said, smiling.

Inquisition over, we breathlessly, reached the top of the hill.

"Wow! Great view. You can see for miles."

"I know, it's fab, isn't it?"

We sat on one of the benches and looked across the London skyline.

"Is that the Gherkin?" asked Hasan, pointing at it.

"I hate that its being called The Gherkin. I bet no one knows its real name, except for the architect."

"Its real name is 30 St Mary Axe, named after the church, St Mary Axe, a medieval relic, knocked down around 1565. The church stood just south of it."

"Crikey, Hasan, you must only be the 'one in a million' who knows its real name. Bit of a mouthful though, isn't it, St Mary's axe. I still don't like The Gherkin though."

We continued to look at the sky line.

"Look! There's the pickled onion," I said, pointing at St Paul's Cathedral.

Hasan laughed. I continued looking at the 'square' buildings either side.

"They are cubes of cheese," I said, pointing at more buildings, and, if you look to the far right, you can just about see a pineapple ring... The London Eye. It's all looking rather like a 1960s finger buffet," I said, giggling.

"Can't see any crisps," responded, Hasan.

"Why do people call it The Gherkin?"

"Because it's shaped like one," said Hasan, with a smile.

I whinged on.

"Gherkins look a bit weak and bendy. Why not 'The Bullet?' or 'The Pod? Can't imagine what foreign visitors to London, must think. Stupid, bloody Gherkin! I blame the press, and while I'm 'on one', have you seen the memorial that's being built for Princess Diana, in Hyde Park?"

"No, haven't seen it yet."

"Don't bother. It is unbelievably disappointing. My heart broke when I laid eyes on it. It's a low, grey, granite, sort of circle, which will eventually contain a bit of water running inside it. It's got hard edges with steps, that look positively dangerous. I wouldn't let a child anywhere near it, let alone walk in the water along the steps. It looks so masculine and uninspiring. I honestly couldn't believe it, when I saw it. I think it's the worst memorial I have ever seen It doesn't reflect her energy or vitality, in any way. It is dull, dull, dull. It's so unworthy. She deserves so much more. Her memorial should have been a glorious, proud, sparkling fountain, something beautiful. Something which reflected her vivacious personality. In my head, I see a large fountain, in the middle of a circle, with little fountains around the edge, to represent her love of children. Maybe the fountains could be of clear water, with white light under them, and in the evenings, the little fountains around the edge could be lit up with different colours. It should be something that people really want to visit, something joyous. I think I might write to Prince William, even if he's not in a position to do anything now, maybe he will give her the memorial she deserves, when he is king."

"I like the fact that you have strong opinions, Gaynor, and your fountain sounds far more appropriate. Shall we walk?"

Moving away from the finger buffet, and our lovely Princess Diana, we continued our walk around the park.

Stroll, chat, stroll, chat, woof, woof.

"Fancy a coffee, Hasan? We still have thirty minutes before the permit runs out."

"Yeah, great, where can we get one?"

"Follow me, just around the corner, on Regents Park Road."

Cappuccinos and chat, water for the dogs, we had managed to get a seat outside a café, just as someone was leaving.

"We should head back to the car now. Traffic wardens hide behind trees and in the bushes around here. We have eight minutes," I said, getting up from my seat.

As we walked towards the car, I spotted something yellow under his windscreen wiper. OMG he's got a ticket! I couldn't find the words to tell him, so waited for him, to spot it.

"What the fuck!"

"Oh, shit, why have they given you a parking ticket?" I said, checking the pay and display permit. "We've got three minutes left!"

"What the fuck's going on? Why have I been ticketed? I don't fucking believe it!"

I walked past the car and along the bend in the road. One… two… three… four. Four cars, all in a row, had been given tickets. At the end of the bay, I saw a yellow sign attached to the lamppost. It wasn't where it should have been. It hadn't been totally removed, probably because it was too secure, but it had been vandalized and pulled to the ground. It was not visible at eye level.

I turned back to see Hasan, banging his forehead on the roof of the Audi. I walked back toward him. "Stop banging your frontal lobe on the car, and come and see this. It's no wonder that you get so many headaches. Why don't you try kicking something instead?"

"Because I'd probably break my foot."

"Come with me," I said, taking him by the arm and walking him back to the lamppost.

He whipped out his new camera phone and took a picture.

"That is your evidence, to contest the ticket," I said, all pleased with myself.

"Knowing my luck, I'll probably be charged with vandalism, as well."

I grabbed him by the shoulders and looked into his eyes. "Don't worry, look, there is a camera, right behind you."

He didn't look behind him, but instead, said, "When you grabbed me by the shoulders and looked into my eyes, I thought you were going to kiss me."

"What! Like this you mean?" I grabbed him and gave him a three second kiss on the lips. Both eyes and mouth closed.

He threw his head back and laughed.

"That's better," I said, walking arm in arm with him back to the car.

On the journey back to mine, I told Hasan that I had kept my knickers up since Christmas, and had no intention of removing them.

"Don't worry, I'll remove them," he said, laughing.

"No, I'm being celibate at the moment. SHE, is in a deep sleep and not to be disturbed."

"No problem," said Hasan, patting my knee.

He dropped me and the dogs home and after a goodbye hug, I sighed, as he disappeared off, up the street. In my heart, I so wished he was ten years older, and me, ten years younger.

THE WANKER IN WHSMITHS

Tuesday, 15th April

Four p.m. I jumped on a bus to pick a few things up from the local shops. Downstairs was full of school kids, so I made my way up top, where there were a few available seats. I plonked myself behind a couple of young girls who were having a conversation.

"We had a seance last night at Oliver's. It was really scary."

"What's a seance?"

"You know, where you sit round a Luigi board and try to contact the dead."

"What's a Luigi board?"

"It's the board you use. It has letters and numbers on, and YES and NO. You put the board on a table or the floor and sit around it with the lights off and ask it questions."

"What like?"

"Is anybody there?"

"How does it answer?"

"You get a glass and place it upside down, in the middle of the board, then everyone puts one finger on the top of it. When you ask a question, the glass moves around the board on its own."

"On its own?"

"Yes, the spirits come through humans."

"So, what happened?"

"Well, there was me, Oliver, Jamie and Sarah all in Olly's bedroom with the lights out. You have to be silent. We each put one finger on the glass and Olly asked the Luigi board a question."

"What did he say?"

"He said, 'Is anybody there?' And the glass moved towards YES. I got really scared."

"Then what?"

"He said, 'what's your name?' Then the glass moved to different letters and it spelt out Robert. Jamie started laughing and said someone was pushing the glass but I don't think they were. I was really scared. Olly told him to shut up and take it seriously."

"Then what?"

"He said, 'when were you born, Robert?' The glass moved to different numbers and it was 1864."

"Then what?"

"Then he said, 'If you are present with us, show us a sign', but nothing happened so Jamie said, "Let me try."

"If there is anyone there, please show us a sign. Suddenly there was a boom, boom, boom! We all jumped out of our skin and Sarah screamed, then Olly said, 'That's my mum banging on the ceiling with a broom because my dinner's ready'. We all fell about laughing. It was good fun we're going to do it again on Saturday if you want to come. We're going to try and get hold of Robert again."

Highly amused, arriving at my stop, I got off the bus and went into WHSmith, to buy a birthday card for my sister. Bending down, I was looking at the cards on the bottom shelf and as I couldn't see them properly, I got down on my knees to get a better look. Suddenly, in my peripheral vision, I was aware of a 'fast' action, rather like a small bird, flapping its wings. I kept my eyes down but looked along the ground to see some sweat pants tucked into a large pair of trainers. No, surely not. I looked from the feet up and saw a youngish bloke with his hand inside his sweat pants having a wank! He saw me looking at him but just carried on. I bolted upright, jumped to my feet, waving my hands, and shouted, at the top of my voice.

"THERE'S A MAN HAVING A WANK IN THE GREETING CARDS AISLE!"

As he ran out of the shop, other shoppers turned toward me and the manager came running over. "Where? Where is he?"

"He's just run out the door."

The young male manager ran to the door, to see the wanker, running down the street. He rushed back past me saying, "Sorry! I need to call the police. Wait there."

Another shop assistant, female, came over to me and asked if I was okay.

"I'm fine, thank you. Just thought you should know and I wanted to embarrass him because he just carried on wanking, when he saw me looking at him."

"Can I ask you what he was wearing?"

"White T shirt, grey sweatpants and white trainers."

"I'm so sorry, he's been in here a few times recently."

I wondered why, if he was a habitual wanker, he always wore the same clothes for his expeditions, why didn't he come in disguise?

"So, he's a regular then?"

"Well, he has been, recently."

The manager came hurrying over. "I'm so sorry, madam. Are you Okay? I've just called the police do you think you could describe him?"

The lady shop assistant answered for me. "It's the same one that was in here last week, grey sweat pants and a white T-shirt."

"Okay, well we already have a good description of him from other shoppers, so I'll take up no more of your time, madam. Thank you for bringing him to our attention, and apologies, again."

Well, I knew I wasn't going to be charged for a greetings card after that. So, I chose three and took them to the pay desk where the manager was standing. "No charge, madam," he said, popping them into a white paper bag and handing them to me. I left the shop, unfazed, somewhat politically incorrect, but slightly amused, and headed up to Sainsburys.

My mind was somewhat preoccupied, with the wanking incident, as I wandered around filling my small basket with bread and fresh fruit. I just needed some nuts then could return home. I couldn't find them, so walked up to a young, male, shop assistant who was busy stacking shelves.

"Excuse me, where are your nuts?"

He burst out laughing.

"Come with me, madam. I'll show you."

I suddenly realized what I had said and thought he might be tempted to take me through the swing-doors to the warehouse.

"Ooops! Said that wrong, didn't I."

"Don't worry, madam. No problem."

Nuts safely in basket, I headed for the checkout. While queuing I was aware of a man in a different queue, who kept looking over at me then turning away. Maybe he thinks I'm Helen Mirren, as people sometimes do, I thought.

Groceries paid for, I left the supermarket and he was standing outside. "Gaynor, is that you?" he said, inquisitively.

I suddenly recognized him from years back. He was a producer at the agency I used to work in. Hadn't seen him for some thirty years and he hadn't really bothered with me in the past. He was very popular with the pretty, young secretaries.

"Yes. It's me. How are you?" I asked, not being able to remember his name.

"You look absolutely fantastic. Have you had surgery?"

"Yes! I had my husband removed," I said, laughing.

"Well, you look really great. It's good to see you again."

"You too but, I'm afraid I've got to dash, meeting up with a friend, and I'm running late."

"No problem. Do you live around here?"

"Yes, just up the road."

"Cool, I'm local so will probably see you again."

"Cool, take care," I responded, hurrying away.

I crossed the road to the bus stop and jumped on the first available bus. Not paying attention, I pulled my travel card from my bag, flashed it at the driver and walked straight into the bus putting it back in my bag.

"Excuse me, madam, you can't travel using that," shouted the driver, as I sat down near his booth.

Crossly, I responded. "And why not? IT'S A NEW CARD! I only bought it, this morning." I marched back to the driver holding up my card clearly. I noticed the back of it. Shit.

"Madam, it's a Pokémon card."

DON'T BE RIDICULOUS

I hadn't seen Bunty for six months and couldn't wait for her to arrive. She had been in Africa, filming, and I had missed her terribly. Even though I had taken my own advice during the last year, rather than hers, the journey I had made, had been taken with choices which were mine and mine alone. I had felt compelled to follow my heart, even though it felt broken at times. The last twelve months, had not only been an adventure, but also cathartic, during which time, I do believe, I had found myself. Or at least, 50% of myself.

Bunty arrived early evening, and I ran downstairs to greet her. We threw our arms around each other, with shrieks of delight.

"Bunteeeeeeee!"

"Hello, darling, so happy to see you, and to be back in UK. I've missed you."

"Me toooooo! Come, I have Champagne waiting."

"Wooohoooo!"

I grabbed the post and we walked up the stairs, into the flat, holding hands. As soon as she was through the door, Daisy and Flo were at her feet, barking with excitement.

"Daisy! Flo!" I've missed both of you, too," she said, bending down to their level and making a fuss of them.

I poured the Champagne.

"First one, down in one?" said Bunty. "I've got two more bottles in my bag."

I nodded enthusiastically, then chinked her glass. "Up your bum, Bunty."

"Up yours," she said, laughing.

With refills, we settled down in the living room and Bunty proceeded to tell me all about her time in the Congo. I found the information both engaging, educational and fascinating. Knowing very little about Africa, I felt I had been given an 'up to the minute' course in geography, culture and customs. It was a world away from how life was lived here, in the UK.

"Enough about me, what have you been up to?" she asked, peering over her specs at me, with raised eyebrows and a naughty smile.

"Hang on, I'm just going to grab more Champagne."

"I've put it in the freezer, it was a bit warm."

"Cool."

I told Bunty about EVERYTHING, including stuff she hadn't been aware of.

I firstly told her about the bad stuff, which had happened with Max, the disappearance of Bill, and such like, then went on to things like the larder incident in 10room, the chewing gum incident, in my bedroom, and Hasan, and the canary.

By the end of ALL my disclosures, she was holding her sore belly, from laughing so much. After pulling herself together, she composed herself, looked at me seriously and said, "Gaynor, you have to write a book."

"Don't be ridiculous! I can't write a book. I've only read two books in my whole life. Pride and Prejudice and Twelfth Night, which I was forced to read at school in English literature. I hate reading."

"You wouldn't be reading, you'd be writing, you used to write ads, didn't you? And you won awards."

"Yes, but that's totally different. Writing a thirty second TV commercial, is a million miles away from writing a book."

"Well, just give it some thought."

"More Champagne, vicar?" I said, picking up the bottle and topping up her glass, knowing her suggestion was way outside my capabilities.

By the time we had finished chatting, we had polished off three bottles of Champagne, so decided to have a bedtime joint, just to wipe us out, completely. Joint smoked, Bunty stumbled off to Ben's room, because he was in Brighton, while I steadied myself, against the walls, which led me to mine. I sat on my bed and opened the letter which had arrived that morning. Inside was a letter of thanks, from The Globe Bar and a cheque for £20,000. Oh my god! Oh my god! Oh my god! I couldn't believe it. I ran onto the terrace and looked up to the heavens.

"Thank you, God. Thank you, God. Thank you for looking after me, God. Thank you, thank you, thank you!"

LOST FOR WORDS

Sunday, 27th April

Eleven a.m. After waking up, in a great space, because of the cheque, I revisited and considered what Bunty had suggested. The trouble was, I didn't feel in any kind of way, at all, that I was a 'literary' person. I rarely went into book shops because I didn't feel I belonged there. On the odd occasion I had visited one, it was to buy books for kiddies, or picture books about art and photography. The other thing I didn't like about book shops, was that they smelt funny. It was as though all those books, sucked the oxygen out of the air. And, worst of all, there was inevitably an area, which smelt 'farty'. I had a theory for that. Bookshops make people want to poo. Books are made from paper, paper comes from trees, does a bear shit in the woods? Yes.

I was, however, flattered, that Bunty had some unwarranted, bizarre confidence in me, that I would have the ability to write a book. She was terribly well read, intelligent and articulate, and always had a book in her bag. I decided, if I were to attempt this colossal feat, I would start with just one chapter. I would write a few pages, about my funny experience in the larder, with Francois. There was one thing I was certain of. If the few pages I was about to write were crap, she wouldn't bullshit me. She'd gently, kindly, tell me it wasn't working.

I had nothing to lose and no expectations whatsoever, so, I got out of bed, sat at my computer, and started writing.

Two hours, and ten pages later, I had finished 'Larder'.

I walked into the living room, to see Bunty, lying on the sofa, reading a book.

Expressionless, I said, "Morning, Bunty. I've written something."

"Where is it? I want to see it... NOW!"

"Okay, just got to go and to print it out. Hang on."

I returned to my bedroom, printed it and returned to the living room. She was already holding out her hand, as I walked through the door. Handing it over, I left the room, went to the kitchen to make tea and toast, then went back to my bedroom and closed the door. Breakfast eaten, I was lying on my bed, stroking Daisy and Flo, when the door flew open. Startled, the dogs jumped up, looking at Bunty, as she waved the pages in the air, raving.

"GAYNOR! YOU HAVE A VOICE! IT'S BRILLIANT! YOU HAVE A VOICE! IT'S SO RARE, PROBABLY BECAUSE YOU HAVE NEVER READ ANYTHING! THERE IS NO INFLUENCE! IT'S JUST YOU, ALL YOU, AND IT'S REAL! YOU HAVE TO WRITE A BOOK! YOU HAVE TO! YOU'RE A WRITER!"

For a few seconds, I was totally lost for words.

"Really? Really? You think it's okay?"

"OK? IT'S FUCKING BRILLIANT! IT MADE ME LAUGH OUT LOUD!"

I felt bemused, elated and gob-smacked, all at the same time.

"It's so engaging and so funny. I want more. You HAVE to write a book."